Media, Technology and Copyright

This book is dedicated to my two wonderful sons, Sam and Ben, everything in their lives that informs them, and some of the things that entertain them.

Media, Technology and Copyright

Integrating Law and Economics

Michael A. Einhorn, Ph.D.

Edward Elgar

Cheltenham, UK • Northampton, MA, USA

Published by
Edward Elgar Publishing Limited
Glensanda House
Montpellier Parade
Cheltenham
Glos GL50 1UA
UK

Edward Elgar Publishing, Inc.
136 West Street
Suite 202
Northampton
Massachusetts 01060
USA

A catalogue record for this book
is available from the British Library

Library of Congress Cataloguing in Publication Data

Einhorn, Michael A.
    Media, technology and copyright: integrating law and economics/
    Michael A. Einhorn.
        p.   cm.
    Includes bibliographical references and index.
    1. Copyright and electronic data processing—United States.
    2. Copyright—Economic aspects—United States. 3. Intellectual
    property—Economic aspects—United States. I. Title.
    KF3030.1.E38   2004
    346.7304'82—dc22

                                              2003069114

ISBN 1 84376 657 4 (cased)

Printed and bound in Great Britain by MPG Books Ltd, Bodmin, Cornwall

Contents

Preface

This book will apply economic reasoning to a number of issues in American copyright law with regard to media, entertainment, and technology. In analyzing markets and financial accounts, economic theory orders thinking, conceptualizes problems, and permits nuanced decision-making. During the course of my professional career as a professor, professional consultant, and testifying expert, I became increasingly convinced of the great power that economic analysis had in promulgating wise court decisions in antitrust law, and beneficial regulatory reform. I also became increasingly disturbed about its frequent lack of application in the copyright arena.

The copyright arena now often ignores key economic factors that rational decision making should consider.

As a professional participant in this judicial and legislative theater, I put forth my thoughts in several lectures and law review articles that form the foundation of this book. Throughout my work, I enjoyed interacting with a great number of individuals in the legal community who were interested in new insights of an economist. There seemed to be a broad understanding, even among the opinionated, that pragmatic economic analysis could serve a useful purpose in the debate.

In addition to my ongoing reading of briefs and articles, a number of scholars affected my attempt to appreciate the nuances of both sides of the debate. I have especially benefited from conversations with Jane Ginsburg, Wendy Gordon and Diane Zimmerman, who have affected my thinking to a considerable degree. I also have had input from Allan Adler, Fritz Attaway, June Besek, Andrew Bridges, David Carson, Robert Clarida, Jeffrey Cunard, Edward Davis, Janet Fries, Eric German, Arthur Greenbaum, Rob Kasunic, Kenneth Kaufman, William Landes, Lawrence Lessig, Arnold Lutzker, Christopher Newman, William Patry, Lawrence Pulgram, Ira Rothken, Michael Remington, Shira Perlmutter, Bruce Rich, Keith Sharfman, Cary Sherman, Greg Welch and conference and seminar participants in New York, Chicago, Philadelphia, San Francisco, Palo Alto and Los Angeles.

I have also benefited from my family's willingness to indulge my many months of research and time spent at the computer. I look forward to rejoining them more now as the summer begins.

Michael Einhorn

1. Introduction

1.1 ECONOMICS AND COPYRIGHT

Copyright for original works is now protected in the US by the Copyright Act of 1976, which is now codified in Title 17 of the US Code.[1] Section 102 of the Act extends copyright protection to original works of authorship that are fixed in any tangible medium of expression.[2] Eight identified works of authorship include material of literary, musical, dramatic, choreographic, pictorial/sculptural, audiovisual, sound recording or architectural nature.[3] Section 106 grants to copyright owners generally exclusive rights to make reproductions, prepare derivative works, distribute copies, make public performances and publicly display controlled works.[4] However, the Act elsewhere provides important restrictions on the exercise of these rights, including fair use,[5] term duration,[6] the idea-expression dichotomy,[7] the first sale doctrine[8] and exemptions for libraries,[9] education[10] and the blind and the handicapped.[11]

The economic justification to protect with copyright an artistic work or software is reasonable. A large fraction of production costs must be incurred upfront, with considerable expense and effort to create and work up for market. Without copyright protection, the resulting product is nonexcludable, in the sense that later access to content can be available to all who see or hear it. While free reproduction, performance and display may benefit users, such takings can expropriate from creators due rewards for invested efforts. In time, the danger of expropriation compounds and reduces the incentives to create content in the first place. One general economic remedy for the economic problem then is to establish property rights through protective social agreements – i.e., copyright.[12]

Economists then generally defend some form of copyright as a collective arrangement[13] that provides incentive and security for artists, writers, publishers and programmers.[14] That is, copyright protection creates a legal right against unsigned parties that is made viable by a legislative compact that no one individual could effectively negotiate and enforce. When producer rights are secure, additional incentives for yet more creation presumably follow. Indeed, the stated purpose for the US patent and copyright system supports an economic instrumentalism based on incentive,[15] which varies philosophically from a European perspective that recognizes the concept of an inalienable moral right that is attributable to the author's inner personality.[16]

However, copyright presents two key countervailing concerns. In exercising or protecting their copyrights, rights owners may increase unit prices above the level of short-run marginal cost (i.e., zero), which is the economically efficient price in static market equilibrium.[17] Moreover, in pursuing payment for access, rights owners may impose additional transaction costs for search and negotiation in a manner that may discourage a number of uses that are otherwise economically efficient.[18]

The conceivable inefficiencies of copyright may realistically be compounded when owners have access to protective legal instruments. If so empowered, owners may uneconomically extend term duration,[19] establish overlapping rights, and otherwise garner rents for existing works without creating additional incentives. Subsequent to production of a protected work, the institutions of intellectual property (IP) can provide rent-seeking opportunities for spinoff activities that are entirely *ex post* and unproductive of real incentives. All things considered, an overly protective process can actually reduce the cumulative knowledge that can be shared among the common citizenry and the creative community.[20] Such concerns about undue protection have inspired academic calls for an 'information commons' – 'a rich public domain of materials whose copyright has expired presumably creates a freely useable set of information that an individual can draw upon for any purpose whatsoever.'[21]

However, copyright owners may rely upon considerable market contingencies to counter their academic critics in several important respects. First, the capabilities of the Internet have greatly reduced the costs of monitoring use and transacting for permissions.[22] Second, licensing agents have designed a wide range of contracts and institutional arrangements to accommodate ease of use at a zero unit price; a reasonable fee is instead extracted upfront from each user based on total sales revenue, size of establishment or number of licensed sites, *inter alia*.[23] Third, there are coordination economies to be had by avoiding overuse of particular artistic properties, e.g., screenplay writers who transcribe original books may reasonably be required to obtain permission so as to ensure coordinated development and profitable release of the movie and possible sequels.[24] Finally, the control over secondary products may enhance original incentives, e.g., the producer of a console for videogames may increase expected profits and lower its introductory price if it can sell or license complementary games at protected prices.[25]

The tensions and contradictions of copyright now devolve into an international dialog that can be aided by the complementary disciplines of law and economics. The legal process is pure social convention; it maintains its societal order largely through interpretations of statutory wording, legislative intent, and judicial precedent. Economics is presumably social science; it purports to conceptualize processes and predict reality without any necessary deference to previously enacted laws. If legal and economic considerations are in balance, the legal stratum must ride atop the scientific, i.e., social procedure must in the end be based upon actual reality.

1.2 LAW AND ECONOMICS

Starting in the 1950s from the intellectual collaboration of the University of Chicago's Edward Levi and Aaron Director, the discipline of 'law and economics' has moved from classroom dialog and academic journal to the abiding economic philosophy of the Antitrust Division, the minds of several appellate judges,[26] at least one best-selling political work,[27] and the course catalogs of the nation's best law schools. In antitrust, the Chicago School contributed in the past three decades to a string of economically sensible cases regarding merger,[28] vertical restraint,[29] and predatory pricing.[30] These cases elevated market efficiency above judicial interpretations of legislative intent,[31] that had aimed instead to protect small producer interests.[32] Economic considerations also made their way into key patent cases that defined the 'but for' world that damage experts must properly consider when estimating economic harm resulting from a patent infringement.[33] Adding economic reasoning to a structural inquiry then gives courts 'breathing room to consider common-sense facts related to efficiency, as well as to think about what sorts of behavior would be rational in the relevant market'.[34]

Lawyers and trial judges must condition their actions with an awareness of economic efficiency and how free markets operate. Imagine the following situation. A rancher lives next door to a farmer, and his cattle trespass and ruin the farmer's crops. The farmer sues to enjoin the rancher, and the court deliberates to create a just solution. What to do?

R.H. Coase suggested that parties ideally might be left to barter indefinitely to determine who is willing to pay whom for the right to continue or stop a particular action.[35] For if an injunction were instituted inefficiently for the plaintiff, the defendant could pay the plaintiff voluntarily to lift the injunction, and the resulting settlement terms could then be structured to leave both parties better off. By contrast, no such accommodative exchange is possible if the starting position is already efficient. In this ideal market theater, courts may award verdicts, but any legal result will be irrelevant to the eventual outcome that will (and should) prevail if property rights can be exchanged in costless transactions.

However, the ideal Coase Theorem generally depends on three conditions:

1. There are no transaction costs – e.g., haggling, holdout, cheating and other

negotiating difficulties – between contending parties that impose costly delays or foreclose settlements entirely.[36]

2.   There are no excluded 'third parties' who lack court standing. Otherwise, the benefit or cost of market externalities are not properly represented or valued in the later transactions.

3.   There is no market power, i.e., the parties value the contested resources at true economic value and not as strategic instruments that can raise prices, deter entry or affect rival choices.

There are four conceivable options should any supporting condition fail. First, courts may measure respective costs and benefits of each alternative outcome and choose a winner based on a rational-comprehensive[37] analysis of all factors involved. In the above example, either the farmer or the rancher may be determined to suffer the greater economic or moral loss.

Second, legislatures can impose a general levy upon the products that are used for or related to tortious activities. For example, all cattlemen in the county may pay a head tax on cattle to cover possible damages resulting from overgrazing. The revenues garnered from such levies can be used to compensate victims for demonstrated or estimated losses.

Third, the defendant may be required to compensate the plaintiff for imposed costs,[38] e.g., the rancher may be required to compensate the farmer for lost crops resulting from overgrazing. In such an instance, the plaintiff will be made whole for his losses, and the rancher's activity will continue only if his private benefit exceeds the damages that he imposes and pays for. Optimal liability rules can then be used if the appropriate measure of damages can be accurately assessed, and no additional punitive restitution is deemed necessary.

Finally, judges can mandate specific preventive actions to limit harm. If efficient, the legal system would place responsibility on that party who could prevent the trespass most cheaply.[39] For example, the farmer may be required to put up a fence. However, there is no economic reason why courts must limit liability solely to one provider;[40] a bilateral resolution would be particularly compelling if different preventive methods could resolve different aspects of the same problem, or otherwise improve economic efficiency or perceived fairness.[41] Alternatively, the court may order one party to undertake the investment, and order the other to compensate her.

Each of the four specified options presents problems:

1.   A rational comprehensive approach requires the courts to identify all relevant effects and perform a global cost–benefit analysis. This may include estimating the net social values of certain considerations and contingencies, as well as their likely probabilities. Such comprehensive

analysis is particularly difficult in the digital marketplace, where so many contingencies are open-ended.

2. General levies have the unfortunate distinction of being placed on non-infringing parties, and raising the product prices to a particular consumer regardless of his likelihood of imposing harm. Moreover, levies also provide no incentive for potential trespassers to limit their harmful activities.

3. Though economically attractive, liability rules still require accurate measurement of prospective damages. If careful measurement is not possible, parties may have incentives to misrepresent relevant magnitudes in order to extract more favorable terms.

4. Efficient fence-protection may require technological assessments, and may additionally impose considerable financial responsibilities upon the non-offending party. Though cross-compensation is possible, the relevant magnitudes may be difficult for a court to determine, or others to discern objectively.

1.3   INNOVATION AND COMPLEXITY

As an economic concern, this book considers how markets and institutions may allocate property rights in intellectual property to competing ends. In the paradigm of Schumpeterian capitalism, these processes are part of a social mechanism that enables the process of 'creative destruction' of new ideas, creations, and processes of production and distribution.[42] Economic efficiency is here gauged by the production of new innovations, rather than by the microeconomic consideration of aggregate social welfare at any one moment. Indeed, to provide the spur for innovation, we often permit the short-run inefficiencies of monopoly power.

However, law is also an investment in harmonious social process, and rules must be designed to assure predictable – if not perfect – resolution of conflicts. Satisfactory legal governance must recognize the complexity of systems where resources are scarce, technology evolving, surveillance imperfect, intelligence widely distributed and information open-ended. As a social contrivance for managing complexity, common law is incrementalist and experimental – restricting considerations, limiting information, forsaking measurement and attempting to learn by doing.[43]

In integrating law and economics, we are then engaged in a 'science of the artificial',[44] which generally comprises the symbols, controls and responses for resolving immediate threats and moving the system toward a long-term order. The intelligence of the system is gauged by the efficiencies and general 'wisdom' of the outcomes achieved in common and statutory law.

1.4　THE DIGITAL WORLD

One short decade ago, the copyright issue occupied the attention of no more than a few individuals in a world of media built around printing presses, celluloid film, record vinyl and analog broadcasts. Photocopiers were more distributed, particularly in libraries and workplaces, but not commonplace in private homes. Video and audio recorders made imperfect copies that were made most often for self-use; general copying for lending and distribution to friends and strangers had been deterred by the physical inferiority of sequential copying and the physical difficulty of widely distributing tape copies.

Copyright issues moved to center stage in the policy arena with the advent of digital technology and the capacity of the Internet to move audio, video, text and numeric data from point to point in a short amount of time. As digital technology develops further, cinema fans will access movies at any hour, music fans may sample or download tunes from an historic catalog, art lovers may cybertour any great museum in the world, and e-book purchasers may replace visits to libraries and bookstores with convenient downloads. Hyperbolically, 'in this vast intellectual commons, nothing will ever again be out of print or impossible to find; every scrap of human culture transcribed, no matter how obscure or commercially successful, will be available to all'.[45]

However, technology also presents a 'danger' for content producers. As the many users of Napster first demonstrated,[46] copying material to a computer hard drive can be the first step in making content available for unauthorized distribution to any computer on the planet. Illegally distributed copies then may reasonably be expected to substitute for legal purchases, and to harm producer incentives in the process. Consequently, due account should therefore be taken of the differences between digital and analog private copying and a distinction should be made in certain respects between them.

The digital network can then be conceived of as a disk. Copyrighted material is transmitted between users through the interior, while material on the circumference moves to other devices using off-network operations. With some exceptions, transfers through the interior can be observed and measured, and are therefore conducive to licensing and sales. By contrast, transfers around the circumference are less easily discerned, and subject more readily to fair use and first sale considerations.

1.5　ORGANIZATION OF THE BOOK

The book is organized as follows. Chapter 2 reviews fair use, and suggests that the present legal regime provides a complex test that creates uneconomic uncertainty for producers of transformative works that imbue copyrighted works with entirely new meaning (e.g., through satire, lecture, critical narrative and parody). Distinguished from superseding and derivative infringements that displace original sales and disrupt the coordination of sequential releases (e.g., books, screenplays), transformative works are seen as spinoff activities that are unrelated to original creation or product development. The chapter contends that courts can improve certainty by more precisely defining such transformative uses, and implementing liability rules to compensate rights owners for actual damages or reasonable royalties.

Chapter 3 considers the economics of digital rights management (DRM), which entails technologies for securing and widening the property rights that original owners may have over content distributed on the Internet. Digital rights management encourages production by improving security and widening the range of consumer choices. Accordingly, protections in the Digital Millenium Copyright Act that outlaw devices to circumvent DRM have a reasonable economic basis.

Chapter 4 considers the issues of contributory infringement and file-sharing, as heard in litigation involving Napster, Madster, Grokster and Morpheus. Courts are found to have resolved Napster efficiently by imposing upon both sides the obligation to institute protections against later infringement, but declining otherwise to shut down Napster. However, ongoing industry litigation against subsequent file-sharing services may be ignoring the unpleasant market reality that more powerful file-sharing technology may follow if one is outlawed.

Chapter 5 discusses the problems of the anti-commons – overlapping and cumbersome rights – that inhere in the market for digitally transmitted music. While the structure of copyright implicates a collection of rights that has some basis in analog law, the structure has less validity in digital markets. As a consequence of the administrative overlay, the resulting licensing arrangements for digital audio transmission are inefficient. The chapter suggests ways to improve economic efficiency by reducing the number of transactions and administrative reviews.

Chapter 6 considers the related topic of publicity rights, which extends to celebrities the rights to control how their names and images are used in media communications. The chapter concludes that celebrities need strong protection against impersonations and digital clones that can substitute for their professional performances. Additionally, producers cannot be permitted to expropriate celebrity names, nicknames and, possibly, phrases in a manner that could imply endorsement. Publicity rights in other respects, particularly with regard to mass merchandise, are found to be excessive. Publicity rights also present a concern for copyright owners, as the resulting regime may lead to another overgrowth in the anti-commons.

Chapter 7 considers economic issues related to software, data and cyber-search. Courts are found to have generously granted fair use protection to users of software interfaces, and to have ignored the potential for licensing arrangements or pricing adjustments to have resolved matters with less expropriation. Courts in both copyright and antitrust law have opposed a number of competitive business models in high-tech markets that actually benefit users and hasten the penetration of new platform technologies. Nonetheless, a case is made for fair use for some data spinoffs that do not affect primary incentives, and for consumer devices where the transactions costs of licensing in private homes may be prohibitive.

Chapter 8 considers the issue of open source software as an innovation in the power of IP protection. Open source software is seen as a highly functional adaptation of copyright law that may enhance cooperative production by reducing transaction costs and eliminating the threat of expropriation. The outcome is a system that greatly increases producer incentives to create in an accommodative and open-ended fashion.

NOTES

1. Pub. L. No. 94-553, 90 Stat. 2591 (1976) (codified as amended at 17 U.S.C. §§ 101–1101).
2. 'Now known or later developed, from which they can be perceived, reproduced, or otherwise communicated, either directly or with the aid of a machine or device' (17 U.S.C. § 102).
3. Ibid.
4. 17 U.S.C. § 106. Also, in the case of sound recordings (otherwise unprotected in the performance right), to perform the work publicly by means of a digital audio transmission.
5. 'The fair use of a copyrighted work ... for purposes such as criticism, comment, news reporting, teaching ... scholarship, or research, is not an infringement of copyright' (17 U.S.C. § 107). The four statutory criteria for fair use are discussed in detail in Chapter 2.2.
6. For known works created after January 1, 1978, copyright endures for a term equal to 70 years after the death of the last surviving author (17 U.S.C. § 302(a)–(b)). For anonymous works, pseudonymous works and works made for hire, copyright endures for 95 years after first publication, or 120 years after creation, whichever expires first (17 U.S.C. § 302(c)).
7. Per full statutory wording, copyright protection does not extend to any 'idea, procedure, process, system, method of operation, concept, principle, or discovery, regardless of the form in which it is described, explained, illustrated, or embodied in such work' (17 U.S.C. § 102(b)).
8. The first sale doctrine extends to a lawful private owner the right to sell or otherwise dispose of a copyrighted work. This does not include the right to make reproductions (17 U.S.C. § 109(a)).
9. With restrictions, libraries may reproduce or distribute single copies of works to interested readers and requesting libraries, and up to three copies (including digital) for preservation of unpublished works or legitimate replacement or reformatting of published ones (so long as a replacement cannot otherwise be obtained at a fair market price) (17 U.S.C. § 108).
10. With restrictions, performances or displays of lawfully made works by instructors or pupils in the course of face-to-face teaching activities are copyright exempt, as are transmissions of non-dramatic literary or musical works. Performances of non-dramatic works are similarly exempt for religious services, non-profit establishments, small eating and drinking

establishments, government organizations, record stores or uses for the blind and handicapped (17 U.S.C. § 110).

11. 17 U.S.C. § 121.

12. O.E. Williamson, 'Transaction Cost Economics: The Governance of Contractual Relations', **22** *Journal of Law and Economics* 233 (1979).

13. See generally M. Olsen, *The Logic of Collective Action* (Cambridge, MA: Harvard University Press, 1972).

14. Brief for G.A. Akerlof et al. as Amici Curaie, U.S. Court of Appeals for the D.C. Circuit, *Eric Eldred* v. *John D. Ashcroft*, May 20, 2002 ('The main economic rationale for copyright is to supply a sufficient incentive for creation [and] an economically mindful author will recognize this and invest in creation only if the expected returns [exceed] the upfront investment. [However] without legal protection, an author cannot prevent others from appropriating the fruits of the initial investment' at 4).

15. The Constitutional purpose of copyright is to 'promote the progress of science and the useful arts, by securing for limited times to authors and inventors the exclusive right to their respective writings and discoveries' (U.S. Constitution, art. 1, § 8, cl. 8). The Supreme Court further affirmed: 'The sole interest of the United States and the primary object in conferring the monopoly lie in the general benefits derived by the public from the labors of authors' (*Fox Film Corp.* v. *Doyal*, 286 U.S. 123, 127–38 (1932); *U.S.* v. *Paramount Pictures*, 334 U.S. 131, 158, 68 S. Ct. 915, 92 L. Ed. 1260 (1948). The 'economic philosophy behind [the Constitutional] clause … is the conviction that encourage of individual effort by personal gain is the best way to advance public welfare' (*Mazer* v. *Stein*, 347 U.S. 201, 219, 74 S. Ct. 460, 471, 98 L. Ed. 930 (1954)).

16. In the continental approach, the 'fruits of intellectual creativity are associated with the author in a peculiar intimate way' (L. Weinreb, 'Copyright for Functional Expression', 111 *Harvard Law Review*, 1149, 1226 (1998)) and therefore implicate a property right to the product in a manner that may be independent of social utility (*Bleistein* v. *Donaldson*, 188 U.S. 239 (1903)).

17. Supra note 14, Section I.B.

18. Ibid., Section II. Economists believe that when market price is set equal to short-run marginal cost, an exchange will take place if and only if consumer value exceeds producer cost. This maximizes aggregate social welfare and is viewed as economically efficient.

19. *Eldred* v. *Ashcroft* 537 U.S. (2003). In dissent, Justice Breyer challenged the 7–2 majority regarding copyright, arguing that protection is constitutionally justified only in so far as it provides the incentive for new production. At II.C.

20. Suzanne Scotchmer, 'Standing on the Shoulders of Giants: Cumulative Research and the Patent Law', 5 *Journal of Economic. Perspectives* 29 (1991); R. Nelson and R. Merges, 'On Complex Economics of Patent Scope', 90 *Columbia Law Review* 839.

21. Howard Besser, 'Intellectual Property: The Attack on Public Space in Cyberspace', *Processed World* (2001); see also D. Lange, 'Recognizing the Public Domain', 44 *Law and Contemporary Problems* 147 (1981); Y. Benkler, 'The Battle over the Institutional Ecosystem in the Digital Environment', 44 *Communications of the ACM* **2** (2001); L. Lessig, *The Future of Ideas: The Fate of the Commons in a Connected World* 249–61 (New York: Basic Books, 2002).

22. E.W. Kitch, 'Can the Internet Shrink Fair Use?', 78 *Nebraska Law Review* 880, 881–3 (1999); T.W. Bell, 'Fair Use vs. Fared Use: The Impact of Automated Rights Management on Copyright's Fair Use Doctrine', 76 *North Carolina Law Review* 557 (1998).

23. R.P. Merges, 'Contracting into Liability Rules: Intellectual Property Rights and Collective Rights Organizations', 84 *California Law Review* 1293, 1326 (1996).

24. E. Kitch, 'The Nature and Function of the Patent System', 20 *Journal of Law and Economics* 265 (1977); S. Ghosh, 'The Merits of Ownership', 15 *Harvard Journal of Law and Technology* 453 (2002).

25. See Chapter 7, section 2.

26. Guido Calabresi (Second Circuit); Richard Posner, Frank Easterbrook (Seventh Circuit); Alex Kozinski (Ninth Circuit).

27. R.A. Bork, *The Antitrust Paradox* (New York: Basic Books, 1976).

28. *U.S.* v. *General Dynamics Corp.*, 415 U.S. 486 (1974) ('Congress indicated plainly that a merger had to be [economically] viewed, in the context of its particular industry' at 498).

29. *Continental TV, Inc.* v. *GTE Sylvania, Inc.*, 433 U.S. 36 (1978) ('we are convinced that the need for clarification of the law in this area justifies reconsideration' of *Schwinn* [infra note 32], at 47).

30. *Matsushita Elec. Indus. Co.* v. *Zenith Radio Corp.*, 475 U.S. 574 (1986) (affirming summary judgment that dismissed claim that Japanese firms had conspired to price predatorily); *Brooke Group, Ltd.* v. *Brown & Williamson Tobacco Corp.*, 509 U.S. 209 (1993) (imposing a rigorous plaintiff requirement for tests of predatory pricing based on considerations of average incremental cost and the likelihood of later market recapture).

31. The 1960s economic ideology of the Supreme Court can be traced to legislative intent behind the Cellar-Kefauver Amendments to the Clayton Act, which were passed in 1950. (15 U.S.C. § 18). 'Small, independent decentralized business of the kind that built up our country ... first, is fast disappearing, and second, is being made dependent upon monster concentration. It is very difficult now for the small business to compete against the financial, purchasing, and advertising power of mammoth corporations' (95 Cong. Rec. 11484).

32. *Brown Shoe Co.* v. *U.S.*, 370 U.S. 294, 315 (1962) ('The dominant theme pervading Congressional consideration of the 1950 amendments was a fear of what was considered to be a rising tide of economic consideration in the American economy'); *U.S.* v. *Philadelphia National Bank*, 374 U.S. 321 (1963) ('Intense Congressional concern with the trend toward concentration warrants dispensing, in certain cases, with elaborate proof of market structure, market behavior, or probable anticompetitive effects' at 363); *U.S.* v. *Arnold Schwinn & Co.*, 388 U.S. 365 (1967) (it was unreasonable for a manufacturer to 'restrict and confine areas or persons with whom an article may be traded after the manufacturer has parted with dominion over it' at 379). For condemning mergers where post-merger market shares were as low as 7.5 and 4.5 percent respectively, see *U.S.* v. *Von's Grocery Co.*, 384 U.S. 270 (1966) and *U.S.* v. *Pabst Brewing Co.* 384 U.S. 546 (1966).

33. Sophisticated economic reasoning appears in *Windsurfing International, Inc.* v. *AMF Inc.*, 782 F. 2d 995 (Fed. Cir. 1986); *Polaroid Corp.* v. *Eastman Kodak*, 1990 U.S Dist. 17968 (E.D. Mass. 1990); *In the Matter of Mahurkar Double Lumen Hemodialysis Catheter Patent Litigation*, 831 F. Supp. 1354 (7th Cir. 1993); *Grain Processing Corp.* v. *American Maize Products Company*, 185 F. 3d 1341 (Fed. Cir. 1999).

34. D. McGowan, 'Innovation, Uncertainty, and Stability in Antitrust Law', 16 *Berkeley Technical Law Journal* 729, 762 (2001). Indeed, 'an antitrust policy divorced from market considerations would lack any objective benchmarks' (*GTE Sylvania*, supra note 29, at 47).

35. R.H. Coase, 'The Problem of Social Cost', 3 *Journal of Law and Economics* 1 (1960).

36. As distinguished from 'thick' markets with many buyers and sellers where prices serve as reasonable benchmarks. See O. Williamson, *The Mechanisms of Governance*, 55–61 (Oxford: Oxford University Press, 1996).

37. Infra note 43.

38. G. Calabresi and D. Melamed, 'Property Rules, Liability Rules, and Inalienability: One View of the Cathedral', 85 *Harvard Law Review* 1089, 1106–10 (1972).

39. Harold Demsetz, 'When Does the Rule of Liability Matter?', 1 *Journal of Legal Studies* 13, 27–8 (1972). For application to torts, see Guido Calabresi and John T. Hirschoff, 'Toward a Test for Strict Liability in Torts', 81 *Yale Law Journal* 1055, 1060 (1972); W.E. Landes and R.A. Posner, *Economic Structure of Tort Law*, ch. 1 (Cambridge, MA: Harvard University Press 1987)

40. See Demsetz and Calabresi and Hirschoff in note 39; S.G. Gilles, 'Negligence, Strict Liability, and the Cheapest Cost-Avoider', 78 *Virginia Law Review* 1291 (1992).

41. Bilateral care rules applied to property disputes were suggested first by M.J. White and D. Wittman, 'Long Run versus Short Run Remedies for Spatial Externalities: Liability Rules, Pollution Rules, and Zoning', in *Essays on the Law and Economics of Local Governments* 33 (D.L. Rubinfeld ed., Washington, DC: Urban Institute, 1979).

42. J.A. Schumpeter, *Capitalism, Socialism, and Democracy* (New York: Harper Brothers, 1947).

43. For extensions to the political process, C.E. Lindblom, 'The Science of Muddling Through',

19 *Public Administration Review* 79 (1959). Lindblom compares incrementalism favorably with rational-comprehensive policy that is elegant but often impractical; rational comprehensive policy tries to consider and weigh all factors, gather all relevant information, measure all relevant quantities and willingly jump to extreme positions as logically justified.

44. See generally, H. Simon, *The Sciences of the Artificial* (Cambridge, MA: MIT Press, 1996).
45. C.C. Mann, 'The Heavenly Jukebox', *Atlantic Monthly*, September (2000).
46. *A&M Records, Inc.* v. *Napster, Inc.*, 114 F. Supp. 2d (N.D. Cal. 2000); *A&M Records, Inc.* v. *Napster, Inc.* 239 F. 3d 1004 (9th Cir. 2001).

2.   Fair use and economic analysis

2.1   INTRODUCTION

This chapter will apply economic reasoning to the judicial principle of fair use that is now often applied in matters involving unauthorized takings of copyrighted works. The four activating principles of fair use, as instituted in 17 U.S.C. § 107, are found to be ambiguous and subjective, and therefore creative of legal uncertainty for producers of secondary transformative works that may add new meaning to a copyrighted work. As 'the [Constitutional] goal of copyright, to promote science and the arts, is generally furthered by the creation of [such] transformative works',[1] the resulting loss of artistic investments and social criticism here can be considerable.

The difficulties of the fair use doctrine are best illustrated in the recent case of *SunTrust Bank* v. *Houghton Mifflin*, which involved the publication of an unauthorized sequel to the Civil War classic, *Gone with the Wind* (*GWTW*), that was entitled *The Wind Done Gone* (*TWDG*). Based on definitions of parody and satire, as well as standard legal considerations of market substitution, excessive borrowing and 'conjuring up', the District Court preliminarily enjoined the new book because the author's stated intent implicated a general criticism of Southern history, and therefore went beyond the proper domain of parody often protected by fair use.[2] On appeal, the Circuit Court vacated the resulting preliminary injunction after finding that *TWDG* was a specific criticism of the depiction of slavery and race relations in *GWTW*,[3] and that the Supreme Court decision of *Campbell* v. *Acuff Rose* was ambiguous on what kind of parody should be protected.[4] The case finally settled in May, 2002 for an undisclosed amount. Had the matter continued, the work might yet have been ruled an infringement and punitive damages might yet have been assessed on the publishers.

Legal theorists may now debate the wisdom of the decision. For market advocates with a less metaphysical bent, *SunTrust* was a waste. The great contest between free speech and copyright was played before two Federal Courts constrained by the present fair use doctrine. Whatever the elegance of the legal arguments, the truth is that two American courts seriously deliberated whether to enjoin the publication of a novel, and could not find unambiguous guidance from the Supreme Court regarding whether or not to do so.[5] Indeed, however nuanced the fair use doctrine may appear, judges must often choose between the same two discomfiting options – injunction and free use.[6] The outcome should be particularly disconcerting to any economically attuned observer who believes that clear signals provide the best incentives for producers of artistic work, and for investors in general.

While we seek to facilitate transformative use, there is no apparent equitable reason why primary rights owners should not be paid for use of their material.[7] Indeed, a number of prominent legal authorities, including Circuit Court Judges Pierre Leval and Alex Kozinski, have suggested that the copyright system is prone to too many injunctions and that courts may facilitate exchange by setting reasonable royalties.[8] These judicial points also appear in *Campbell* v. *Acuff Rose*; i.e., the 'goals of copyright law, "to stimulate the creation and publication of edifying matter", are not always best served by automatically granting injunctive relief when parodists are found to have gone beyond the bounds of fair use'.[9]

I suggest a modification of Title 17 to provide an option to facilitate exchange in rights for transformative works. First, a new statutory category of 'transformative' works would be established for material that adds sufficient new meaning to copyrighted material, and might reasonably include parodies, satires, criticisms, comments, news reports, research articles, classroom materials and sequels or adaptations. Second, transformative users of copyrighted works may forego the fair use claim in favor of an arbitration procedure that would base compensation on existing market benchmarks. Rate arbitration could only be operational for works that are demonstrably transformative, but may include some material that does not now qualify for traditional fair use. This creates greater legal assurance that transformative works are produced and that copyright owners get paid for their contribution.

2.2 FAIR USE AND TRANSACTION COST

As the introduction to Chapter 1 elaborates, copyright entails two economic phenomena. First, artistic works and software entail substantial investments that primary creators must undertake initially; unchecked imitation can dissipate producer profits and financial incentives. Copyright protection then encourages artistic production by protecting against the dissipation of just deserts and financial incentives for a period of time.

However, copyright may also depress uses by secondary creators who might base their works on some amount of original material. To the point, while 'knowledge and learning are promoted by the creation of more works, knowledge and learning are also promoted by a greater ability to access and to use the works of others'.[10] 'It is not enough then to say that intellectual property law favors "creators" – for here we have creators on both sides of the equation.'[11]

It is then economically improper to protect the exclusive interests of either primary or secondary producers.[12] The tension between respective gains and losses in a particular case is better resolved through a nuanced approach that considers the particular circumstances of a contended use.[13] Good jurisprudence regarding copyright must then consider the basic nature of the use, market definition, transactions costs, externalities, behavioral incentives and equitable compensation. As distinguished from the continental regime of moral rights awarded to the creator of the work, the broad exercise of copyright in the US must then be weighed in an 'equitable rule of reason' that balances contending positions of user and producer.

Beginning with Section 107, Chapter 1 of the Copyright Act specifies restrictions aimed to balance user and buyer rights. The fair use limitations on copyright appear in Section 107,[14] which extends the 'privilege in other than the owner of a copyright to use the copyrighted material in a reasonable manner without his consent, notwithstanding the monopoly granted to the owner'.[15] The introduction of Section 107 clearly establishes that transformative works (i.e., new meanings) are the primary concern of the fair use doctrine: 'the fair use of a copyrighted work … for purposes such as criticism, comment, news reporting, teaching (including multiple copies for classroom use), scholarship, or research, is not an infringement of copyright'.[16]

The four factors to be considered for identification of fair uses are:

1. The purpose and character of the use, including whether such use is of a commercial nature or is for nonprofit educational purposes.[17]
2. The nature of the copyrighted work.[18]
3. The amount and substantiality of the portion used in relation to the copyrighted work as a whole.[19]
4. The effect of the use upon the potential market for or value of the copyrighted work.

Damage estimates can reasonably include displaced unit sales and licensing opportunities.

Legal justifications for 'fair use' now bear an economic nuance that tends to focus on the transactions costs that are implicated in the use of protected work. Two academic articles contributed notably to this transformation. When negotiations are costless, wrote Nobel Laureate economist R.H. Coase in 1960,[20] disputants could be trusted to efficiently resolve commercial disputes through multilateral bargaining without need for legal stricture. However, the powerful capability of the market is diminished when transaction costs are positive,[21] or when economic benefits or costs redound to third parties who are excluded from representation in the exchange.

Coase's notion of transactions costs came to the copyright theater in 1983, two decades later, when Wendy Gordon related the friction of market exchange to fair use. Professor Gordon argued that 'an economic justification for depriving a copyright owner of this market entitlement exists only when the possibility of consensual bargain has broken down in some way'.[22] Extending Gordon, Edmund Kitch and Tom Bell later observed that automated rights management may reduce the transactional difficulty and the implied economic rationale for fair use.[23]

This modification presented by Kitch and Bell led to allegations that Professor Gordon's economic analysis of transactions costs is overly focused on bilateral exchange, to the exclusion of merit goods that may present wider public gains.[24] While concerns regarding a narrow application of rights management to fair use are valid, such a reading of Gordon's analysis is not correct. In economic analysis, Gordon's transactions costs also include identifying third-party beneficiaries of public goods who might not be represented at the bargaining table, and monetizing their resulting gains. In this respect, we must distinguish between difficulties that result from the inherent friction of negotiation and the harm resulting from excluded third parties, respectively termed 'no consent' and 'implied consent'.[25]

2.3 THE MARKET RESPONSE

An analysis of transactions cost is also incomplete if it fails to recognize how owners may respond to assigned property rights with modified business practices, institutions or technologies. This leads to another of Professor Gordon's points; fair use – if applied too broadly – could sap the incentive to develop the institutional mechanisms needed to reduce transactions costs and accommodate paid exchange.[26] With greater specificity,

> to award fair use without regard to the possibility of imminent change in the market structure might be to make permanent an otherwise curable market failure and thus potentially to insulate a new and valuable use from the stimulus of consumer demand ... To persuade users to proceed through the device, copyright owners might well need a ... declaration that the uncompensated use, previously minor and left unfettered, constituted an infringement of copyright.[27]

As noted in Chapter 1, markets, organizations, jurisprudence and political process are interlocking components of an inherent social logic that accommodates innovation, production and distribution. Creators, publishers, negotiating agents, and monitoring organizations then engage in routines, practices, contracts and enforcement as tactical operations in order to actualize this logic. Judicial and legislative processes and results should then be appreciated as catalysts that can induce changes elsewhere in the logical stratum. The bounds of property rights must then be carefully defined to provide room for evolving market and technology.

There are a number of ways that a free market will come to facilitate copyright beyond the legal grant.

Self-Help and Collectives

With self-help practices, copyright owners may sometimes appropriate for themselves a share of social gains by increasing prices generally or discriminatorily. In the latter respect, movie studios may charge video stores more for tapes, and publishers of professional journals and books may require libraries to pay more for subscriptions than individual buyers.[28] More general ways of appropriating gains from property rights may include strategic contracts,[29] license innovations (such as seat licenses now used for software[30]) and different service versions[31] (such as per transaction or blanket licenses offered by LEXIS-NEXIS[32]).

Licensing collectives can then facilitate market exchange when transaction costs between any two players are high.[33] These agencies (which include, *inter alia*, copyright collectives, rights clearance organizations and 'one stops'[34]) negotiate licenses, monitor use and collect royalties on behalf of rights owners. Indeed, the ability of licensing agencies to respond to newly enforced property rights was a primary issue in the landmark case of *Williams and Wilkins* v. *US*.[35] In this landmark decision, photocopying by the defendants National Institute of Health and National Library of Medicine was awarded fair use because it was unclear 'whether a ... clearinghouse system can be developed without legislation, and if so whether it would be desirable'.[36] However, Chief Judge Cowen in his dissent argued that the very presence of a plaintiff award 'may very well lead to a satisfactory agreement between the parties for a continuation of the photocopying by the defendant upon payment of a reasonable royalty to plaintiff'.[37]

Exemplifying the point, the US Congress first extended copyright protection to non-dramatic public performances of musical compositions in 1897. However, since music use in non-dramatic settings was exclusively live and often spontaneous, the newly granted performance rights were difficult to enforce. Unauthorized performances consequently were quite frequent. With no extraneous government effort, several prominent songwriters in 1914 established the American Society of Composers, Authors, and Publishers (ASCAP), a nonprofit cooperative agency for the monitoring and collection of performance royalties. ASCAP instituted a system of blanket licenses that enabled music halls, movie theaters and other licensees to perform any registered composition in its entire catalog for a specified contract period. It distributed blanket revenues to its members based on a monitored count of public performances.

The potentiality of appropriative copyright institutions was also recognized in 1995 in *American Geophysical Union* v. *Texaco*.[38] Publishers of scientific journals brought a class action suit against the Texaco Corporation, whose 400 to 500 scientists had engaged in unauthorized photocopying of journal articles while performing professional research. The Circuit Court concluded that copying had ambiguous effects in displacing journal subscriptions.[39] However, the court also found that publisher revenues could conceivably increase through greater opportunities for licensing, document delivery services and royalties that could be administered through the Copyright Clearance Center (CCC), an institution established in 1978 to assist in the collection of licensing fees from photocopiers.[40] Per *Texaco*, a copyright holder then is 'entitled to demand a royalty for licensing others to use its copyrighted work ... and the impact on potential licensing revenues is a proper subject for consideration in assessing the fourth [fair use] factor'.[41] The effect of strong court decisions that upheld copyright for photocopied works in facilitating the institutional rise of the CCC is documented in legal research by Kenneth Crews.[42]

New Technologies

As an engineering application of self-help, content owners may activate new technologies to protect material and augment legal prosecution. *Technological self-help* would generally implicate 'an expanding set of devices, software code, and systems designed to protect content from unauthorized copying and to facilitate electronic commerce'.[43] While the use of computer code is sometimes opposed as an intrusion upon consumer rights,[44] a substitution of code for law is often an efficient monitor, as technology may be a less expensive means for protecting content than ongoing surveillance and litigation. This is particularly likely when infringement produces ongoing damages that may redound through widespread digital copying and the ongoing disruption of legitimate market participants.

Self-help technological protection of copyrighted content began in January, 1986, when cable broadcasters (e.g., HBO and Showtime) encrypted over-the-air broadcast signals in order to force satellite dish owners to pay subscription fees to defray the costs of uninterrupted programming captured previously for free use.[45] After signals were encrypted, dish owners were forced to pay for the necessary decoding equipment. Congress itself later moved to protect the encryption technology from unauthorized circumvention.[46] Enacted in Title 47 of the US Code, the new statutory rules for access protection disallowed unauthorized access to the work in the first place. Notably, access protection rules were legally different from copyright, which protected the underlying work from infringing acts identified in 17 U.S.C. § 106.

Statutory Response

In addition to protecting the integrity of established 'self-help' technologies, law can also be used proactively to protect owner rights, particularly if enabling institutions cannot be anticipated to arise. This more directed legal strategy was deployed most extensively in the statutory framework of the Audio Home Recording Act of 1992,[47] which concerned the sale of digital audio tapes and home recorders that can perfectly copy music from CDs and other digital tape. In combined legislative action, Congress imposed levies[48] on the sale of digital audio tapes and home recorders, established a Serial Copy Management System that was to be installed to prevent the making of serial digital copies of sound recordings,[49] and outlawed its subsequent circumvention.[50] As a proactive strategy similar to the access protection of satellite signals, the Digital Millenium Copyright Act[51] of 1998 outlawed the circumvention of access protection technologies designed to protect content on the Internet,[52] as well as the commercial trafficking of devices that could be used to circumvent either access[53] or copy protection.[54]

In summation, it is the openness and interactivity of the logical interface – composed of procedural, organizational, technological and legal elements – that often enables property rights to be enforced. This openness of process can sometimes produce unforeseen outcomes, but is to be preferred to administrative decisions based on rational-comprehensive considerations.[55]

However, an open system poses an uncertainty to the fair use provisions in copyright law that should not be overlooked. Through the market harm criterion of Section 107, the primary fair use factor attempts to determine actual or potential damages to rights owners that result from infringement. With an incomplete and open logical interface, judgments under this criterion sometimes implicate far more subjectivity than many may acknowledge. Perhaps a less ambiguous manner of implementing fair use protection is to define and establish more forthrightly a domain of underlying use rights that must be protected. We now turn to this discussion.

2.4   ECONOMICS AND FAIR USE

Courts now implement the four-part test of Section 107 with a 'sensitive balancing of interests'[56] that weights and resolves opposing factors into a blunt vector of 'yes' or 'no' that frequently reduces to injunction or fair use. As there are no precise definitions to these considerations, what is ostensibly a sensitive balance is actually quite often an arbitrary one.

As alluded, the market harm test is very subjective. To avoid market harm (per *Campbell* v. *Acuff Rose*), a defendant must prove that there is no market for either unit sales or use-licensing of a particular work.[57] This evidently requires, *ab initio*, a proper definition of a market, and a subsequent finding that the defined entity does not exist for the application at hand.

No clear definition of a copyright market has ever been stated, nor is it evident what such a definition might look like. The implicit notion of a market generally used in copyright law does not comport with either basic economic theory or antitrust law, which considers actual or potential co-habitation of *economic markets* by two different identified *goods or services* that are reasonable substitutes for one another (most often measured by high cross-price elasticities of demand[58] or the reasonable potentiality of competitive entry[59]).

However, this economic definition of a market based on entry and substitution is not easily extended to *copyright markets*, where a protected work frequently has no real legal substitutes, actual or potential. Rather, legal analysis in copyright law implicates co-habitation of copyright markets by comparing different *kinds of exchanges* that may come of a protected work. Definitions of economic and copyright markets then implicate two entirely different conceptual frames. And while economic/antitrust definitions implicate consumer or producer behavior that is often quantitatively discernible – if not statistically measurable – copyright definitions are considerably more subjective.

As a second consideration, market analysis in copyright law now considers not only demonstrable actual exchanges, but also those that are *likely* to be developed.[60] In this regard, an assessment of likelihood must determine which conceivable events can reasonably be expected to evolve and which are largely imaginable. An appropriate market definition would then require some delineation of standards useful toward market definition. However, establishing such standards for a copyright market can be a tall order, even for bilateral transactions, due to the openness and inherent unpredictability of responses within the logical interface.

The Ambiguities of Market Harm

The problem of economic definition in copyright markets can be illustrated through a number of practical examples:

1. Bilateral transactions: a conceptual difficulty of market definition in a matter of bilateral exchange appeared in *Ringgold* v. *Black Entertainment*

Television, where artist Faith Ringgold sued a television network for using a poster of her work in the visual background of a program. Holding for the defense, the District Court found that the program's use did not create a market substitute and would not therefore affect the artist's ability to license her work elsewhere.[61]

The Circuit Court reversed after Ms Ringgold claimed that she had been *asked* on a number of occasions to license her work.[62] However, Ringgold did not claim to have actually *concluded* any such transaction for the work in question.[63] This outcome could have been an indication that exchange was possible but *not particularly likely*, an intuitive indicator of *market failure*. In upholding Ringgold, the court found potentiality of market exchange to be based on the act of 'asking', rather than in the likelihood of any action actually arising.

2. Licensing institutions: when licensed uses have not yet congealed, the resulting market definition is heuristic and often circular. A dissent in *Texaco* identified the problem: 'the [required] market will not crystallize unless courts reject the fair use argument ... but, under the statutory test, we cannot declare a use to be an infringement unless ... there is a market to be harmed'.[64]

    The *Texaco* dissent brought forth considerable more uncertainty about the likelihood that viable licensing arrangements would eventually result in a manner that would accommodate Texaco's actual needs. The CCC licensed only 30 percent of Texaco's journals in use, and the CCC's per transactions and blanket license had particular features that might have interfered with likelihood of licensing had Texaco tried.[65] Whether the shortfall of content and the ease of licensing might have changed was, to the dissenters, anyone's guess. There was no great assurance that licensing procedures would accommodate every reasonable concern.

3. Excluded beneficiaries: Professor Gordon warns that a 'potential user may wish to produce socially meritorious new works by using some of the copyright owner's material, yet be unable to purchase permission because the market structure prevents him from being able to capitalize on the benefits to be realized'.[66] Particularly in cyberspace, the licensing of a shared project among a distributed base of noncommercial users may be quite difficult. That is, an informal association of permanent or transitory 'cyber-pals' would face the daunting task of assigning licensing costs to contributing participants, who may have different degrees of commitment and willingness to donate to the project. Market failures in club or public goods can result if each consumer acknowledges personal gain but fails to internalize the broader gains of other parties in the common-use coalition. As a practical matter, it would be difficult to gauge what licenses will be negotiated in the first place, and which will remain sustainable through

subsequent strategizing by individuals who attempt to reduce their contributions.

4. Business models: it is difficult to judge market harm when business models are unformed or evolving. Both the District and the Circuit Court recognized the complications of disrupted business models in the *Napster* cases, where unauthorized individuals reproduced and distributed through the Internet the contents of copyrighted sound recordings.[67] The defense had contended that the Napster system could actually have stimulated record sales and improved profits.[68] For their part, the labels presented evidence that confirmed their *intent* to enter the digital services market, and argued that their *prospective* business models would be hurt.[69] The court was evidently invited to a fair bit of subjective consideration regarding actual and imaginable events.

5. Widespread harm: in examining market harm, courts in copyright cases also consider how unrestricted and widespread conduct similar to the defendant's would adversely affect the potential market for the original work.[70] This consideration explicitly moves the notch from demonstrated likelihood (however judged) to mere possibility. There is nothing particularly economic or rational about considering harms from conceivable events without due regard to their respective costs and eventual practicality.

Secondary Categorizations

Given the ambiguities of market harm, it may be appropriate to replace the existing fourth criterion of Section 107 with a clause that directly implicates three types of use, as identified and defined below. We must recognize that market forces and interfaces may evolve differently with respect to statutory protections for each.

Courts have distinguished three categories of secondary use of copyrighted materials: (1) *superseding* works that directly supplant original sales,[71] (2) *derivative* works that recast copyrighted material to a new medium 'that creators of original works would in general develop or license others to develop [in] traditional, reasonable, or likely to be developed markets'[72] and (3) *transformative* works that 'add something new, with a further purpose or different character, altering the first with new expression, meaning, or message'.[73]

In clear statutory framing, Section 101 of the Copyright Act defines the term 'derivative'.[74] Derivative works may include, *inter alia*, translations, musical arrangements, dramatizations, fictionalizations, motion picture versions, sound recordings, art reproductions, abridgments or condensations.[75]

Two definitions can be added to Section 101. Redacting the Supreme

Court's definition[76] and wording in 17 U.S.C. §107,[77] a transformative work could be similarly defined in the following manner: 'A *transformative* work is a work that adds new meaning to previous copyrighted content. Transformative works would include satires, parodies, criticisms, comments, book reviews, classroom materials, news articles, research, and sequels and adaptations that add substantial new meaning to existing characters and plots.'

Finally, an additional definition of superseding could be added to Section 101: 'A *superseding* work is a direct reproduction or performance of a work that is expected to directly substitute for actual sales or existing licensing opportunities.'

Each kind of copying presents different market consequences. Substantially similar reproductions and performances of copyrighted material may supersede or displace sales and licensing of the original product, and may create immediate financial distress. Derivative copies tend to interfere with an owner's actual or potential ability to produce work in predictable applications that have wide market appeal. When the use is transformative and accordingly implicates substantially new meaning, 'market substitution is at least less certain, and market harm may not be so readily inferred'.[78] From an economic perspective, these distinctions are of primary importance.

2.5   SUPERSEDING WORKS

In substituting one reproduction or performance technology for another, superseding copying can admittedly be economically efficient in the short run.[79] That is, copying in pirate factories or user hard drives may indeed lower production costs, drive prices toward marginal cost and lead to more efficient modes of product delivery. However, primary rights owners can be harmed in the process unless they can expropriate some gains. There is then no compelling reason why copyright should be relaxed in favor of a superseding technology, even if it is ostensibly more efficient. In a free market, copyright owners would yet have the financial incentive to adopt the more efficient production technology themselves (if unpatented), license the more efficient delivery technology (if patented), or merge or enter into a joint venture with more efficient operations.

Alternatively, copy technologies may have higher production costs than the original technology. Despite production inefficiency, these copies may survive in the market because they can underprice original product; copyists need not recover the sunk costs necessary to produce intellectual property in the first place. Although infringing production would push market prices in the direction of marginal cost, copyists nonetheless would be substituting into a less efficient production technology while simultaneously draining off contributions made toward sunk cost recovery. As both producer surplus and social welfare decline when copying is allowed, the case for copyright protection here is even more compelling

The potential for substitution and sales displacement in copyright law can be related practically to product attributes and consumer tastes in the market at hand. Among *extrinsic considerations*,[80] potentially infringing products may be gauged for sufficient similarity to underlying works; extrinsic considerations may include, *inter alia*, product design, material, subject matter and setting. By contrast, *intrinsic considerations* focus on the response and impressions of the intended user base.[81] Intrinsic considerations would include customer demographics, tastes and conceivable responses to differences in product quality or price. While the potential for infringement can be found when two works are sufficiently similar,[82] the ultimate determinant of substitutability must be the behavior of prospective buyers.

The Fourth Circuit performed in 2001 a thoughtful economic analysis in *Lyons Partnership L.P.* v. *Morris Costumes*,[83] where infringement involved the commercial rental of a dinosaur costume that resembled the famous television character 'Barney'. After the District Court found that evidence failed to support the idea that the costumes were sufficiently similar to cause confusion among the adults who actually rented them, the Circuit Court remanded with instructions for an injunction.[84] Evidence confirmed that younger children often could not tell the difference between the costumes; purchasing adults then expectedly would substitute between the two on many occasions.

In the Circuit Court opinion,

> the relevant question that courts must ask in determining whether a work has been copied is not whether society as a whole would perceive the works to be similar in an aesthetic sense, but rather whether the works are so similar that the introduction of the alleged copy into the market will have an adverse effect on the demand for the protected work.[85]

Consequently, 'the economically important views are those of the young children ... Even if adults can easily distinguish between costumes, a child's belief that they are one and the same could deprive Barney's owners of profits'.[86] Considering again the anticipated responses of young children, similar approaches regarding audience perception, market definition, and sales displacement appeared in *Ideal Toy Corp.* v. *Fab-Lu Ltd.*[87] and *Medias & Co., Inc.* v. *Ty, Inc.*[88]

The three decisions pass the litmus test for sound economic reasoning. Each considered product characteristics, intended consumers, the practical nature of decision-making and the resulting likelihood of product substitution by the copy. Each step of the process admits room for important evidence and obliges litigants to recognize important commercial consequences. Plaintiffs might have improved their case had they provided more direct evidence (e.g., surveys) to confirm empirically that adult buyers would switch to product look-alikes if they felt children would not notice. For their part, defendants might have questioned the absence of such evidence.

No Market Substitution

The famous case of *MCA* v. *Wilson* represents a good example of a failure to consider properly the nature of competition and product substitution.[89] Appearing in an adult musical *Let My People Come* in the New York night club, The Village Gate, actors performed and recorded 'The Cunnilingus Champion of Company C', which was a bawdy rendition of the wartime classic 'Bugle Boy' with the same underlying melody.

Upholding the District Court, the Second Circuit in 1982 ruled that the two songs qualified as competitors in the entertainment field and that 'Champion' was therefore an infringement. In the court's notion of competition, both songs were performed on the stage, marketed in record stores and sold in printed copies; the songs were therefore market rivals.[90] Testimony, accepted as credible by the trial court, indicated that 'Champion' was made to sound like 'Bugle Boy' to create publicity.

By economic standards, these songs assuredly were not competitors. Real competition between two products depends upon the willingness of prospective buyers to interchange them. A sophisticated dissent made the proper economic points:

> The issue is not whether the parody uses the same media as the copyrighted work – most parodies do – but whether it is 'capable of serving as a substitute for the original' (A. Latman, *The Copyright Law*, 215 (5th ed. 1979)), which depends on demand and product overlap rather than on the market in which the two products are vended. Applying this correct standard, it is eminently clear that the two works respond to wholly differing demands and that a customer for one would not buy the other in its place. A raucous and explicitly sexual satire is not a substitute for the innocence of Bugle Boy.[91]

More than a decade later, Alan Katz and Chris Wrinn wrote a book *The Cat NOT in the Hat* that depicted the events of the O.J. Simpson trial using the famed poetic doggerel of children's author Dr Seuss. Nothing was taken from original Seuss but trademarked illustrations (most famously, the elongated hat) and the author's poetic style. After the District Court enjoined the book's cover and illustrations based on trademark dilution, the Ninth Circuit Court in 1995 went further to establish harm to the copyright.[92]

The court held that Katz and Wrinn made 'no effort to create a transformative work with new expression, meaning or message'.[93] Though the two authors copied none of Seuss's words and the plaintiff did not attempt to prove displaced sales, the court inferred market harm from lost goodwill and reputation that could accrue to the dead author's estate.[94] Unsubstantiated as a practical matter by empirical evidence, this potential loss of goodwill was held to outweigh unrecovered expenses that redounded to the publisher, as well as the consumer loss resulting from a suppressed product.[95] Here too, the imagined market harm has no relation to likely consumer behavior. There was no evidence presented, nor does it seem likely, that the Seuss book would have lost readership or goodwill among its primary intended audience of school children, teachers and parents.[96]

2.6 DERIVATIVE WORKS

Turning to derivative works, secondary copies do not necessarily supersede sales of original materials, and at times actually may promote them. However, in adapting the basic message of a copyrighted work for representation in a different media (e.g., books to screenplays, prints to T-shirts), derivatives take substantially from the heart of a copyrighted product and may interfere with the primary owner's rights to penetrate the new market himself. Consequently, the danger of unauthorized derivative uses may affect how a copyrighted work is subsequently developed, and conceivably how it is originated.

Courts generally have upheld the right of copyright owners to receive payments for derivative uses of their works and have explicitly rejected the suggestion that a positive impact on primary sales of their works negates entitlement.[97] Indeed, 'a speculated increase in ... sales as a consequence of ... infringement would not call the fair use defense into play as a matter of law. The owner of the copyright is in the best position to balance the prospect of increased sales against revenue from a license'.[98] The Supreme Court made the point more concretely; even if a 'film producer's appropriation of a composer's previously unknown song ... turns the song into a commercial success, the boon to the song does not make the film's ... copying fair'.[99] This ruling adheres to the basic point of Coase that a fair market value can generally be established in negotiations.[100]

However, the appropriate legal means for protecting derivatives has been sometimes contested. Judge Alex Kozinski and attorney Christopher Newman suggested that injunctions on derivative works could be abandoned in favor of liability rules that would establish reasonable royalties based on market benchmarks or demonstrated damages,[101] and attorney Judith Bresler now proposes limited considerations for derivative works of fine art.[102] Indeed, courts themselves have recently acknowledged the conceivable usefulness of liability rules to facilitate copyright transfer to derivative compilations in *New York Times Co.* v. *Tasini*,[103] and *Greenberg* v. *National Geographic Society*.[104] The proponents of expedited licensing do have a point; immediate injunctions discourage or suppress some secondary applications, and it is unclear whether derivative license revenues will increase the likelihood of any primary investment, which must often quicken well before secondary markets congeal.

Conceding dubious incentive effects on most primary investments, William Landes and Richard Posner point out that copyright protection in derivative markets enables *coordination effects* that permit more efficient development of the product sequence.[105] For if secondary rights are exclusively controlled for a time, major producers – such as movie studios and record labels – can be expected to synchronize better their production and marketing operations. Without protection of derivatives, primary producers might purposely but inefficiently delay product launches simply to ensure that secondary products are lined up for immediate release and entry. Alternatively, primary producers may close gaps by speeding up secondary production. Made necessary by the lack of copyright protection, the resulting strategizing may nonetheless be economically inefficient.

Seminal articles by Arnold Plant[106] and Stephen Breyer[107] unwittingly illustrate the issue. Both articles seem to suggest that copyright for books can be abandoned if original publishers can warehouse large inventories for the purpose of deterring or competing vigorously with eventual copyists. Of course, such pre-emptive stockpiling represents a considerable expense that may reduce substantially the profitability of book publishing in the first place. The process would also heighten publisher risk, as the additional costs of stockpiling might not be recovered if subsequent sales underperform initial expectations. The additional costs posed by preemptive strategizing and lack of coordination also undermine Stewart Sterk's economics-based suggestion that derivative rights are justified *only* when projected returns from the original work cannot recover production costs, and the ensuing returns from the license are sufficient to make up the deficit.[108]

There are two additional reasons why property rules are generally preferable to liability rules for licensing of derivative works. First, the ensuing rules will have precedential value. For example, if Warner Bros. were permitted to take the Harry Potter novels for their highly successful movies, all movie producers – as well as game, doll and clothing manufacturers – would also come to claim easy access to a whole drove of subsequent best-selling content from Potter, possibly including sequels. If derivative markets are not protected, market onslaught by such secondary works would be overwhelming but would promulgate no real efficient deployment of cultural resources. Second, derivative infringements now entail new digital uses. It may then be particularly impractical to establish the necessary license benchmarks here. It would often require consideration of imaginary or emerging business models in markets that have yet to congeal.

To the point of the discussion, 'concerns are deeper than just audience confusion. Intellectual property law is also concerned with the chaos that can occur with multiple authors pursuing their vision of some common material. Hence, copyright law serves to give the author exclusive right to control all derivative work'.[109] With legal protection of derivative works, the copyright holder may 'curb the development of such a derivative market by refusing to license a copyrighted work or by doing so only on terms the copyright owner finds acceptable'.[110]

However, while copyright must extend to derivative works to allow coordination economies in the initial years, there is no theoretical reason why all forms of derivative protection must necessarily run the full lifetime of the original copyright. Indeed, considerable social gains could be had if the right to produce some derivative works (particularly movies, plays and book sequels) could be spun off at some earlier point. This temptation nonetheless raises three practical concerns. First, a protected class of derivatives must be carefully defined, e.g., would space shifts, compilations, abridgements, translations, screenplays, sequels and hard merchandise equally qualify for reduced protection? Second, the primary owner must be entitled to moral rights of attribution and integrity that may permit her to identify or disassociate with the new work.[111] Third, to avoid the legal difficulty of later uses of a split copyright, the secondary user can have no copyright in a derivative work. An expedited derivative use must then be awarded the limited status that is now granted to a secondary mechanical reproduction of a musical composition, which can be taken from a previously recorded work without permission but enjoys no copyright protection.[112]

2.7 TRANSFORMATIVE WORKS

In contrast to superseding works that reduce original sales and derivative works that displace predictable licensing opportunities, transformative uses may build on previous works to create an understood context from which advocates may more powerfully criticize or comment on social beliefs and institutions, e.g., the reuse of a patriotic or religious melody can add punch to a criticism aimed at a government or church. Sometimes tasteless, transformative uses have included a number of song parodies,[113] a comedic reuse of a photographic pose,[114] a music collage involving a U2 recording,[115] the Seussian *Cat NOT in the Hat*,[116] adult versions of Disney,[117] a burlesque of the movie *Gaslight*,[118] a satiric sequel of *Gone with the Wind*,[119] and postmodern visual art that appropriated recognized images for social criticism.[120]

As mentioned, the use of implanted public icons may actually increase the emotional impact of political and social comment, particularly if explored by artists and musicians not given to scholarly or prosaic expression. For example, Alice Randall criticized southern history and racial attitudes in *Gone with the Wind* far better as an author than she might have as an historian, and Jimi Hendrix protested militarism far better with his Woodstock version of 'The Star Spangled Banner' than he could ever have in a speech or leaflet. In this respect, the Supreme Court held that a restriction on the form of communication – regarding a T-shirt that said 'Fuck the Draft' – amounted to a restriction on speech itself by defusing the speaker's anger.[121] It is then unrealistic to contend that transformative artists who access a work do so simply to 'avoid the drudgery in working up something fresh',[122] or that they may otherwise find an equally effective weapon by finding a different original that would be willingly licensed.[123]

A parody that pokes fun at an original work is a quintessential example of a work with a new meaning. Indeed, Justice Souter ruled in *Campbell* v. *Acuff-Rose*,[124] that a parody of Roy Orbison's 'Pretty Woman' shed light on the blandness and easy sexuality of the earlier work and, as a comedic form of criticism, is transformative.[125] The judge distinguished between a critical work and other derivative works generally protected by copyright; critical transformations suppress demand while derivative works usurp it.[126] Considering prospective transactions costs, Souter stated that 'the [limited] likelihood that creators of original works will license critical reviews or lampoons of their own productions removes such uses from the very notion of a potential licensing market'.[127]

Though protective of parody, courts have generally held that transformative works that use existing works as weapons to direct criticism at institutions and social norms do not qualify for fair use. In *Williams* v. *Columbia Broadcasting Systems*,[128] defendants used the comic figure of Mr Bill to ridicule attitudes in the US Navy. Holding for the plaintiffs, the court ruled that a transformative work 'does not gain protection of the fair use doctrine if it merely uses the protected work as a means to ridicule another object [citing *Campbell* v. *Acuff Rose*, 510 at 580]'.[129]

The idea that a targeted parody of the original work is appropriately exempt, while more general satiric or critical use is not, is consistent with Richard Posner's distinction between 'target' and 'weapons' applications; the former criticizes the original work while the latter uses the original to criticize something else.[130] Posner, too, would protect only the parody, as he contends the satiric use would predictably be licensed in a voluntary transaction and therefore 'there is no objection to letting the market make the tradeoff'.[131]

Posner's distinction regarding the transactional ease of licensing satire seems contrived. Parody or satire, copyright owners can be expected to strongly resist licensing secondary uses involving sexual or lowbrow comedy, political content, artistic style, musical idiom or cultural/historical criticism that they find tasteless, disrespectful, inartistic or impolitic. They may invoke some expanded idea of moral rights beyond the limited rights of attribution and integrity that the copyright statute now extends in 17 U.S.C. § 106(a). As such, transactions costs may be equally formidable obstacles that block a wider variety of transformations. From an economic perspective, the case for a balanced resolution of these alternative forms of expression may resolve negotiating difficulty and reduce producer uncertainty.

The Supreme Court itself is ambiguous on the distinction regarding the special protection of parody. Indeed, the Supreme Court acknowledged the potential for a wider definition of fair use in *Campbell* v. *Acuff Rose*, albeit fleetingly in a footnote.[132] Yet the court elsewhere makes a distinction: 'parody needs to mimic an original to make its point, and so has some claim to use the creation of its victim's imagination, whereas satire can stand on its own two feet and so requires justification for the very act of borrowing'.[133] This dictum would form the foundation for the later ruling in *Williams* v. *Columbia Broadcasting System*.[134]

Economic Analysis

Any process that awards injunctions against transformative works with new meaning necessarily suppresses new product and, in so doing, produces outcomes that are economically inefficient. If published, such works would widen consumer choice, contribute to political awareness and heighten cultural sensibility. Moreover, transformative works with new meanings tend to reach largely new audiences, and do not predictably displace sales of primary goods or interfere with later undertakings of derivative licenses. Accordingly, it is unlikely that any creator's incentive to produce primary work depends on whether a small class of transformative uses can be published or not, or that an idiosyncratic use will cause producers to modify their coordination tactics or business models.

Other aspects of the present fair use test are problematic for transformative undertakings. Though Congress 'eschewed a rigid, bright line approach to fair use',[135] the present doctrine of fair use treats a commercial nature as a negative factor. Carrying a negative factor, commercial publishers who are unsure of clearing this and other legal hurdles may shy away from publishing transformative works. By contrast, a facilitating attitude toward commercial presentation may actually encourage wider production and dissemination of artistic comment and criticism.

As a third complicating consideration, creators and publishers may face a daunting criteria in the third fair use factor, which is related to the allowable amount and substantiality of the taking. Courts now do not require that takings for parody be minimal; rather, a non-minimal taking is permitted to present a reasonable 'conjuring up' of a copyrighted work to make its wit recognizable.[136] However, the application of the 'conjuring up' rule can be highly subjective and is economically problematic; additional material that exceeds the necessary conjuring may broaden or deepen the punch of a critical work. Moreover, works that borrow excessively create tedium and may suffer harsh review and reduced demand. The market then has forces that constrain conjuring to efficient levels that widen the appeal of a secondary work.

As a famous example of the last point, a published comic book in 1978 showed famous Disney characters engaged in sex and drug use. Although a parody, the work was enjoined nonetheless because the defendants took more 'than was necessary to place firmly in the reader's mind the parodied work and those specific attributes that [were] to be satirized'.[137] In attempting to gauge the reader's mind, the court here failed to consider the possibility that the added material could have actually been humorous to the intended audience, and therefore capable of increasing the appeal of the new product. As a general consideration, the matter begs a rule that would allow a broader variety of uses than the present fair use rule.

The upshot is clear. As illustrated by the legal banter in *SunTrust*,[138] present legal distinctions regarding commerciality, conjuring, and parody/satire are often ambiguous and may then depress incentives for presentation or publication of speech and expression. Moreover, as overseers of creative processes, transformative artists and publishers should be encouraged to offer their best interpretation rather than mince words with clipped messages that may diminish intended meaning, market appeal, and a strong adherence to the First Amendment.[139]

2.8   ECONOMIC DAMAGES

Infringements of copyright are often stopped through the issuance of preliminary injunctions. Generally, the single most important prerequisite for the issuance of a preliminary injunction is the showing of irreparable harm.[140] While courts outside of copyright cases have found that contended irreparable harm must be 'likely and imminent, not remote and speculative', and that the injury must be something beyond simple monetary damages,[141] the task in copyright is considerably less onerous. In the copyright domain, 'a showing of a prima facie case of copyright infringement or reasonable likelihood of success on the merits usually raises a presumption of irreparable harm for preliminary injunction purposes'.[142] The requirements to make a prima facie case are simple; plaintiff must show copyright ownership, and that defendants have engaged in unauthorized copying or violated exclusive owner rights.[143] Moreover, 'once a prima facie case of copyright infringement is established, the allegations of irreparable injury need not be very detailed because such injury is *generally assumed* [emphasis added].[144]

From an economic perspective, there is no reason to believe that acts of unauthorized copying necessarily lead to *irreparable* market harm to the original rights owner. Nonetheless, the use of injunctions and statutory damages may be economically justified for superseding and derivative applications. Superseded businesses may be hurt to the core by repeat infringement, which can be widely distributed in a worldwide market. *Ex post* economic damages would be difficult for plaintiffs to measure and courts to confirm.[145] Moreover, measuring damage to actual and potential markets from derivative infringements would be equally, if not more, difficult, as these markets may take some time to congeal.

Per 17 U.S.C. §504, may reasonably award for copyright infringement either actual damages or defendant profits, or statutory damages.[146] Judge Richard A. Posner offers a sophisticated rationale for the compensation structure:

> If the infringer makes greater profits than the copyright owner lost ... the owner is allowed to capture the additional profit even though it does not represent a loss to him. It may seem wrong to penalize the infringer for his superior efficiency and give the owner a windfall. But it discourages infringement. By preventing infringers from obtaining any net profit, it makes any would-be infringer negotiate directly with the owner of a copyright that he wants to use, rather than bypass the market.[147]

From a perspective of short-run allocative efficiency, any compensation that exceeds actual damages deters efficient transfers that would otherwise take place. Posner correctly points out that the higher penalty is nonetheless useful to dissuade brazen and repeated violators who may otherwise profit from infringement, but who scoff at negotiating. This could be noticeably found among famous artists who may prey upon unknown writers. From a long-run perspective, the additional protection is economically efficient if it can provide greater security and stimulate additional production.

Granting the need for strong deterrence of superseding and derivative works, we must nonetheless acknowledge that transformative works may be dissuaded if punishment is excessive. As a vehicle for new meaning, transformative work incorporates considerable social value. Moreover, higher transactions costs can be reasonably expected for transform use, as engaged parties attempt to assess the relative added worth of a work with little chance of displacement, but some considerable taking of moral right.

Based on a distinction by Haddock and McChesney,[148] copyright judges may well distinguish transformative works based on a distinction in tort law between trespass and nuisance.[149] There is no balancing in trespass of relative costs and benefits; the defendant will be subject to liability regardless of whether he caused actual financial harm to the other party. Courts in trespass actions then award injunctions and punitive damages and make no exception for *de minimis* harm. By contrast, nuisance is actionable only if demonstrable harm outweighs utility gained; paid damages are based on economic loss. In nuisance cases, 'failure to show actual damages ... usually results in the denial of all relief because of the failure to satisfy the "substantial harm" requirement for liability'.[150] So long as damages are paid, injunctions are rare.

The authors point out that assets which can be appropriated through efficient negotiation are best protected by property rules, while those that may encounter predictable licensing difficulties should be subject to liability rules and *ex post* compensation. The key determinant would be the expected transactions cost needed to obtain agreement. Based on expected transactions costs, it is then entirely reasonable to consider different means of compensating rights holders, depending on whether or not copying is transformative, market exchange is not predictable and negotiation is 'thin'.

The distinction regarding transactions costs can implicate transformative works. In view of predictable negotiation difficulties, courts may forego injunctions and limit plaintiff awards for transformative infringement to actual damages or reasonable royalties, which correspond to demonstrated lost profits or foregone license fee.[151] Plaintiff rights to receive statutory damages for transformative uses may be entirely restricted.[152]

From a short-run economic perspective, efficient compensations for transformative uses are efficiently based upon actual damages. Moreover, if transformative infringements are compensated with amounts that exceed the true social cost (i.e., actual damages), it is difficult to believe that such confiscatory assessments will elsewhere stimulate more primary works or facilitate their coordination. Rather, higher prices may actually depress the level of transformative creation. Accordingly, compensation here would reasonably be based on the short-run optimum, i.e. identifiable actual damages.

2.9   THE LIABILITY OPTION

I shall now argue that Section 107 might be improved if Congress establishes *optional liability rules* that secondary users may attempt to invoke for some uses that are demonstrably transformative, but do not qualify for fair use. Tbough problematic, fair use is not to be eliminated.

The motivation for a liability rule is based on the economic and political notion that transformative works must have more protective certainty and a widened market outlet. Moreover, there is a moral notion that primary rights owners are equitably entitled to just deserts for contributions made to the value of a work,[153] but are not entitled to direct or censor the work of others. In implementing liability rules, we can arbitrate royalties elsewhere as in the present copyright system.[154] The suggested process is also similar to common procedure in patent law, where injunctions are rare and patent infringement cases are generally resolved with court-determined royalties that are based on 15 judicial criteria.[155]

The suggested modification of Section 107 would require two key modifications in Title 17: i.e., a list of qualifying transformative works must be defined and administrative procedures must be established.

Definitions

We must modify Section 101 to establish a definition of transformative works that must be coverable through liability rules. Stated above, a statutory definition would establish a precise list of uses that qualify as transformative.[156] This statutory definition would parallel the statutory definition of derivative works that now appears in 17 U.S.C. § 101.

A necessary factor to determining what is a transformative element in the list of uses is the infusion of new meaning, rather than artistic creativity per se. The concept of 'new meaning' evidently admits some subjective judgment, but is preferable to other related concepts that have been used or suggested elsewhere as a justification for fair use. Suggested vagaries from judges and writers have included allowances for 'productive copying',[157] 'socially laudable purposes',[158] copying for 'a different purpose from the original',[159] 'the prevailing understanding of the community',[160] or 'customary practice'.[161] With this imposing lineup, 'one cannot help but suspect that, as a test, "transformative in purpose" provides little more guidance to a judge than would be supplied by his or her own set of personal values'.[162] Seemingly confirming the last point, Judge Leval stated in *Texaco* that photocopying of a single article might be fair if a scientist could avoid carrying a whole journal, but would not be fair if used to save space in one's filing cabinets.[163] As a final point, the 'community understanding' and 'customary practice' standards of Lloyd Weinrib provide no ethical vision and would apparently justify unauthorized downloading of music files on college campuses where social mores may be less accommodative of copyright law.

The purpose of the statutory definition of transformative works then is to include as many works that are practical, without necessarily committing to all possibilities. Even if not now qualified for fair use, a libertarian may hope at least that all satires, parodies and criticisms can qualify for consideration under an optional liability rule. However, framers may need to distinguish satires and parodies that directly modify the copyrighted work from critical compilations of primary material that is itself quoted directly. In the latter case, it may be necessary to limit such secondary takings to not allow reproductions (i.e., public performance, display and streaming), so to eliminate the threat of a simpler commercial compilation based on a collection of existing material. Framers must also decide how to handle transformative uses for advertising, where cartoons, jingles, character names, etc., are used to convey a commercial message that does not shed new meaning on the work or the surrounding culture. As evidenced by the 'Rocky', 'Godfather', and 'Harry Potter' sequences, sequels may also be particularly difficult to gauge for transformativeness; sequels may then appropriately remain as derivative works.

Arbitration

The administrative process for royalty setting can be modeled upon arbitration procedures negotiated between ASCAP and the US Department of Justice.[164] We may allow new arbitration procedures to be implemented through statutory terms in Section 107.

Any user of a copyrighted work may request arbitration from a designated magistrate to determine a reasonable royalty for a particular use of a previously published work:

1. The prospective user must submit a written request to the copyright owner or her designated agent.
2. The request must be activated before the initiation of any litigation regarding the particular use.
3. Upon receipt of a written request, the copyright owner must within sixty days advise the user in writing of a reasonable license fee, or the information that it would require to make such a determination.
4. If the parties are unable to reach agreement within sixty days from the date when the request is received, the user may apply to the court for a determination of a reasonable fee retroactive to the date of the request.
5. If legally agreed upon, the court may attempt to resolve disputes through arbitration instituted under the jurisdiction of a specially appointed court magistrate.
6. A magistrate shall determine actual damages or reasonable royalties based on prevailing market rates established for similar uses of the copyrighted material. A court expert may be appointed.
7. Arbitrators may establish no fee for any secondary work unless it is listed as transformative, as defined by 17 U.S.C. § 101.

8. Arbitrator decisions regarding the nature of the transformative work may be appealed to the District Court at large.
9. Arbitrator decisions regarding the size of the adjudicated royalty may not be appealed.

Per the terms of item 6, arbitrators (or their experts) may set licensing fees in a number of manners, beginning with actual financial harm or lost licensing fee. The plaintiff is obliged exclusively to prove the former. Regarding lost license fees, arbitrators and experts may obtain data from licensing databases, such as the Royalty Source Intellectual Property Database,[165] which gathers data on licensing from public financial records, news releases and other articles and references. Parties may also subscribe to periodicals and organize conferences related to the matter of licensing, which might be organized by professional organizations such as the Licensing Executives' Society.

Instead of gathering data and appointing results, arbitrators alternatively may deploy procedures that are now used in buyout valuations among joint ventures. One suggested method is as follows.[166] Each disputant must retain a valuation expert to value the work in question, or measure the resulting market harm. If the two valuations are within a designated percentage of one another, the average of the two is a conclusive value. Otherwise, a third valuation is necessarily performed by an appointed third party. The appropriate valuation is the average of the third valuation and the disputant fee that is closest to it.

Were they adopted, liability rules based on reasonable royalties or actual damages might have been reasonably deployed in a number of cases. For example, in *SunTrust*,[167] the District Court recognized that the copyright owners administered a well-established market for licensed sequels that could have been extended to provide a reasonable royalty benchmark for *The Wind Done Gone*.[168] Alternatively, using data from the Royalty Source Intellectual Property Database, this author suggests that characters or plots of existing works are appropriately licensed with royalties that range between 8 and 10 percent of book revenues.[169]

As another example, a reasonable apportionment of royalties for reproductions and performances of recognized melodies in transformative musical compositions would be evenly divided between the original composer and the new lyricist. This would award equally the contributions made by the composer of the melody and the transformative lyricist who creates the imaginative change in words that sells the work to a new audience.

As a general rule, arbitrated licensing fees can be expected to range between 5 and 10 percent of the new sales price. Admittedly, a number of allowed uses may go badly compensated for lack of a good benchmark (although no price seems as deliberately ignorant of the market as the present choice of null or infinite price – i.e., fair use and injunction). This said, business practices and institutions will have the greatest opportunity to fill out only if exchangeable property rights are first defined, possibly with court encouragement. By establishing respective rights for creators to exchange in free or administered markets, courts then establish the requisite institutional support for complementary databases and negotiating agents. Arbitration of reasonable royalties then provides the greatest opportunity and incentive for these logical operations to 'thicken'.

2.10   AN INFORMATION COMMONS?

The issue of fair use – particularly on the Internet — is related to the academic vision of an 'information commons' – i.e., 'a rich public domain of materials [with] a freely useable set of information that an individual can draw upon for any purpose whatsoever'.[170] While presenting a captivating vision, the academic advocates of an information commons often ignore the harmful market consequences of the behaviors that they would protect as 'fair', and often seem hostile to the general idea of copyright. If free takings are to continue, advocates must appreciate the nuances of property rights, market exchange and the particular technology at hand.

Licensing and Noncommercial Uses

As a key means of enabling human communication, digital technology allows users to transform and combine artistic and literary material into new presentations, or otherwise comment on it through email, web site, or cyber-chat. Licensing requirements in a number of these team applications would be idiosyncratic. Historically, licensing agencies have confined themselves to individual and period-specific applications related to a single work, or a body of related works. For large and frequent users in businesses and public institutions, adaptive licensing mechanisms resulted from the continued efforts and negotiations of related parties determined to spend the time necessary to make the system happen.

However, it is not clear what kind of licensing infrastructure could be expected to prevail for content in open-ended communities of noncommercial netizens. For such applications, particular uses of works may be repeated once or a small number of times. It is arguable whether accommodating negotiations would be practical, whether intermediary institutions would evolve, whether the resulting licensing structure would be efficient or whether members of open groups would willingly pay fees for every application. The resulting system, or lack of system, may deter teams of noncommercial users from making interesting adaptations and uses of other material. The Internet would then lose some of its best capabilities to enable group communications among a networked population.

Cyber-Art

Interesting challenges to fair use involve fan fiction,[171] multimedia art,[172] song 'mashups',[173] and edited movies.[174] Aided by a computer network, a distributed base of users can freely post material on web sites, or modify open source files bearing programmed text, art or music. While commercial users should be expected to pay license fees for their artistic efforts in these new areas, careful exemptions in statute and common law might be worked out for noncommercial interactive work

As a first matter, the noncommercial web posting of original fan fiction involving some copyrighted characters and universes provide opportunity for considerably new expression and impose little direct market harm upon original right owners. Since the transactions costs of licensing different contributions here seems prohibitive, noncommercial fan fiction may then reasonably qualify for fair use in most instances.

Noncommercial multimedia art might also be reasonable fair use if reproductions are saved back to one web site. This enables users to access the material, stream content and make additional contributions without capturing a permanent copy. This restriction would seem necessary, otherwise, 'artists' can design and distribute multimedia art throughout the web without restraint.

Song 'mashups' and edited movies are more problematic. Without careful definition of legal practices, a 'mashup' could involve a large sampling of the core of one song, with beginning and end material taken from a second. Movies would suffer from the same editorial encroachments. It would appear that some clear limits be established on the permissible taking (e.g., percentage of total) from a particular song or movie.

Chat Rooms

As another matter for a commons, we can ponder the ability of the Internet to enable cyber-discussion of prominent news issues by citizens who might otherwise lack the ability to write a well-researched critical piece.

Advocates of an 'information commons' might start out by specifying rules to enable the common use of news articles from diverse newspapers. Evidently, cyber-discussion of news stories would allow informal associations of citizens the right to exchange views on breaking news or to criticize the bias of the primary source. However, District Courts have rejected noncommercial takings of both news and content posted for cyber-chat after finding that the original copyist simply posted great amounts of material without adding substantial commentary.[175] Logically, if material can be so posted in the stated hope that criticism follows, there is no limit to the amount of takings from the original.

Accordingly, advocates of a commons may do best by offering to newspapers a voluntary contract, much like an open source license,[176] which permits a group of private citizens the right to make available the entire content of an unaltered news article for purposes of cyber-chat among its membership. At least four conditions would be needed to make the offer attractive to copyright owners. First, a limited number of takings from a newspaper or periodical would be allowable. Second, the permitted reproduction can be posted for some number of days to a web site, but cannot be distributed to potential respondents via email nor otherwise made available for reproduction on hard drives. Third, users might reasonably be required to hyperlink to the newspaper URL (web site address) if free access is available.

Finally, the contributing newspaper must necessarily receive – without payment – the right of first refusal for the resulting cyber-session (with user anonymity protected). This would include the right for the user to reframe it and make the content available for later commercial gain in a proprietary archive. By archiving public conversations with newspapers, we extend the public record for later researchers. We here provide to the newspaper some compensation for maintenance of the archive, as well as for the copyright to the original material.

2.11   CONCLUSION

As more information is learned, initial categorizations of works for fair and expedited use may prove problematic, and the borders that delineate rights and exemptions for particular protections can then be suitably modified. The perspective on the role of law and economic policy-making is purposely incrementalist and experimentalist; the game is open-ended and relevant information is slowly revealed in the play. It is an appreciation of this interactive logicality that safeguards the system, and is a concept that an economist would endorse.

NOTES

1.   *Campbell* v. *Acuff Rose*, 510 U.S. 569, 580 (1994); 114 S. Ct. 1164.
2.   *SunTrust Bank* v. *Houghton Mifflin*, 136 F. Supp. 2d 1357, 1372 (2001).
3.   268 F. 3d 1257, 1268–9 (11th Cir. 2001).
4.   Supra note 1.

5. 'The [Supreme] Court suggests that the aim of parody is "comic effect or ridicule", but it then proceeds to discuss parody more expansively in terms of its "commentary" on the original. We choose to take the broader view' (supra note 3, at 1272).

6. A. Kozinski and C. Newman, 'What's So Fair about Fair Use?', *Journal of the Copyright Society of the U.S.A.* 513, 525 (2000).

7. Such expansion of the right to receive compensation for the use of intellectual property is particularly appropriate in commercial markets, where market prices signal value and implicitly assign producer resources among contending uses. *See also* P. Goldstein, *Copyright's Highway: From Gutenberg to the Celestial Jukebox* (Palo Alto, CA: Stanford University Press, 1994); J.C. Ginsburg, 'Authors and Users in Copyright', 45 *Journal of the Copyright Society of the U.S.A.* 1 (1997); R.P. Merges, 'The End of Friction? Property Rights and Contract in the Newtonian World of On-Line Commerce', 12 *Berkeley Technology Law Journal* 115 (1997).

8. P.N. Leval, 'Toward a Fair Use Standard', 103 *Harvard Law Review* 1105, 1132 (1990) ('there may be a strong public interest in the publication of the secondary work [and] the copyright owner's interest may be adequately protected by an award of damages for whatever infringement is found'); A. Kozinski and C. Newman, supra note 6 ('The best way to promote production of valuable intellectual works is to give authors and inventors the ability to demand and receive compensation for the values they create ... The best way to do this is to grant property rights that give their products exchange value.')

9. Supra note 1, at 578, n. 10.

10. L.P. Loren, 'Redefining the Market Failure Approach to Fair Use in an Era of Copyright Permission Systems', 5 *Journal of Intellectual Property Law* 1, 6 (1997).

11. M.A. Lemley, 'The Economics of Improvement in Intellectual Property Law', 75 *Texas Law Review* 989, 996.

12. 'Without a legal monopoly too little of the information will be produced, but with the legal monopoly too little of the information will be used.' (R. Cooter and T. Ulen, *Law and Economics* 145 (Reading, MA: Addison-Wesley, 1988)).

13. 'Because intellectual property rights impose costs upon the public, the intellectual property laws can be justified by the public goods argument only to the extent that they do on balance encourage enough creation and dissemination of new works to offset these costs. One of the reasons that intellectual property rights are limited in scope, in duration, and in effect is precisely in order to balance these costs and benefits' (supra note 11, 997).

14. 17 U.S.C. § 107 (2000).

15. *Rosemont Enterprises Inc.* v. *Random House Inc.*, 366 F. 2d 303, 306 (2d Cir. 1966), *cert. denied*, 385 U.S. 1009, 87 S. Ct. 714, 17 L. Ed. 2d 546 (1967).

16. 17 U.S.C. § 107 (2000).

17. The purpose and intent implicates the introduction to Section 107, which identifies a category of uses of key concern to the drafters of the Copyright Act. The distinction regarding commerciality may sometimes be ambiguous. *See Worldwide Church of God* v. *Philadelphia Church of God, Inc.*, 227 F. 3d 1110 (9th Cir. 2000), *Marobie-FL, Inc.* v. *National Assoc. of Fire Equipment Distributors*, 983 F. Supp. 1167 (N.D. Ill. 1997).

18. 'The scope of fair use is more limited with respect to non-factual works than factual works; the former necessarily involves more originality and creativity than the reporting of facts' (*New Era Publications* v. *Carol Publishing Group*, 904 F. 2d at 157). 'Factual works are believed to have a greater public value and unauthorized uses of them are more readily tolerated by copyright law' (*Salinger* v. *Random House, Inc.* 811 F. 2d at 96).

19. Generally, 'the larger the volume (or the greater the importance) of what is taken, the ... less likely that a taking will qualify as a fair use' (Leval, supra note 8, at 1122). However, 'there are no absolute rules as to how much of a copyrighted work may be copied and still be considered a fair use' (*Maxtone Graham* v. *Burtchaell*, 803 F. 2d 1253 (2d Cir. 1986), *cert. denied*, 481 U.S. 1059, 107 S. Ct. 2201, 95 L. Ed. 2d 856 (1987)).

20. Ronald H. Coase, 'The Problem of Social Costs', 3 *Journal of Law and Economics* 1 (1960).

21. Transaction costs would broadly include drafting, bargaining, performance safeguarding, renegotiation, monitoring and enforcement. See O.E. Williamson, *The Economic*

Institutions of Capitalism 20–22 (Glencoe, NY: Free Press, 1985).

22. Wendy J. Gordon, 'Fair Use as Market Failure: A Structural and Economic Analysis of the Betamax Case and Its Predecessors', 82 *Columbia Law Review* 1600 (1982). The author continues: 'Only where the desired transfer of resource use is unlikely to take place spontaneously, or where special circumstances such as market flaws impair the market's ordinary ability to serve as a measure of how resources should be allocated, is there an economic need for allowing nonconcensual transfer' (ibid., 1615). A similar point is made by W.M. Landes and R.A. Posner, 'An Economic Analysis of Copyright Law', 18 *Journal of Legal Studies* 325, 357 (1989).

23. E.W. Kitch, 'Can the Internet Shrink Fair Use?', 78 *Nebraska Law Review* 880, 881–3 (1999); T.W. Bell, 'Fair Use vs. Fared Use: The Impact of Automated Rights Management on Copyright's Fair Use Doctrine', 76 *North Carolina Law Review* 557 (1998).

24. 'Overly influenced by market failure theory and misled by evidence of licensing practices, courts have failed to distinguish between markets that should belong to authors and those that should not … . A fair use may be seen not as an encroachment on the rights of an owner, but rather as a use that does not belong to the owner to begin with' (M. Africa, 'The Misuse of Licensing Evidence in Fair Use Analysis: New Technologies, New Markets, and the Courts', 88 *California Law Review* 1145, 1150, 1152–3 (2000)).

25. A.P. Winslow, 'Rapping on a Revolving Door: An Economic Analysis of Parody and Campbell v. Acuff Rose', 69 *Southern California Law Review* 767, 783 (1996). Lydia Loren succinctly characterizes 'implied consent' as a market outcome where 'significant external benefits associated with a particular use that cannot be internalized in any bargained-for exchange; … uses … have significant external benefits that are spread across society as a whole' (supra note 10, at 6). 'Implied consent' could arguably include 'the prevailing understanding of the community' and 'customary practice' (L.L. Weinrib, 'Fair's Fair: A Comment on the Fair Use Doctrine', 103 *Harvard Law Review* 1137, 1143–4, 1160 (1990)).

26. Gordon, supra note 22, 1620–21; Landes and Posner, supra note 22, at 358.

27. Ibid., Gordon.

28. Stanley J. Liebowitz, 'Copying and Indirect Appropriability: Photocopying of Journals', *Journal of Political Economy*, 945 (1985).

29. *Pro CD* v. *Zeidenberg* 86 F. 3d 1447 (7th Cir. 1996).

30. E.g., see http://www.cyber-matrix.com/pcprices.html

31. C. Shapiro and H.R. Varian, *Information Rules*, 53–82 (Barton, MA: Harvard Business School Press, 1999).

32. http://www.lexisnexis.com/productsandservices/featured.asp

33. Robert P. Merges, 'Contracting into Liability Rules: Intellectual Property Rights and Collective Rights Organizations', 84 *California Law Review* 1293, 1326 (1996).

34. *Copyright collectives* negotiate contracts on behalf of their rights holders, e.g., in photo-reproduction or musical performances. *Rights clearance centers* grant licenses based on individual terms specified by the owner. '*One-stop-shops*' are coalitions of separate collective management organizations which offer centralized sources for a number of related rights, e.g. photos and music, that would be particularly useful in multimedia production. At http://www.wipo.org/about-ip/en/about_collective_mngt.html (visited June 26, 2001).

35. 487 F. 2d 1345 (Ct. Cl. 1973).

36. Ibid., 1360–61.

37. Ibid., 1372.

38. 802 F. Supp. 1 (S.D.N.Y. 1992), *aff'd*, 60 F. 3d 913 (2d Cir. 1994), *cert. dismissed*, 516 U.S. 1005 (1995). *See also Basic Books, Inc.* v. *Kinko's Graphics Corporation*, 758 F. Supp. 1522 (1991), *Princeton University Press* v. *Michigan Document Service*, 99 F. 3d 1381, 1389 (6th Cir. 1996) (en banc) (rejecting the idea that commercial course packs at universities were transformative since the course packs substituted for purchase of individual books and had 'the intended purpose of supplanting the copyright holder's commercially valuable right').

39. Ibid., 928 ('evidence is not resounding for either side').

40. Ibid., 928–9. Since 1978, the Copyright Clearance Center has issued licenses to large institutional copiers on a blanket (i.e., flat fee) and per transaction basis. Blanket fees for a particular licensee are based on estimated copying levels from surveyed companies in the related industry. Transactional fees can be based on a common page rate or a more specific charge related to the exact material that is copied. By serving as a central clearinghouse, the CCC economizes on transactions costs and provides requisite authorities for reproductions in a cost-effective manner.

41. Ibid., citing Campbell, supra note 1, at 1178, *Harper and Row Publishers Inc.* v. *Nation Enters.*, 471 U.S. 539, 568–9 (1985); *Twin Peaks Productions, Inc.* v. *Publications International Ltd.*, 996 F. 2d at 1377; *D.C. Comics Inc.* v. *Reel Fantasy Inc.*, 696 F. 2d 24, 28 (2d Cir. 1982); *United Telephone Co. of Missouri* v. *Johnson Publishing Co., Inc.* 855 F. 2d 604, 610 (8th Cir. 1988).

42. K.D. Crews, 'Copyright at a Turning Point: Corporate Response to the Changing Environment', *Intellectual Property Law* 277 (1996).

43. K.W. Dam, 'Self Help in the Digital Jungle', 28 *Journal of Law and Economics* 393 (1999).

44. L. Lessig, *Code and Other Laws of Cyberspace* (New York: Basic Books, 2001), 100–108.

45. D. Philp, 'Who Owns Satellite Transmissions?', at www.cs.dartmouth.edu/~dphilp/paper2.html (retrieved February 12, 2003).

46. 47 U.S.C. § 553a.

47. Pub. L. 102-563, 106 Stat. 4237 (1992).

48. 17 U.S.C. § 1003-1004. The royalties are to be established and apportioned by arbitration panels that are appointed by the US Copyright Office (17 U.S.C. § 800). Equipment levies are also more broadly implemented in other countries, such as France (where analog and digital media are taxed), Italy (where analog and digital media and audio equipment are taxed), and Germany (where analog and digital media, and audio and video equipment are taxed), but the concept is the same.

49. *See generally* 17 U.S.C. § 1002.

50. 17 U.S.C. § 1002(c).

51. Pub. L. No. 105–304, 112 Stat. 2860 (1998).

52. 17 U.S.C. § 1201(a)(1).

53. 17 U.S.C. § 1201(a)(2).

54. 17 U.S.C. § 1201(b).

55. See generally C.E. Lindblom, 'The Science of Muddling Through', 19 *Public Administration Review* 79 (1959). Lindblom identifies rational comprehensive policy as administration that tries to consider and weigh all factors, gather all relevant information, measure all relevant quantities and willingly jump to extreme positions as logically justified.

56. Supra note 1, at 584, quoting *Sony Corp.* v. *Universal City Studios, Inc.*, 464 U.S. 417, 454, 194 S. Ct. 774, 795 (1984).

57. 'Since fair use is an affirmative defense, its proponent would have difficulty carrying the burden of demonstrating fair use without favorable evidence about relevant markets' (supra note 1, at 590).

58. 'The outer boundaries of a product market are determined by the reasonable interchangeability of use or the cross-elasticity of demand between the product itself and substitutes for it' (*Brown Shoe* v. *U.S.* 370 U.S. 294, 325; 82 S. Ct. 1502, 1523; 8 L. Ed. 2d 510 (1962)); *see also U.S.* v. *E.I. du Pont de Nemours & Co.*, 351 U.S. 377, 400 (1956).

59. *U.S.* v. *Falstaff Brewing Corp.*, 410 U.S. 527 (1973).

60. Supra note 1, at 1178.

61. 1996 WL 535537 at * 4 (S.D.N.Y. 1996).

62. 126 F. 3d 70 (2nd Cir. 1997) sourcing Affidavit of Faith Ringgold, P/P 13–14.

63. Ibid.; *see also* supra note 24, at 1161.

64. 60 F. 3d 913, 934 (J. Jacobs, Dissent).

65. Ibid.

66. Supra note 22, at 1631.

67. *A&M Records, Inc.* v. *Napster, Inc.*, 114 F. Supp.2d (N.D. Cal. 2000), 239 F. 3d 1004 (9th

Cir. 2001).
68. For example, see Defense Report of Peter S. Fader.
69. The argument was made principally in confidential expert testimony submitted by David Teece.
70. Supra note 1, at 590.
71. *Folsom* v. *Marsh*, 9 F. Cas. 342 (No. 4,901) (CCD Mass. 1841).
72. Supra note 2, at 592.
73. Ibid., 579; the decision quotes Leval, supra note 8, at 1111.
74. 17 U.S.C. § 101 (2000).
75. Ibid.
76. Supra note 2. ('Is the work superseding or does it instead add something new, with a further purpose or different character, altering the first with new expression, meaning or message; it asks, in other words, whether and to what extent the new work is transformative [quoting Leval, supra note 8, at 1111]).
77. 17 U.S.C. §107.
78. Supra note 1, at 591.
79. S.R. Besen, 'Private Copying, Reproduction Costs, and the Supply of Intellectual Property', RAND Report No. N-2207-NSF (1984).
80. *Sid & Marty Krofft Television Productions, Inc.* v. *McDonalds Corp.*, 562 F. 2d 1157, 1164 (9th Cir. 1977)
81. Ibid., 1164; *International Luggage Registry* v. *Avery Products Corp.*, 541 F. 2d 830, 831 (9th Cir. 1976); *Harold Lloyd Corp.* v. *Witwer*, 65 F. 2d 1, 18–19 (9th Cir. 1933). *Twentieth Century Fox Film Corp.* v. *Stonesifer*, 140 F. 2d 579, 582 (9th Cir. 1944).
82. *Bleistein* v. *Donaldson Lithographing Co*., 188 U.S. 239, 250, 23 S. Ct. 298, 47 L. Ed. 460 (1903) (circus posters); *Sunset House Distributing Corp.* v. *Doran*, 304 F. 2d 251, 252 (9th Cir. 1962) (plastic Santa Claus); *King Features Syndicate* v. *Fleischer*, 299 F. 533, 534 (2nd Cir. 1924) (doll).
83. 243 F. 3d 789 (4th Cir. 2000).
84. Ibid., 801.
85. Ibid., 803.
86. Ibid.
87. 261 F. Supp. 238, 241–2 (S.D.N.Y) 1966), *aff'd* 360 F. 2d 1021 (2d Cir. 1966).
88. 106 F. Supp. 2d 1132 (D. Colo. 2002).
89. 677 F. 2d 180 (2nd Cir. 1982).
90. Ibid., 185.
91. Mansfield, Dissent, ibid., 188–90.
92. *Dr. Seuss Enterprises* v. *Penguin Books*, 109 F. 3d 1394 (1995).
93. Ibid., 1399.
94. Ibid., 1403.
95. Ibid., 1406.
96. The Seuss decision is criticized in T. Ochoa, 'Dr. Seuss, The Juice, and Fair Use: How the Grinch Silenced a Parody', 45 *Journal of the Copyright Society of the U.S.A.* 546 (1998); G.K. Jung, 'Dr. Seuss Enterprises v. Penguin Books', 13 *Berkeley Technical Law Journal* 119 (1998); M.L. Shapiro, 'An Analysis of the Fair Use Defense in Dr. Seuss Enterprises v. Penguin', 28 *Golden Gate University Law Review* 1 (1998); J.M. Vogel, 'The Cat in the Hat's Latest Bad Trick', 20 *Cardozo Law Review* 287 (1998).
97. The present defining case would seem to be *On Davis* v. *The Gap, Inc*., 246 F. 3d 152 (2nd Cir. 2001) (upholding the idea that plaintiff's distinctive eyewear was a properly licensed item in the clothing advertisements in which it facilitated a visual draw).
98. *D.C. Comics, Inc*. v. *Reel Fantasy, Inc*., 696 F. 2d 24, 28 (2d Cir. 1982).
99. Supra note 1, at 591, n. 21.
100. Supra note 20.
101. Supra note 6, at 525.
102. J. Bresler, 'Begged, Borrowed, or Stolen: Whose Art is it Anyway?' presented to the New York Chapter of the Copyright Society of America, January 16, 2003.
103. 533 U.S. 483; 121 S. Ct. 2381; 150 L. Ed. 2d 500 (2001). The *New York Times* had

constructed a digital database of its previously published newspaper articles without consent of the contributing writers. Agreeing with the Second Circuit 205 F 3d 161 (2nd Cir. 2000) that the use was not suitably protected as an unmodified revision of a licensed periodical, the Supreme Court left remedies to the District Court with an obvious point: 'if necessary, the court and Congress may draw on numerous models for distributing copyrighted works and remunerating authors for their distribution' (at 519, 2393–4, 541).

104. 244 F. 3d 1267 (11th Cir. 2001). The Eleventh Circuit found that National Geographic had similarly infringed upon the rights of photographers by reproducing material in its digital service. On its remand, the Court wrote: 'In assessing the appropriateness of injunctive relief, we urge the [District] court to consider alternatives, such as mandatory license fees, in lieu of foreclosing the public's computer-aided access to this educational and entertaining work' (at 1276).

105. Landes and Posner, supra note 22, at 353–5.

106. A. Plant, 'The Economic Aspects of Copyright in Books', 1 *Economica* 167 (1934).

107. S. Breyer, 'The Uneasy Case for Copyright: A Study of Copyright in Books, Photocopies, and Computer Programs', 84 *Harvard Law Review* 281 (1970).

108. S.E. Sterk, 'Rhetoric and Reality in Copyright Law', 94 *Michigan Law Review* 1197, 1215–16 (1996). (An author who earns $8 million per book 'obviously does not need income from a movie or television-drama licensing to cover her original cost of production'.)

109. S. Ghosh, 'The Merits of Ownership', 15 *Harvard Journal of Law and Technology* 453 (2002).

110. *UMG Recordings* v. *MP3.com, Inc.*, 92 F.Supp. 2d 349, 352 (S.D.N.Y. 2000).

111. 17 U.S.C. § 106(a).

112. 17 U.S.C. § 115.

113. Elsmere infra note 126 ('I Love New York'); *MCA* v. *Wilson*, supra note 89 ('Boogie Woogie Bugle Boy'); *Fisher* v. *Dees*, infra note 126 ('When Sonny Sniffs Glue'); *Grand Upright Music Ltd.* v. *Warner Bros. Records, Inc.* 780 F. Supp. 182 (S.D.N.Y. 1991) ('Alone Again Naturally'); *Campbell* v. *Acuff Rose*, supra note 1 ('Pretty Woman').

114. *Annie Leibovitz* v. *Paramount Pictures Corp.*, 137 F. 3d 109 (2nd Cir. 1998).

115. *Island Records and Warner-Chappell Music Inc.* v. *SST Records* (1991). The case settled; see http://www.atu2.com/news/tdih/search.src?TYEAR=1991&Key (retrieved September 29, 2003).

116. Supra note 92.

117. *Walt Disney* v. *Air Pirates*, 581 F. 2d 751 (9th Cir. 1978); *see also Walt Disney Productions* v. *Mature Pictures Corp.*, 389 F. Supp. 1497 (S.D.N.Y. 1975) (X-rated movies with actors wearing Disney hats and clothing).

118. *Benny* v. *Loew's Inc.*, 239 F. 2d 532 (9th Cir. 1956).

119. Supra note 2–4, and surrounding text

120. Famous examples of appropriation art using copyrighted works (many of which settled out of court) include Andy Warhol's silkscreen prints of Henri Dauman's photograph of Jacqueline Kennedy, painter George Pusenkoff's use of an outline of a nude from a Helmut Newton photograph, Robert Rauschenberg's taking of Morton Beebe's Pull, Susan Pitt's visual adaptation of material from DC Comics, David Salle's taking of visual art from Cockrill and Hughes, Jeff Koon's sculptural reproductions of comic strip drawings by James Davis and photographs by Art Rogers and Barbara Campbell, and Damian Loeb's appropriation of photography by Lauren Greenfield. William M. Landes, 'Copyright, Borrowed Images, and Appropriation Art: An Economic Approach', 9 *George Mason Law Review* 1 (2000). *See also Rogers* v. *Koons* 960 F. 2d 301 and *United Feature Syndicate, Inc.* v. *Koons*, 817 F. Supp. 370 (S.D.N.Y. 1993).

121. *Cohen* v. *California*, 402 U.S. 15, 25, 91 S. Ct. 1780, 1789; 29 L. Ed. 2d 284, 294 (1971). Neil W. Netanel, 'Copyright and a Democratic Civil Society', 106 *Yale Law Journal* 283 (1996). ('It should not be forgotten that the Framers intended copyright itself to be the engine of free expression.')

122. Supra note 1, at 1172.

123. As argued by J. Bisceglia, 'Parody and Copyright Protection: Turning the Balancing Act

into a Juggling Act', 34 *Copyright Law Symposium (ASCAP)* 1, 25 (1987)).
124. Supra note 1, at 578.
125. Ibid.
126. *Fisher* v. *Dees*, 794 F. 2d 432 (9th Cir. 1986); *Elsmere Music Inc.* v. *National Broadcasting Company*, 482 F. Supp. 741 (S.D.N.Y. 1979), *aff'd* 623 F. 2d 252 (2nd Cir. 1980).
127. A potential licensing market would include 'only those [markets] that creators of original works would in general develop or license others to develop' (supra note 1, at 591).
128. 57 F. Supp. 2d 961 (C.D. Cal. 1999).
129. Ibid., 968–9.
130. R.A. Posner, 'When is Parody Fair Use?', 21 *Journal of Legal Studies* 67, 70–72 (1992).
131. Ibid., 73.
132. 'When there is little or no risk of market substitution ... taking parodic aim at an original is a less critical factor in the analysis, and looser forms of parody may be found to be fair use, as may satire with less justification for the borrowing than would otherwise be required' (supra note 1, at n. 14).
133. Supra note 1, at 585.
134. Supra note 128 and surrounding text.
135. Sony, supra note 56, at 449, n. 31
136. Elsmere Music, supra note 126, at 253, n. 1; *Fisher* v. *Dees*, supra note 126, at 438–9.
137. *Disney* v. *Air Pirates*, supra note 117.
138. Supra note 2–4 and surrounding text.
139. The connection between copyright and the First Amendment is made tellingly by M. Nimmer, 'Does Copyright Abridge the First Amendment Guarantees of Free Speech and Press?' 17 UCLA *Law Review* 1180, 1199 (1970). *See also* E.K. Ames, 'Note, Beyond Rogers v. Koons: A Fair Use Standard for Appropriation', 93 *Columbia Law Review* 1473, 1475–6 (1993): 'Art created from existing imagery is a valid form of criticism and comment should be protected by copyright law against suits for infringement. To do otherwise is to chill unnecessarily the development of artistic expression and to grant an individual copyright holder undue power over the secondary artist's choice of source material.'
140. *Bell & Howell: Mamiya Co.* v. *Masel Supply Co.*, 719 F. 2d 42, 45 (2d Cir. 1983).
141. *NAACP* v. *Town of East Haven*, 70 F. 3d 219, 224 (2d Cir. 1995); *JSG Trading Corp. Tray-Wrap, Inc.*, 917 F. 2d 75, 79 (2d Cir. 1990) (holding that 'possibility' of harm is insufficient).
142. Supra note 88, at 1139 (D. Colo. 2002)
143. *Hasbro Bradley, Inc.*, v. *Sparkle Toys, Inc.*, 780 F. 2d 189, 192 (2d Cir. 1985); *Sandoval* v. *New Line Cinema Corp.*, 973 F. Supp. 409, 412 (S.D.N.Y. 1997).
144. *Hofheinz* v. *AMC Productions*, 147 F. Supp. 2d 127, 134 (E.D.N.Y. 2001); sourcing *ABKCO Music Inc.* v. *Stellar Records*, 96 F. 3d 60, 64 (2d Cir. 1996).
145. *Country Kids 'N City Slicks, Inc.*, v. *Sheen*, 77 F. 3d 1280, 1288–9 (10th Cir. 1996).
146. A Circuit Court has also upheld the value of infringer's use as a permissible basis for estimating actual damages, while distinguishing this value from total infringer profits and the list price of the infringer's product. *Deltak, Inc.*, v. *Advanced Systems, Inc.*, 767 F. 2d 357, 361 (1985).
147. *Taylor* v. *Meirick*, 712 F. 2d 1112, 1120 (1983).
148. D.D. Haddock and F.S. McChesney, 'Do Liability Rules Deter Takings?', in *The Economic Consequences of Liability Law: In Defense of Common Law Liability* (eds R.E. Meiners and B. Yandle, New York: Quorum Books, 1991), 29–59.
149. T.W. Merrill, 'Trespass, Nuisance, and the Costs of Determining Property Rights', 14 *Journal of Legal Studies*, 13, 18 (1985). Trespass applies to invasions of space by unauthorized persons and tangible objects, while nuisance applies more to indirect interferences that affect the enjoyment of that space (e.g., noise, odor, pollution). The principal distinction between trespass and nuisance is the standard of care applied to determine whether the interference is actionable; i.e., whether Marshall may enjoin and/or received damages from the action of Taney, or Taney may practice his intrusion without exclusion from Marshall. To establish an actionable trespass, Marshall must show that

Taney has invaded his space.

150. Ibid.

151. *On Davis* v. *The Gap, Inc*. 246 F. 3d 152 (2nd Cir. 2001).

152. Copyright plaintiffs may press for actual or statutory damages (17 U.S.C. sec 504(a) (2000)). Higher statutory rewards are possible if the plaintiff can demonstrate willfulness (17 U.S.C. 504(c)(2)(2000)). A plaintiff must make a choice between actual or statutory compensation only before the final verdict is rendered. This may encourage the defendant to settle, but may actually serve as a disincentive to the plaintiff, as it leaves the possibility of more money on the table. The presence of statutory royalties provides incentives for rights owners to gamble for higher compensation unrelated to the actual market value of the misappropriation. Furthermore, the additional uncertainty of higher statutory damages can serve as an additional deterrent on the publication of the transformative work.

153. W.J. Gordon, 'An Inquiry into the Merits of Copyright: The Challenges of Consistency, Consent, and Encouragement Theory', 41 *Stanford Law Review* 1343, 1353 (1989).

154. Rate Courts now set license fees for performance licenses for ASCAP and BMI. Copyright Arbitration Royalty Panels now set license fees for performances in jukeboxes, secondary mechanical reproductions, and distant retransmissions of cable and satellite content

155. *Georgia Pacific Corporation* v. *United States Plywood Corporation*, 318 F. Supp. 1116, 1120 (S.D.N.Y. 1970). *See also Atlas-Pacific Engineering Co*. v. *Ashlock*, 339 F. 2d 288, 290 (9th Cir. 1964); *cert. denied*, 382 U.S. 842, 86 S. Ct. 55, 15 L. Ed. 2d 83 (1965). ('There is a variety of possible elements of damages for patent infringement, such as the profits made by the infringer, the actual damage to the patentee, or a reasonable royalty.')

156. Supra notes 76–7 and surrounding text.

157. Which may include, *inter alia*, copying to prepare lecture notes, to enrich professional understanding, improve citizen awareness, personal entertainment, or space or time-shifting (Sony, supra note 56, at 455, n. 40).

158. Sony, supra note 56 at 478–9 (Blackmun, J. dissenting).

159. 802 F. Supp. 14–15 (1994).

160. Weinrib, supra note 25.

161. Ibid.

162. D. Zimmerman, 'The More Things Change, The Less They Seem "Transformed"; Some Reflections on Fair Use', *Journal of the Copyright Society of the U.S.A.* 251, 262, n. 55 (1998). ('To the best that I can determine, they are uses the court in question likes.')

163. 802 F. Supp. 14–15 (1994).

164. U.S. Department of Justice, Antitrust Division, Second Amended Final Judgment, at http://www.usdoj.gov/atr/cases/f63000/6395.html (retrieved May 5, 2001).

165. AUS Consultants, Moorestown, NJ (http://www.royaltysource.com).

166. Keith Sharfman, 'A New Procedure for Resolving Valuation Disputes', unpublished manuscript, Rutgers University School of Law (2003). Sharfman contends that variations of such methods are now used for buyout valuation in joint ventures by Merck/Schering and Verizon/Vodaphone.

167. Supra notes 2–4 and surrounding text.

168. The 'fair price to be paid for the right to publish a sequel to the work has already been set by two publishers who have agreed to pay, or paid, substantial advances and royalties for the right to create its sequels' (supra note 3 at 1373–4, n. 12).

169. In 1999, Brighter Child Interactive acquired rights to use the characters from the television program *Adventures with Kanga Roddy* in connection with its interactive software production. In 1997, Kideo Productions Inc. acquired the rights to publish personalized storybooks using Disney Standard Characters for a $25000 upfront and a 10 percent royalty rate. The license contract specified a $20000 upfront payment plus a royalty amount based on 8 percent of net revenues. In the same year, ClubCharlies.com Inc. acquired screenplay rights to an original story plot entitled 'The Misadventures of Charlie Chance'; rates were $150000 upfront and 10 percent of net revenues (supra note 165).

170. H. Besser, 'Intellectual Property: The Attack on Public Space in Cyberspace', *Processed World* (2001); *see also* D. Lange, 'Recognizing the Public Domain', 44 *Law and Contemporary Problems* 147 (1981); Y. Benkler, 'The Battle over the Institutional

Ecosystem in the Digital Environment', 44 *Communications of the ACM* 2 (2001); L. Lessig: *The Future of Ideas: The Fate of the Commons in a Connected World* 249–61 (New York: Basic Books, 2002).

171. 'All manner of vignettes, short stories, and novels based on the universes described in popular books, TV shows, and movies' (Ariana Eunjung Cha, 'Harry Potter and the Copyright Lawyer', at http://www.washingtonpost.com/wp-dyn/articles/A7412-2003June17.html (retrieved June 30, 2003)). For example, the web site 'fanfiction' has stories for over 150 movies, with 'X-men' attracting over 2500 at http://www.fanfiction.net/subcats.php?categoryid=205 (retrieved June 29, 2003). For a directory of all fan fiction on the web, see http://www.fanfictionlinks.com (retrieved June 29, 2003).

172. Where users might combine two or more content sources for integrated presentations, post modern appropriations, collages or morphs.

173. Computer generated works containing two or more different songs (ibid.). *See also* http://mike.whybark.com/archives/000705.html (retrieved June 29, 2003).

174. With alternative endings or deleted characters (ibid.).

175. *Religious Technology Center* v. *Lerma*, 1996 U.S. Dist. LEXIS, 15454, 1996 WL 633131 (E.D.Va. 1996), *Religious Technology Center* v. *Netcom On-Line Communications Services, Inc.*, 923 F. Supp. 1231 (N.D. Cal. 1995); *Los Angeles Times* v. *Free Republic*, 2000 U.S. Dist. LEXIS 5669 (C.D.Cal. 2000). These decisions follow Supreme Court dictum: 'whether a substantial portion of the infringing work was copied verbatim from the copyrighted work is a relevant question ... for it may reveal a dearth of transformative character of purpose' (supra note 2, at 587–8).

176. See chapter 8.

3. Digital rights management, licensing and privacy

3.1 INTRODUCTION

Digital rights management (DRM) entails the operation of a control system that can monitor, regulate and price each subsequent use of a digital file that contains media content or software. Electronic access can be administered through rendering software tied to a protected work, and can be complemented with encryption, digital signatures, watermarking or hardware programming. Depending on the price that a user pays, owners of protected works may limit use by number of plays, duration of access, temporary or partial uses, and the number and location of computers on which the file may be accessed.

Digital rights management and access control is legally different from copyright, which protects the underlying work from unauthorized reproduction, distribution, derivation, public performance or display.[1] Copyright protection is principally limited by term duration,[2] fair use,[3] the first sale doctrine,[4] the idea–expression dichotomy,[5] and exemptions for libraries,[6] classrooms and distance learning,[7] and the blind and the handicapped.[8] In contrast, access protection entails technological procedures that shield a copyrighted work from the attempt to copy. Access protection then is technology protection, akin to measures that disallow 'black boxes' to decode scrambled cable signals or devices that circumvent the Serial Copy Management System.[9] As such, access protection might not be subject to the same legal limitations and user rights now established in traditional copyright.

The case for legal access protection was set forth initially by the Clinton Administration's White Paper, *Intellectual Property and the National Information Infrastructure*, which argued for laws that would forbid the use of technologies that could be used to circumvent it.[10] The White Paper was a key influence behind the subsequent Digital Millenium Copyright Act of 1998 (DMCA),[11] which Congress enacted to 'facilitate the robust development and worldwide expansion of electronic commerce, communication, research, development and education' by 'making digital networks safe places to disseminate and exploit copyrighted materials'.[12] In so doing, the USA more than met its treaty commitments that had been established under Article 11 of the World Intellectual Property Organization (WIPO) Copyright Treaty and

Article 18 of the WIPO Performances and Phonograms Treaty, which specified that parties must provide 'adequate legal protection and effective legal remedies against the circumvention of effective technological measures' used by authors, performers, or producers of phonograms 'in connection with the exercise of their rights'.[13]

Under Section 1201(a)(1) of the DMCA, 'no person shall circumvent a technological measure that effectively controls access to a work protected under this title'.[14] Section 1201(a)(2) further disallows the manufacture, import, offering, provision, or other trafficking of devices that could be used for the purpose of circumventing access protection.[15] Section 1201(b) additionally bans related devices that may circumvent copy controls, but does not outlaw the actual act of circumvention.[16] The remainder of Section 1201 sets forth qualifications that attempt to mitigate the restrictiveness of the anti-circumvention clauses.

The nation's four national academies (National Academy of Sciences, National Academy of Engineering, Institute of Medicine, National Research Council) sounded a more cautionary note regarding access protection with the publication of *The Digital Dilemma: Intellectual Property in the Information Age*.[17] The report echoed earlier legislative concerns that the resulting legal framework would create a 'pay-per-use' society, eliminate fair use and put into place a regime of superdistribution where copyright owners would attach fees to each subsequent copy of any original download.[18] The four academies also feared that digital protection may lead to loss of historic records, the deliberate non-sharing of content, constraints on audience activities and access times, and general difficulties that may result as digital presentation of information comes to replace offline production.[19]

The controversy over access protection also emerged full force in Europe. Adopted in September, 2000, the Common Position of the European Parliament and the Council of the European Union stated: 'In order to avoid fragmented legal approaches that could potentially hinder the functioning of the internal market, there is a need to provide for harmonized legal protection against circumvention of effective technological measures and against provision of devices and products or services to this effect.'[20] Less restrictive than the DMCA, Article 6 of the subsequent EU Directive directed the members of the European Union to provide adequate legal protection against the circumvention of technological measures, as well as the manufacture, import, distribution, sale, rental and advertisement of devices for the provision of such services.

This chapter examines access protection from an economic perspective. By reducing the dangers of unauthorized reproduction and distribution of copyrighted works, access protection may actually provide greater incentive for digital presentation. Access protection may also enhance the range of service offerings and provide to consumers more kinds of versions. Particularly for academic and library uses, content suppliers can be expected to provide consortium services that provide accommodative licensing arrangements. Personalization techniques will make it possible to accumulate information on prospective buyers in order to reduce search costs.

Nonetheless, policy-makers might conceive of certain areas in which the DMCA can be modified to allow a wider domain of user rights. As a general approach, the Copyright Office and Congress may reasonably examine rules that affect peripheral (i.e., non-network) digital appliances to determine whether any provide 'significant noninfringing uses' (e.g, 'first sale' rights) could offset conceivable harms from copying in local neighborhoods. However, it is far too early to allow general circumvention devices to be marketed over the Internet, as the circumvention could lead to viral reproductions that could destroy markets for new works.

3.2   ACCESS PROTECTION IN CONSUMER MARKETS

We first consider the economics of access protection in the domain of entertainment and artistic content now offered for final sale to home consumers.

Professor Peter Jaszi of the Digital Future Coalition observed critically of access protection that 'technologies now exist that permit information proprietors to continue to regulate 'access' to digital copies of content after those copies have been lawfully acquired'.[21] Professor Jaszi notwithstanding, this technical ability to protect against subsequent access to content files, even if lawfully acquired, may actually be quite reasonable. The pejoratively termed 'persistent access control'[22] (which is not synonymous with obligatory pay-per-use; see below) seems a practical way of stopping digital copyists from making unauthorized viral distributions of copyrighted material.

As more uses of digital technology emerge, the enabling networks will evolve due to positive synergies between increased content and buildout of available content and hardware. For example, as more users have access to preferred titles and genres of digital music, more player software will be installed. As the installed base of player software expands, more music content can be profitably digitized and transmitted. The availability of more content will lead yet more users to install more software, which will encourage production and digitization of yet more content, etc. The outcome presents an example of a system of network goods that increase in value as the size of the overall system expands.[23]

Because no one provider will produce all hardware or software, the benefits of these positive synergies between content and equipment cannot be monetized by any one player and will redound principally to consumers. However, the continuing development of ongoing network effects depends critically upon the willingness of content owners to make material available for digital distribution; serious reductions in network synergies can result if a few key providers were to decline to distribute content through emerging digital platforms. This makes access protection a critical element of a network strategy. Beyond the means of any one player to implement, rules for access protection collectively resolve the problem by enforcing compliance among people who individually may have reasons to circumvent controls.[24]

With strong access protection, publishers conceivably may encumber or eliminate how consumers make or distribute personal copies now protected by 'fair use'[25] or 'first sale'.[26] As will be discussed below, legal reform may be appropriate in some instances. However, the value of desirable consumer uses is implicitly monetized in the purchase price of any product, including a copyrighted work.[27] As a result, producers who institute restrictive rules or technologies, or otherwise fail to appreciate the importance of customer ease, might actually reduce market demand for new products and the resulting prices.

Consumer Choice and Versioning

Professors Carl Shapiro and Hal Varian coined the phrase 'versioning' to represent the ability to charge different prices for different kinds, levels and combinations of (online) product.[28] For example, the right to download, copy or lend a legally accessed movie or sound recording may be priced differently than the right simply to download content without making further transmissions or reproductions. Accordingly, a digital rights system that establishes a menu of optional rights[29] allows the rights owner to price individual components and extract different payments from different kinds of users.[30]

Overall, versioning is a market-based equivalent to offering more personalized options to individual users. The concept is not new to the digital era. Magazine publishers make content available for subscriptions and single copies, and studios make movies available in first-run theaters and video stores. Versioning, then, allows consumers the choice of a number of service options rather than the confinement of any one.

Evidently, resale or arbitrage between low- and high-end markets cannot be permitted if versioning is to operate effectively. Besides stopping viral reproduction, access protection and digital rights management then provide a more positive benefit: that is, by stopping resale or redistribution of content from one market to another, access protection and digital rights management widen consumer choice and promote product diversity.

Versioning is profitable because producers recognize that variations in customer demands can be priced differently for greater gain. Discriminating producers who can extract greater revenue from across the user spectrum will have more incentive to produce and release more content. The prospective menu of differing versions and prices is particularly defensible in content industries, where much of the production costs are sunk costs that often cannot be recovered if only one version is made available. This explains why studios make films available through a number of viewing 'windows' – each with a different price – that span theaters, pay-per-view cable, video rental, basic cable and network television.[31]

The effect of versioning upon users is bifurcated. The largest and most intense users of any product can be expected actually to pay more than under uniform prices.[32] This is because discriminating producers may extract incremental consumer value by charging higher prices for deluxe services, without worrying about attrition among less intense users. These customers may gain nonetheless, as suppliers also have greater financial incentives to innovate with deluxe features if they can be additionally compensated.

Smaller users will more assuredly gain. This is because producers may actually lower prices for limited basic services without worrying about an offsetting revenue loss among high-end users that will be on a different version. Using personalization techniques (see below), content owners may actually be able to identify prospective first customers and extend to them low-price introductory offers that time out after a specified period. Consequently, many low-end purchasers formerly excluded entirely from purchase may now enjoy a 'no frills' basic or introductory version.

With versioning, diverse user rights to access, make and/or lend copies can be monetized and made available as service options. Were a slate of options presented (enabled by access protection), we would have a market test of just how important traditional rights of 'fair use' and 'first sale' are to buyers of copyrighted works, and to what degree consumers may prefer discounted purchases to buyer 'protections' that would otherwise be obligatory.

The Music and Digital Rights Management Services

In the past year, a number of new music subscription services have arisen that enable listeners to legally stream and download catalogs of recorded music. Economists uniformly welcome the opportunity for new services to compete for market share. The success of digital rights management may be a key factor in determining their eventual success.

The five major labels[33] that now distribute 85 percent of records sold in the USA launched two competing joint ventures in December, 2001. First to launch, MusicNet now distributes songs from Warner Music, BMG, EMI,

Universal and major independent, Zomba, with delivery technology made available from Real Networks.[34] Now owned by Roxio (May 2003),[35] market rival Pressplay now uses content from Sony, Vivendi Universal, BMG, EMI, Zomba and eight smaller independent labels, along with transmission technology from Microsoft, 'burning' software from Roxio, distribution agreements with Yahoo! and Microsoft, and a prospective tie-in with Napster.[36] Interesting independent services in the USA include Listen.com,[37] Full Audio,[38] Emusic.com,[39] PulseOne,[40] MusicMatch,[41] Liquid Audio (now closed)[42] and a number of interesting niche applications.[43] In contrast with the above monthly subscription services, Apple's Music Store now offers to Mac users individual downloads with more liberal burning capabilities;[44] Microsoft will now follow. Intriguing ideas from Europe include Vitaminic,[45] OD2[46] and Wippit.[47]

There are five points to be made regarding the nature of market competition among the services. First, the resulting market spectrum ranges from 'pay-per-use' to diverse subscription options; the contending music services then offer a slate of differentiated versions with varying features regarding permanence of ownership, service length, pricing, bundling, partnerships and marketing strategy. To profit, each online provider will need to distinguish its particular services, attract a base market segment and successfully innovate further to widen its appeal. With no abiding market certainty, rival incumbent providers will come to 'learn by doing' the particular services and features that consumers most want.

Second, the gain in portability and buyer convenience made possible by permanent downloads and burns may be a necessary service if interactive music services are to distinguish themselves from file-sharing that implicitly offers unlimited download and burn capability.[48] However, permanent fixations pose a greater target for copyright infringers who can more readily break protection in order to reproduce and digitally distribute copyrighted songs. Unauthorized copying will disrupt business models, reduce license fees and hinder service buildout through legitimate services.

Third, the constellation of present offerings now illustrate the market potential for different product versions enabled by gradations in price. Both MusicNet and Pressplay originally only rented music; i.e., they allowed full sampling through streams and downloads, but ended access to all previously downloaded music at the termination of service (except for a limited number of burns that require an additional fee). Basic listeners of MusicNet services purchased through Real Networks now may pay a monthly fee of $4.95 to stream 100 songs and download 100 more, $9.95 for a combined package with additional Net radio services,[49] and $19.95 for a Gold Pass subscription with sports, entertainment and news programming.[50] By contrast, AOL offers basic MusicNet service (20 streams, 20 downloads) for $3.95 per month, unlimited streams and downloads for $8.95, and ten additional burns for $17.95.[51] AOL Time Warner also sells individual downloads.[52]

Pressplay users may choose among Basic ($9.95 for 300 streams and 30 downloads), Silver ($14.95 for 500 streams, 50 downloads and ten burns), Gold ($19.95 for 750 streams, 75 downloads and 15 burns) and Platinum services ($24.95 for 1000 streams, 100 downloads and 20 burns).[53] The company offers to annual subscribers a plan for unlimited streams and downloads for $179.40 per year.[54] Emusic also sets different subscription prices depending on user willingness to commit to a contract length.[55]

With considerable jukebox functionality but limited burning, these rental services contrast with 'pay-per-burn' services like Apple's Music Store, where users may download individual tracks after hearing a 30 second sample. Downloaded tracks may be burned to CDs and iPods for an unlimited number of times, and transferred to three other computers. While Music Store can be useful in selling Apple's OS X and iPods, the wider appeal of the company's light version of DRM will now be tested; Microsoft now will provide to content owners its Windows Media technology as a secure system and will give away DRM software to promote Windows upgrades.[56] Apple will also need to decide whether to program for non-iPod players and release a version of its jukebox software for the pesonal computer (PC).[57] For its part, Microsoft plans to develop software that will tether and clock music downloads on portable devices, thereby allowing subscription services to offer unlimited rights in a wider range of uses.[58]

Fourth, DRM technology enables distributors to give away promotional products, or price music below cost. For example, the Pressplay service now offers a 14-day free trial subscription of 200 streams and 20 downloads;[59] Gateway customers may also buy personal computers or 40 GB hard drives pre-loaded with 2000 Pressplay songs with a free subscription period.[60] In order to sell its subscription services, Listen.com now makes burns available at 49 cents per track, which is below acquisition costs of 60 to 75 cents per track.[61] After settling a law suit regarding its original data shield,[62] SunnComm now offers a more user-friendly data shield – Promoplay – which gives a CD buyer the opportunity to upload and email a copy of a song to a friend without additional charge.[63] European buyers of OD2 were treated to a Digital Download Day that allowed them to download or listen to three albums worth of tracks for a $5.33 credit.[64] These services extend trial periods and user rights beyond what 'bricks and mortar' stores may otherwise allow, and would not be commercially possible but for the DRM strategies that protect against unauthorized reproduction and distribution.

Fifth, enabled by various formats of DRM, competition in the market is a

clear indication that innovative business models are now being tested. While
the Apple Music Store's first month was impressive (2 million downloads),[65]
the fact remains that subscription services can expose listeners to a much
wider range of sampling and innovative listening. Due largely to the broadcast
bottleneck, 2 percent of releases now account for 80 percent of industry sales;
this suggests the presence of considerable promotional slack that can be filled
by a more informative service.[66] This point is illustrated further by recent
numbers from Listen.com, where the average user listens to about 200
different songs per month, but only 13 percent opted for even one burn.[67]
Services can add text material, video, concert promotions and merchandise
sale to widen their appeal as information clearinghouses. Made possible by
new formats of DRM, innovations in the market can then combine elements of
a download store and subscription plan.

3.3   ACADEMIC MARKETS

We now consider how access protection may affect demand for and usage of
copyrighted materials by libraries, schools and research institutions, which are
'knowledge factories' that work up and produce more intellectual property.
Generally speaking, 'a system of property rights that might seem natural
would be to protect the first innovator so broadly that licensing is required
from all second generation innovators who use the initial technology. But such
broad protection can lead to deficient incentives to develop second generation
products'.[68]

The Academic Product

The potential for digital technologies to improve user convenience and the
general quality of research and teaching is evident. Academic researchers may
have convenient home and office access to favored journals and necessary
articles at a moment's notice. With proper authorization, a researcher may
automatically email a selected article to a group of co-workers at different
universities without making physical copies. A researcher who views a
particular article may view ongoing commentary, embedded hyperlinks to
referenced articles and content filtering based on his online behavior or the
preferences of similar users in a particular network.[69] If use is tracked through
personalization technology, a researcher may receive email suggestions
regarding what books or articles should be read next. Teaching gains can be
considerable, both with web-enhanced content in a traditional course and more
comprehensive digital interfaces of distance learning that will extend the
geographic domain of college instruction.[70] The capabilities of digital

technology will multiply yet further with the further deployment of voice recognition and video capability.

Like small users of home entertainment, institutions of modest means may actually benefit from 'versioning' as new markets congeal for basic or introductory services.[71] Simultaneously, publishers may increase prices for deluxe services.[72] As mentioned above, price discrimination and versioning are particularly defensible in industries with high fixed costs of production. This is the case in scholarly publishing, where editorial and production fixed costs account for 70 percent of the total costs of publication.[73]

Nonetheless, researchers and educators are concerned that access protection may actually threaten their ability to perform important complementary activities, such as partial copying,[74] criticisms and parody,[75] searching,[76] dissemination and transformation. Five commenting library associations made the point:

> Technological measures define a user's 'accessing a work' as not only initial access, but accessing for purposes of printing, copying, extracting or even viewing or reading. Thus, the library patron who is using a lawfully acquired work and who circumvents a technological measure for certain types of lawful, copyright uses, could be exposed to prosecution under Section 1201(a) because each 'use' requires an additional 'access' under the control of the technological measure.[77]

The willingness of any person, or group of people, to invest hours needed to work up inputs into classroom or research product depends on ease of use, the presence of risk and the ready interaction between members of a research team or classroom. Consequently, researchers may conceivably be dissuaded from initiating cooperative activities in the first place if access protection is a hindrance. Furthermore, a demonstrated negative effect upon research could dissuade libraries from investing in the startup costs of new technology, network distribution, customer support personnel and file storage systems.[78]

Nonetheless, the expressed concerns of many critics might be ignoring market reality. Professor Jeffrey Mackie-Mason of the University of Michigan found that higher inconvenience or user cost of access – subsuming money, time and effort – had a significant depressive effect upon the number of digital articles that university researchers access.[79] In this respect, publishers who raise costs fail to accommodate key user needs; price gouging on complementary products will reduce demand for product and lower the market price. It would then be a generally bad market decision for a publishing house to attempt to affix library lending fees, deny permission to archive, refuse rights to reserve use, implement cumbersome passwords, restrict browsing, disallow academic criticism and fail to make promotional material available for preliminary review. Indeed, since terms can be negotiated, a Yale University librarian approvingly notes: 'In many cases, librarians ask that the publisher reinstate the "public good" clauses of the Copyright Act into the electronic content license, allowing fair use copying or downloading, interlibrary loan, and archiving for the institutional license and its customers.'[80]

Content providers can be trusted to monetize their investments through starting prices and gradations for more deluxe features. However, if content (e.g., data) is publicly available, competitive forces and the threat of new entry may constrain anti-consumer behavior. Finally, the editors of a scholarly journal, who find it incumbent to maximize readership in order to disseminate new ideas and attract interesting manuscripts, may choose to switch publishers if readers become dissatisfied. Accordingly, though some unfortunate examples can be expected to continue,[81] content suppliers would be better advised to attempt to devise profitable licensing strategies that provide things that users want most, i.e. ease of use. Markets generally ensure this outcome.

Licensing Arrangements

Of particular importance in the next few years will be the capacity of licensing contracts and copyright institutions to expedite arrangements for making digital content available to online users. This capacity evolves from the workings of a free market. As a general rule, digital markets will evolve gradually in a manner that will reduce transactions costs and enable use.

A useful instrument that will serve a central role in academic and general applications is the site license. For periodic fees, site licensors offer unlimited access at any designated computer location with no additional charge per individual transaction. Rights owners may then obtain access control without a metered pay-per-use that critics fear.[82] Rights owners will price usage efficiently at short-run marginal cost (i.e., zero) and have correct incentives to reduce non-monetary transactions costs in order to stimulate demand.[83]

As a prime example of site licensing, college library subscribers to Elsevier's Lexis Nexis Division now offer to online users simultaneous unlimited access to the company's 1200 scholarly journals. Fees are paid on a per-student basis with optional sublicenses for offcampus users. The access mechanism is protected through IP validation, which allows access only to computers with Internet Protocol addresses that subscribing institutions supply beforehand. Summarizing the company's position, Karen Hunter of Elsevier understands the drawbacks of pay-per-use and superdistribution:

> Elsevier's goal is to give people access to as much information as possible on a flat fee, unlimited use basis. [Elsevier's] experience has been that as soon as the usage is metered on a per article basis, there is an inhibition on use or a concern about exceeding some budget allocation.[84]

In a licensing variation, SilverPlatter – which makes available 250 online databases – allows academic libraries to choose from a menu of subscription fees based on the number of allowed simultaneous users. SilverPlatter points out that its modularity meets the varied needs of differently sized institutions.[85] The company's testimony before the Copyright Office in 2001 illustrates an example for an industry that seems to have encountered and resolved at least some licensing difficulties in a market-based fashion. 'Five years ago, database producers typically had geographic restrictions on their products, limited to a particular computer, or a particular building. The market resisted this, and now it is routine to see database publishers ... making their products available to authorized users ... from anywhere in the world.'[86]

More generally, database providers seem to have modified their revenue models since the 1970s, moving from pricing schemes based on minutes of connect time (which was unpredictable and which discouraged browsing) to new systems that may include free access to offline hits and prints, as well as online displays.

Transactional difficulties may result if the licensing of a one-time or a limited number of specific uses cannot be efficiently forged into a site-based contract. Here we can expect pay-per-use, short-period (e.g., hourly, daily) licensing and other forms of modular or transactions-based licensing to continue to emerge. The Internet is particularly suited for this role, as it can monitor the use of individual takings by distributed viewers.

In the academic world, the College Division of Houghton Mifflin conducted a pilot program with Copyright Direct, a permissions tool of Yankee Rights Management, to provide to users access to online material in a real-time basis. The Division also had worked with Reciprocal to provide 'secure containers' to permit related information on relevant rights and permissions to be carried online with the related content.[87] Finally, journal publishers may make content available through generalized subscriptions that permit access to bundles with a prespecified number of individual articles. This generalized subscription model was found to be a particularly popular alternative to traditional subscription, as few readers take the time to read everything in a particular issue of an academic journal.[88]

Licensing Organizations

Licensing could prove more difficult when cooperation of several different content providers is necessary to a particular project, as would be the case – for example – in a film course. In such situations, each content provider may have incentive to hold out for a greater share of the licensing take.[89] However, before reassigning property rights by administrative fiat, we should here recognize the great potential for consortia, subscription agents, copyright collectives, rights clearance centers and 'one-stop shops'[90] to negotiate complex contracts that accommodate online requests and facilitate collection when sole source or single use licensing is impractical.[91] Through digital technology, transactional licensing though these organizations will move from a domain of letters, emails and faxes to full online functionality where relevant information is submitted – and permissions obtained – through web interfaces.

Promising improvements in licensing technology are emerging. In addition to blanket licenses that provide unlimited rights to text reproductions based on industry type and staff size, the Copyright Clearance Center in the USA now offers transactional services for its catalog of 1.75 million text works controlled by 9600 owners.[92] The Center's Academic Permission Service has licensed academic course packs since 1991, and the Center's Electronic Course Content Service has accommodated electronic course packs since 1997.[93] In June, 2001, Rightsline.com began to offer one-stop online licensing to 1160 diverse members of the International Licensing Industry Merchandisers' Association, including a wide range of properties in film, music, sports and publications.[94] The Media Image Resource Alliance now provides online access to licenses for over 60000 photographs.[95] Info2clear in Europe provides online licensing for text reproductions that may eventually implicate choice of language.[96] At the LIBLICENSE web site, university librarians can propose online contract modifications that may meet specific user needs.[97]

A Guiding Philosophy

Three quotes from three authorities may represent best the true state of the license market and copyright clearance. The vice-chairman of the International Federation of Reproduction Rights Organizations, Professor Daniel Gervais of the University of Ottawa, offers an important caveat to rights owners who see licensing and access protection primarily as protectionist instruments that would curtail user rights:

> The basic question boils down to this: is the provider's mandate to minimize unauthorized uses or is it to maximize authorized uses? To limit unauthorized reuse, negative licensing tools are used: encryption, digital containers, and others that limit the options available to the user ... by physically preventing uses that the rights holder wants to prohibit ... Positive licensing, on the other hand, assumes that users find what they want and are given an easy option to determine terms of use, both at the time they acquire the content and later on ... [Positive licensing] allows users to acquire the content on appropriate terms (and at the right price) and then acquire new rights as their needs change and grow.[98]

To my mind, it is not difficult to reconcile Professor Gervais's remarks with those of Professor Laura Gasaway of the University of North Carolina, a strong advocate of library interests:

> For several decades, libraries have been signing licenses to make information available online to their users; there has been no thought or debate that non-public domain databases should be provided free ... What librarians staunchly advocate is that individual users should not have to pay for information obtained from their public libraries ... So, statements such as 'information wants to be free' may simply mean free to the individual, not free to the library.[99]

The appropriate synthesizing remarks on the matter belong to Ann Okerson, Associate Director of the Yale University Library, who now stands by the present relevance of comments she made in 1997 regarding the efficiency of markets and licensing:

> The market has brought librarians and publishers together; the parties are discovering where their interests mesh; and they are beginning to build a new set of arrangements that meet needs both for access (on the part of the institution) and remuneration (on the part of the producer) ... [Price issues notwithstanding], libraries are able to secure crucial and significant use terms via site licenses, terms that often allow the customer's students, faculty, and scholars significant copying latitude for their work ... at times more than what is permitted via the fair use and library provisions of the Copyright Act of the U.S.[100]

3.4 PRIVACY

A final concern with digital rights management is the capacity for online businesses to record individual transactions to construct dossiers and data bases on online purchases of individual consumers. Sometimes enhanced by data overlays from offline sources, collected information may include, *inter alia*, shopping preferences, surfing behavior, membership information, household income, domicile, financial details, health information, marital history, and car and home ownership.[101]

In the offline world, customer profiling is now made routine through supermarket savings cards, white pages, surveys, contest entries, financial and census records, motor vehicle data, credit card transactions, phone records, credit records, product warranty cards, subscriptions and public records.[102] However, digital technology – aided by digital rights management – makes data collection, personalization and concentration considerably more efficient and thorough. For example, Experian boasts a consortium database on catalog shopping with 590 titles, 65 million households and 600 million transactions,[103] Claritas offers 62 detailed demographic lists (including Blue

Blood Estates, Young Literati, New Empty Nests, Mobility Blues, Shotguns and Pickups, Norma Rae-ville, Mines and Mills, and Scrub Pine Flats).[104] The Direct Media List Services enables granular breakdowns from 'Catholics who subscribe to Newsweek' to 'adults above the age of 55 who subscribe to any of Hearst's twelve magazines'.[105] Amazon.com monitors both book purchases and browsing,[106] and extends greater discounts to first-time visitors.[107]

Critics contend that these practices may intrude upon privacy[108] and reduce trust in digital commerce.[109] Indeed, 89 percent of American respondents in a Harris Poll in the year 2000 were uncomfortable with web tracking where responses were combined with user identities, while 88 percent supported 'opt in' requirements that would oblige web sites to secure positive consent before gathering data from a particular visitor.[110] Moreover, 62 per cent of Americans who did not shop online in the year 2000 did not do so because of concerns regarding privacy and security of their personal information.[111]

There are five economic distinctions that must be drawn about the private gathering and concentration of market information. First, free markets work better when search and information costs can be reduced.[112] With easy information, supplying producers and retailers may more easily reach prospective buyers, and vice versa.[113] Digital techniques and sales agents that accommodate easy exchange of information then lubricate transactional mechanisms and enhance economic efficiency.

In this respect, the right to economic privacy is essentially the right to conceal information from other parties in the market.[114] Moreover, the right to proscribe data gathering is the power to require others to withhold information as well. If market information is less available, buyers and sellers must spend more time and effort trying to communicate with one another. Much like unlisted telephone owners, online privacy imposes a cost on the market by reducing information flow.

Second, a good number of consumers will find data collection and profiling to be a convenient part of online shopping. Put metaphorically, 'some people may be troubled if a pizza delivery firm keeps a record of their address and favorite toppings; others may feel it saves them time'.[115] With transactional ease, a buyer from Domino's may order a pizza anywhere in the USA without ever having to reenter a credit card number or food preference. As data profiling increasingly builds on previous information, the collective savings in time and energy may be more profound.

Third, contemporary advertising now appears most intrusive precisely because advertisers lack personal information on their prospective buyers. National advertisers of beers, cars and refrigerators now hawk their wares on television, radio, newspapers and magazines based on imperfect conjectures regarding who represents their best prospective buyers. A good number of ad purchases are wasteful, and a large number of viewers find media advertising annoying or useless. Internet advertising targeted at specific buyers based on anticipated interest then would be a more efficient way to reach some individuals and avoid others, and would be particularly advantageous for suppliers of niche products who might be able to afford mass marketing media.

Fourth, trust and reliability are monetizable from the consumer end. That is, the loss of consumer trust at a web site can lead to reduced traffic and business revenues. If the demand for privacy is substantial, web sites will have economic incentives to design more sophisticated programs and add-on features. Moreover, online businesses may find it in their collective interests to establish standards and safeguards for data gathering. Operators that choose not to participate in privacy programs 'are going to limit their market and the number of people that visit them'.[116]

Fifth, merchandisers may willingly buy data from other web sellers. If monetized, their financial interests provide incentives to others to gather more information and for application service providers to provide more efficient exchange. If consumer data has a residual value in a newly formed secondary market, shoppers that provide information can expect lower prices from retailers and web site operators who are anxious to attract their business and additional worth.

It is appropriate that concerned individuals be allowed to withhold information. However, withholders should expect to pay some premia for online purchases if they fail to contribute additional value to the secondary market. Accordingly, any product would ideally be sold with a choice of prices that vary with the degree to which the operator may subsequently deploy data from an individual buyer. Indeed, any blanket requirement to impose greater privacy standards upon an online business can be expected to increase prices paid by all users.

Ira Magaziner, former policy advisor to President Clinton, set forth four standards for a voluntary code regarding online information and privacy:[117]

1. Sellers and other web site operators must notify visitors of any information that they will collect and how it will be used.
2. A person visiting a web site has the opportunity to 'opt out' of any individual use, as well as all.
3. Visitors may look up the information on himself/herself to ensure accuracy.
4. A seal (e.g., Better Business Bureau) is devised to assure consumers that a visited web site complies with the specified code on gathered information.

Rather than legislate standards, Magaziner would not stop buyers from visiting noncomplying sites. Rather, he would rely upon self-help and market outcomes to determine the overall appeal of market privacy.

In any market, government bodies may ensure additional privacy protection for matters of prime personal concern.[118] Legislatures and regulatory agencies may reasonably enact specific rules against, *inter alia*, misuse of social security numbers,[119] financial and medical records,[120] profiled activities of minors and students,[121] telephone usage or other customer proprietary network information (CPNI),[122] or sales of online content records.[123] Watchdog Electronic Privacy Information Center (EPIC, at http://www.epic.org), lists 21 different specific categories of privacy legislation now in consideration in the state legislatures.[124] In an initiative adopted in 2001, the Federal Trade Commission (FTC) advocated particular reforms for improving privacy enforcement.[125] Law enforcers may prosecute fraudulent representations or other deceptive practices.[126] Courts may establish guidelines for contract liability, tortious defamation and admissibility of evidence gathered under electronic or commercial monitoring.

Beyond specific safeguards, more government regulation about general data collection from online shoppers, such as the FTC's once-advocated privacy standards[127] or a European initiative that would require customers to 'opt in' to a program,[128] may be unnecessary for three key reasons. First, it is unclear exactly what general privacy harms would result on most retail web sites. In this respect, EPIC's own web site unwittingly illustrates the non-issue of general privacy abuse by supermarket loyalty cards:

> Von's Supermarket of California sought to introduce 'loyalty card' records in a court case where a consumer had slipped and injured himself in the store. Von's wished to prove that the customer may have been alcohol impaired, and that his loyalty card would show numerous purchases of alcohol. The evidence was ultimately never introduced ... .[129]

As the quote evidences, many issues can be resolved with specific protections against admissibility of court evidence from shopping records; they do not qualify as generic problems.

Second, specialized web sites (e.g., of extremist or pornographic material) now have considerable market incentives to protect privacy of their visitors. Moreover, wary customers may choose to avoid such sites altogether by confining purchases to 'bricks and mortars' stores. Again, courts or legislatures may choose to restrict the admissibility of shopper evidence gathered by law enforcement authorities or private detectives, or otherwise introduced into a proceeding.

Finally, a number of protections now enable consumer self-help. Watchdog groups, such as EPIC, may monitor commercial web sites and suggest improved language for privacy concerns.[130] For disgruntled shoppers, EPIC's web site provides access to programs that enable 'snoop-proof' email, anonymous remail, anonymous surfing, protection against pop-ups, 'cookie busting', secure instant messaging, encryption, password generators, firewalls and disk file erasing.[131]

In this self-help context, the Platform for Privacy Preferences (P3P) specifies a standard computer-readable language that allows web sites to encode privacy policies.[132] With a standard XML format, P3P allows users to configure browser agents to reflect individual preferences.[133] User preferences can be matched with encoded website warnings that are capable of providing service or warning of a possible discrepancy.[134] Major elements of the P3P protocol would describe contact information, whether users will have access to personal information, categories of collected data, purposes of collection, and organizations having access.[135]

Critics, such as EPIC, caution that P3P will result in a sequence of 'endless popup windows' that will unduly burden users who set high privacy preferences, driving them off the web or forcing them to capitulate to a lesser standard.[136] The Electronic Privacy Information Center would prefer a common legislated privacy standard that would be simpler and more transparent, but more restrictive of information gathering. From an economic perspective, there is no compelling reason to reduce choice by mandating such protective standards, and negate the preferences of many consumers less guarded about their privacy. In simple truth, people who find themselves burdened by the data entry requirements of P3P have other protections and shopping alternatives at their disposal.

3.5   FUTURE MODIFICATIONS OF CIRCUMVENTION RULES

As noted in Chapters 1 and 2, markets, organizations, and law interactively accommodate innovation, production and distribution of intellectual property. Law generally should then be appreciated as a catalyst to stimulate changes, an unguent that can bind disparate actors to a common perspective and a signaling apparatus to enable communications among the players. The terms of property rights must then be carefully defined to accommodate changes in evolving markets and technologies.

In this respect, a Copyright Office statement nicely summarizes its related policy-making rationale:

> When changes in technology lead to the development of new markets for
> copyrighted works, copyright owners and users should have the opportunity to
> establish mutually satisfactory relationships. A certain degree of growing pains may
> have to be tolerated if the government is not to step in prematurely, in order to give
> market mechanisms the change to evolve in an acceptable direction. At some point,
> however, existing but dysfunctional markets may require adjustments in the law.
> Timing is therefore key.[137]

We now turn to the issue of administrative review and accommodation with
regard to the DMCA.

Copyright Office Hearings

In the spring of 2000, the Copyright Office instituted its first triennial review
of the DMCA. Per statutory requirements, the Office sought to assess whether
the conduct ban on circumvention (i.e., Section 1201(a)(1)) was actually
diminishing the ability of individuals to make lawful uses of protected
works.[138] Classes of works so adversely affected were to be exempt from a ban
on use restrictions that was to be otherwise implemented in October, 2000.
Drawing upon a perceived legislative intent of the underlying statute, the
Copyright Office considered only demonstrated adverse impact to 'users of a
particular class of work' that were based on 'the attributes of the works
themselves, and not by reference to some external criteria such as the intended
use or users of the works'.[139]

In this quite restricted domain, the Copyright Office permitted access
circumvention only for (1) compilations of lists of websites blocked by
filtering software,[140] and (2) literary works, programs and databases protected
by access control mechanisms that malfunction in some fashion.[141] The Office
declined to follow comments that suggested exemptions for a wide variety
number of other consumer uses.[142] The Office finished a second triennial
review in October 2003 by exempting two new uses.[143]

From an economic perspective, there are three problematic aspects to the
present administrative process. First, interpreting the intent of Congress, the
Copyright Office has assigned exemptions based on embedded attributes of
specific products without regard to underlying consumer tastes and
capabilities. In economic reality, the benefits and costs of a use allowance in
Section 1201(a)(1) cannot practically be made without regard to the value of
underlying consumer activities[144] and the transactional difficulties of market
exchange.[145] The imposed requirement to consider only entire classes of work
may mean that a number of non-infringing uses will remain illegal because
they implicate a wider class of proscribed works.

Second, the Copyright Office's analysis is confined to demonstrated effects.
This ignores the possibility that a great number of innovative uses or devices

have not yet emerged, and might never emerge, if trafficking and use restrictions are too tight, that is, it is difficult to demonstrate what does not exist. Demonstrated effects then should consider supply-side considerations on future activity as well as present user difficulties.

Third, the Office viewed copy and access protection as two independent domains, with the former beyond the present administrative purview of Section 1201(a).[146] The Office dismissed the problem of copy circumvention, pointing out that there is now no restriction in the DMCA that disallows copying for noninfringing uses of materials that have been lawfully acquired or accessed.[147] However, the Association of American Universities cautioned regarding the bootstrapping of access and usage controls; i.e., access 'controls can be, and increasingly will be, coupled with usage controls ... As technology advances, it will become increasingly difficult to distinguish access control technology from copy control technology'.[148]

Nonetheless, if our economic analysis in the preceding sections is correct, the eventual consequences of the present law may be less problematic than harsh critics imagine. Regardless of how rights are initially assigned, content owners will still have financial incentives to provide enabling technologies and integrate technical functions in order to widen product appeal and accommodate new institutions. For example, network users in time will probably be able to mouseclick to an authorized web site with the additional device power to provide a particular circumvention need (although possibly at a positive price that some fair use advocates may argue is inherently undeserved).

Optimal Intervention

If markets fail in some instances to provide important benefits and direct government intervention therefore is necessary, additional use exemptions can now be incorporated in the remaining body of Section 1201(a). Indeed, the DMCA itself now contains seven specific exemptions for particular uses.[149] However, the addition of new protected uses would require more cumbersome legislation and does not admit continued feedback and ongoing surveillance regarding the outcome.

As a second relaxant, courts might also have the authority to implement in common law a second stratum of highly contextual fair use rules that safeguard particular circumvention rights; under Section 1201(c)(1), 'nothing in [Section 1201] shall affect rights, remedies, limitations, or defenses in copyright infringements, including fair use, under [Title 17]'.[150] However, the wording here is quite ambiguous, and the District Court in *Universal City Studios* v. *Reimerdes* held that users may not now break access protection to enable fair use.[151]

With a more aggressive eye to restoring user rights, Representatives Boucher and Doolittle introduced the Digital Media Consumers' Rights Act (DMCRA).[152] Section 5(b)(1) aims to resolve the conflict between Section 1201(a)(1) and Section 1201(c). The section makes clear that it is legal to circumvent a technological measure in order to gain access to or use a work if the circumvention does not result in infringement of copyright.[153] If enacted, the new provision would allow users the right to defeat circumvention for noninfringing reasons.

Taken by itself, the suggested change attempts to moderate possible overextensions in Section 1201(a)(1).[154] However, it may at times require courts to work through a number of complex legal issues regarding infringement, such as fair use, and therefore may fail to provide clear ongoing administrative signals to the market. Moreover, as a practical matter, few consumers have the technical wherewithal to break access protection by themselves.

In a wider easing, Section 5(b)(2) of the DMCRA would relax further the anti-trafficking provisions of Section 1201(a)(2). To do this, it would modify section Section 1201(c) by adding a new paragraph (5); i.e. it is not a violation of Section 1201 to manufacture, traffick, or make noninfringing use of a hardware or software product that is capable of enabling significant noninfringing use of a copyrighted work.[155] In Representative Boucher's view:

> The section restores the standard set by the U.S. Supreme Court in the 1984 decision of Sony v. Universal City Studios, 464 U.S. 417 (1984) (commonly known as the 'Betamax' case). The provision is intended to ensure that consumers will have access to hardware and software products by which to engage in the activities authorized by the legislation. For example, a person could develop software that would enable him to listen in audio form to the text of an electronic book he has purchased.[156]

Though greatly extensive of consumer rights, Section 5(b)(2) goes too far. By enabling general trafficking of circumvention devices, the act would enable rogue users to obtain technology needed to defeat protection, and then post and distribute copyrighted material throughout the Internet. This would raise considerably the costs of policing the Internet and prosecuting violators, and may discourage a number of interesting investments in content and distribution.

However, a weakened reform of Section 1201(a)(2) might be reasonable, such as a conceivable three-year review of circumvention devices approved by the Copyright Office. This would allow the Copyright Office to conduct public hearings and recommend technologies that meet more precise use restrictions on the network (e.g., tethering). The Office could also review off-network uses in which access protection is embedded (e.g., garage door openers, toner cartridges).[157] The process would readily admit continuing technical input and feedback contrasting notably with present legislative and jurisprudential domains that admit no systematic feedback. However, the Copyright Office would not be statutorily compelled to permit any circumvention device. As one possible example, the Office might approve the trafficking of limited circumvention devices to allow home users to make backup copies of personally owned music files, which the Copyright Office itself recommended to Congress as a suitable reform in the DMCA.[158]

3.6   CONCLUSION

From this economist's perspective, a procedurally rational approach that combines markets, administration, and judicial and legislative oversight should permit for relevant matters the necessary time and information to surface. The incrementalist approach is purposely and wisely limited – restricting considerations, limiting classifications, forsaking measurement, leaving options open and learning by doing. Incrementalists learn which outcomes are 'satisficing' by *not* acting, forsaking the spectacular imagined gains from an immediate fix for the prosaic benefits of slow judgment and reversible errors. Regrettably, the truly relevant information for a more comprehensive approach is often lacking, particularly in the open-ended game called the Internet.[159]

NOTES

1. 17 U.S.C. § 106.
2. For known works created after January 1, 1978, copyright endures for a term equal to 70 years after the death of the last surviving author (17 U.S.C. §302(a)–(b)). For anonymous works, pseudonymous works, and works made for hire, copyright endures for 95 years after first publication, or 120 years after creation, whichever expires first (17 U.S.C. §302(c)).
3. Fair use is a complex subjective matter that requires consideration of four factors: the purpose and character of use, the nature of the copyrighted work, the amount and substantiality of the taking, and the effect of the use upon the potential market for or value of a copyrighted work (17 U.S.C. § 107). The doctrine has been said to be 'so flexible as virtually to defy definition' (*Time Inc.* v. *Bernard Geis Assoc.*, 293 F. Supp. 130, 144 (S.D.N.Y. 1968)).
4. The first sale doctrine extends to a lawful private owner the right to sell or otherwise dispose of a copyrighted work. This does not include the right to make reproductions (17 U.S.C. § 109(a)).
5. Per full statutory wording, copyright protection does not extend to any 'idea, procedure,

process, system, method of operation, concept, principle, or discovery, regardless of the form in which it is described, explained, illustrated, or embodied in such work' (17 U.S.C. § 102(b)).

6. Libraries may reproduce or distribute single copies of works to interested readers and libraries, and up to three copies (including digital) for preservation of unpublished works or legitimate replacement or reformatting of published ones (so long as a replacement cannot otherwise be obtained at a fair market price). Digital copies may not be distributed outside the premises of the library, although physical copies derived from them may. A format is considered obsolete if the machine or device needed for rendering is no longer commercially available (17 U.S.C. § 108).

7. Performances or displays of lawfully made works by instructors or pupils in the course of face-to-face teaching activities are copyright exempt, as are transmissions of non-dramatic literary or musical works. Performances of non-dramatic works are similarly exempt for religious services, non-profit establishments, small eating and drinking establishments, government organizations, record stores or uses for the blind and handicapped (17 U.S.C. § 110).

8. 17 U.S.C. § 121.

9. See 47 U.S.C. § 553a and 17 U.S.C. § 1002(c). See also M. Jackson, 'Technology and the Changing Nature of Copyright Enforcement', unpublished paper, Telecommunications Policy Research Conference, Alexandria, Virginia, September 23–25, 2000.

10. Information Infrastructure Task Force, *Intellectual Property and the National Information Infrastructure: The Report of the Working Group on Intellectual Property Rights*, Washington, DC: U.S. Department of Commerce (177 1995).

11. Pub. L. No. 105–304, 112 Stat. 2860 (1998).

12. S. Rep. No. 105–190, 2 (1998).

13. World Intellectual Property Organization, Copyright Treaty, Article 11; Performances and Phonograms Treaty, Article 18; adopted December 20, 1996, Geneva, Switzerland.

14. 17 U.S.C. § 1201(a)(1)(A). Circumvention means to 'descramble a scrambled work, to decrypt an encrypted work, or otherwise to avoid, bypass, remove, deactivate, or impair a technological measure, without the authority of the copyright owner' (17 U.S.C. § 1201(a)(3)(A)).

15. 'No person shall manufacture, import, offer to the public, provide, or otherwise traffic in any technology, product, service, device, component, or part thereof, that is primarily designed or produced for the purpose of circumventing a technological measure that effectively controls access to a work protected under this title' (17 U.S.C. § 1201(a)(2)). Outlawed devices must be primarily designed to facilitate circumvention, have limited commercially significant impact beyond circumvention, or be marketed with knowledge for use in circumventing a technological measure (17 U.S.C. § 1201(a)(2)).

16. 'No person shall manufacture, import, offer to the public, provide, or otherwise traffic in any technology, product, service, device, component, or part thereof that is primarily designed or produced for the purpose of circumventing protection afforded by a technological measure that effectively protects a right of a copyright owner under this title in a work or a portion thereof' (17 U.S.C. § 1201(b)(1)).

17. Computer Science and Telecommunications Board, National Research Council, *The Digital Dilemma: Intellectual Property in the Information Age*, Washington, DC: National Academy Press (2000).

18. H.R. Rep. No. 105–551, pt 2, 26 (1998).

19. Supra note 17, at 202–3.

20. European Parliament and the Council of the European Union, Common Position (EC) No. 48/2000, 47, 28 September 2000.

21. P. Jaszi, 'Testimony, Exemption to Prohibition on Circumvention of Copyright Protection Systems for Access Control Technologies' (hereafter 'Exemption Hearing'), 64 Fed. Reg. 226, Docket No. RM 99-7, May 2, 2000, at http://www.loc.gov/copyright/1201/hearings (retrieved May 19, 2001).

22. In the language of the American Library Association, persistent access control measures control 'the digital product at every step of the process from initial access to distribution to

re-access to use. These types of systems generally employ one or more forms of encryption to protect the content and associated permission and identification information. Persistent access control systems also require software or hardware methods for enforcing attached usage rules, metering and tracking use, and authenticating users and payment' ('Initial Comments', M.M. Nisbet, American Library Association, et al., #162, Exemption Hearing, supra note 21, 13, at http://www.loc.gov/copyright/1201/comments (retrieved May 19, 2001)).

23. The theory of network goods is more fully discussed in M. Katz and C. Shapiro, 'Systems Competition and Network Effects', 8 *Journal of Economic Perspectives* 93 (1994).

24. M. Olsen, *The Logic of Collective Action*: (Cambridge, MA: Harvard University Press, 1972).

25. Ibid., 5.

26. Ibid., 6.

27. D. Friedman, 'In Defense of Private Orderings', 13 *Berkeley Technology Law Journal* 3 (1998).

28. C. Shapiro and H.R. Varian, *Information Rules* (Boston, MA: Harvard Business School Press, 1999), 53–82

29. 17 U.S.C. § 106(1)–(6).

30. W. Gordon, 'Intellectual Property as Price Discrimination: Implications for Contract', 73 *Chi-Kent Law Review* 1367 (1998). 'Accordingly, judges should watch for situations in which unauthorized use of copyrighted material undermines price discrimination schemes [i.e., versioning] and should be chary of holding such uses fair' (W.W. Fisher, 'Reconstructing the Fair Use Doctrine', 101 *Harvard Law Review* 1661, 1742 (1988)).

31. B.M. Owen and S.S. Wildman, *Video Economics* (Cambridge, MA: Harvard University Press, 1992).

32. A.M. Spence, 'Non linear Prices and Welfare', 8 *Journal of Public Economics* 66 (1979). The resulting price schedule can usually be expected to be volume discounting. That is, producers will generally charge less money for each succeeding unit of production or day of storage.

33. BMG Entertainment, EMI Recorded Music, Sony Music Entertainment, Vivendi Universal Music Group and Warner Music Group.

34. MusicNet is distributed as a software product that allows users to stream or temporarily download a specified number of songs from individual application service providers (ASPs) for a monthly subscription fee. Each ASP may set subscription prices and tailor service features to its individual liking. At first, MusicNet tracks were not downloadable to portable MP3 players or burnable onto CDs (E. Hansen and J. Hu, 'RealNetworks Plugs in MusicNET', *Tech News*, CNET.com, December 4, 2001); L.M. Bowman, 'MusicNet, Pressplay Closing in on Labels', *Tech News*, CNET.com, October 15, 2002.

35. J. Hu, 'Pressplay bid points to Napster remix', *Tech News*, CNET.com, May 19, 2003.

36. *Pressplay* will more aggressively manage the customer interface, directly market online product to consumers, and determine retail fees that partners may charge. The Pressplay service will offer a number of plans, including an annual subscription (price = $14.95/month) that permits unlimited streaming and downloading, as well as 120 free 'burns' that may be supplemented afterward with individual purchases (J. Hu, 'Pressplay Comes to Life after Long Wait', *Tech News*, CNET.com, December 19, 2001); L.M. Bowman (supra note 34). Selected tracks at Pressplay may be transferred to a second computer at no additional charge, but downloads to MP3 players are not permitted. The Pressplay service will also permit playlist sharing, browsing by artist and genre, parental opt outs, and streaming of free '30 second samples'. (J. Borland, 'Pressplay to Offer Unlimited Downloads', *Tech News*, CNET.com, July 31, 2002).

37. Well situated for deals with broadband distributors. *Listen.com* has sound recording licenses with each of the five major labels, distribution partnerships that include Direct TV, Verizon, Charter Communications, Time Warner's RoadRunner and more than 50 webcaster affiliates (J. Borland, 'Listen.com Lands Last Big Five Label', *Tech News*, CNET.com, July 1, 2002). Its Rhapsody service had offered an all-streaming subscription

service (price = \$9.95/month) with unlimited monthly use, but came to permit CD burning. (J. Hu, 'Listen.com Inks Broadband Deals', *Tech News*, CNET.com, July 31, 2002; J. Borland, 'Listen to Offer Legal CD-Burning', *Tech News*, CNET.com, October 23, 2002). It markets service heavily through Internet service providers and is now working with several home-electronics companies to bring music subscription service to home stereos through enabled chips and local area connectivity (J. Borland, 'Listen Aims for Living Room', *Tech News*, CNET.com, January 9, 2003). Real Networks bought the service for \$36 million in late 2003 (J. Borland and S. Olsen, 'RealNetworks seeks Listen.com buyout', *Tech News*, CNET.com, April 21, 2003).

38. *Full Audio* has a cache-download technology that offers superior audio quality and permanent downloads, but not burning or song transfer to MP3 players. The subscription service now has sound recording licenses with Universal, Warner Music, BMG and EMI, and distribution arrangements with Clear Channel Radio and Microsoft's WindowsMedia.com (G. Mariano, 'Full Audio Gets New Music, Funding', *Tech News*, CNET.com, June 18, 2002). The service offers 50 downloads for \$7.49 per month, or 100 downloads at \$14.99 per month. Full Audio also struck an agreement with Warner Music to allow AOL users to download individual tracks for 99 cents apiece (G. Mariano, 'Full Audio Gets New Music, Funding', *Tech News*, CNET.com, June 18, 2002; 'Full Audio Corporation Launches MusicNow Digital Music Subscription Service on Phoenix Clear Channel Radio Stations', MI2N.com, April 18, 2001).

39. *Emusic.com* offers streaming and downloading of a number of MP3s from Universal Music Group for a monthly fee (G. Mariano, 'Universal, Sony to Trim Download Prices', *Tech News*, CNET.com, June 12, 2002). The group recently entered into a business partnership with computer manufacturer Gateway to bundle music service on new computers, and signed similar bundling deals with Hewlett Packard (M. Kanellos, 'Gateway tests Waters of Music Business', *Tech News*, CNET.com, April 26, 2002). A free 30-day trial subscription with 100 free MP3 downloads is now offered (G. Mariano, 'Off-key Efforts Hinder Paid Net Music', *Tech News*, CNET.com, June 5, 2002). Monthly fees for subscriptions are \$14.99 (three month commitment) or \$9.99 (one-year commitment) (G. Mariano, 'Gateway Grooves to Emusic', *Tech News*, CNET.com, April 29, 2002).

40. PulseOne (from Rioport) offers a new 'Direct to Device' technology that enables secure playing of tracks on portable MP3 devices, music phones, digital stereos, and set-top boxes. PulseOne features licensed tracks from Sony, Warner and BMG. Rioport does not sell songs directly but rather offers them for sale through web sites (e.g., BestBuy.com and MTV.com) that use its retail technology (Rioport, News Release, 'Rioport Unveils Industry-First Technology', January 3, 2002; G. Mariano, 'BMG to Offer Tunes on the Go', *Tech News*, CNET.com, January 28, 2002; J. Hu, 'Warner Whistles a New Digital Tune', *Tech News*, CNET.com, September 23, 2002).

41. *MusicMatch* has agreements with BMG, EMI, Warner, and Universal. The service announced in November a new paid streaming service called 'Artist on Demand'. The service fee will be \$6.95 per month or \$59.40 per year. The interactive service will augment *Music Match*'s subscription radio service (Radio MX, \$4.95/mo.) and jukebox software (S. Olsen, 'MusicMatch in Tune with Labels', *Tech News*, CNET.com, November 13, 2002).

42. *Liquid Audio* announced its dissolution in 2002 after selling its encoding patents to Microsoft (J. Hu, 'Liquid Audio to evaporate', *Tech News*, CNET.com, December 6, 2002). An intriguing service, Liquid Audio had packaged music playing software that allowed but controlled copying and transfer of songs. Liquid Audio's service permitted subscribers to download 20 songs per month, burn each song up to three times, and export it to five different portable devices. The company had distribution deals with important retailers – Amazon, Best Buy.com, CDNow, Sam Goody, Barnes & Noble and Sony Music Club. Subsequent to the dissolution, six prominent retailers announced their intention to work together to effectively compete in the digital marketplace through an investment in Echo Networks; the new service will involve streaming, downloading, and music recommendation (M. Kane, 'Liquid Audio finds a Buyer', *Tech News*, CNET.com, June

13, 2002).

43. IMG Entertainment recently bought *Songspy.com* (July, 2002), a legitimate peer-to-peer music service that tracks downloads and pays royalties to artists and labels (Reuters, 'IMG Snaps up Peer-to-Peer Service', *Tech News*, CNET.com, July 30, 2002). Information company Muze streams music samples (G. Mariano, 'Muze Attracts Fourth Major Label', *Tech News*, CNET.com, June 11, 2002). Users of reformed *Scour Exchange* download a limited number of free songs for monthly intervals (L.M. Bowman, 'Sony to Send Songs via Scour', *Tech News*, CNET.com, May 14, 2002). *Streamwaves* offers a streaming service for Christian music (G. Mariano, 'Universal Licenses Music to Streamwaves', *Tech News*, CNET.com, June 4, 2002). *Warner Music* is releasing unprotected MP3 downloads of individual song tracks for 99 cents apiece for AOL subscribers.

44. Tracks in Apple's library can be downloaded for 99 cents, with a 30-second sample period and no subscription fee. Some albums are available for $9.99. With light-handed DRM (called Fairplay), each track can be burned in unlimited amounts to iPods and CDs, and made available to three other Macs on a wireless network called Rendezvous. Apple's compression technology, Advanced Audio Coding, is 30 percent more efficient than MP3, the present standard for free transfer, and has audio quality equal to CDs. MAC users can also designate playlists using jukebox software called *iTunes*, which works seamlessly with the iPod player (J. Borland, 'Apple Unveils Music Stores', *Tech News*, CNET.com, April 28, 2003). Tracks ripped to KaZaa, or other file-sharing services, will not be permitted or have wildly distorted sound.

45. *Vitaminic* uses content solely from independent labels and sells unlimited download services to commercial customers who use free packaged online music to promote interest in their business 'Vitaminic and Verbatim Strike Digital Music Distribution Agreement', at http://www.vitaminic.co.uk, June 24, 2001 (retrieved September 30, 2003)

46. *OD2* (On Demand Distribution) offers an innovative service option for fans of 'world music', where 40 tracks per month can be automatically deleted and replenished by the service itself ('Womad, Realworld, and OD2 in Ground-Breaking Partnership to Launch World's First Music Subscription Services', at http://www.ondemanddistribution.com/eng/home/home.asp, October 18, 2001 (retrieved September 30, 2003)).

47. *Wippit* is a legitimate peer-to-peer service that allows unlimited downloads for an annual subscription, as well as a ring tone service for mobile phones 'Wippit Offers Unlimited Downloads for 10 pounds Per Year', at http://www.wippit.com/download/, October 4, 2001 (retrieved September 30, 2003).

48. Over 80 percent of the online listening audience now uses the music primarily to accompany time spent working on the computer (B. Rose and L. Rosin, 'Internet V: Startling New Insights about the Internet and Streaming' (New York: Arbitron/Edison Media Research, 2000)). This means that webcasters and interactive streaming may be contending for the same listening minutes.

49. J. Borland, 'Net Music Gets AOL Audition', *Tech News*, CNET.com, February 26, 2003.
50. Supra note 34.
51. Supra note 49.
52. J. Hu, 'AOL Fills Bargain Bin with New Music', *Tech News*, CNET.com, June 18, 2002.
53. Supra note 36.
54. J. Borland, 'Pressplay to Offer Unlimited Downloads', *Tech News*, CNET.com, July 31, 2002.
55. Supra note 39.
56. J. Wilcox and E. Hansen, 'Apple's Music: Microsoft's Sour Note?', *Tech News*, CNET.com, April 30, 2003.
57. I. Fried, 'Apple Plants Seed of iTunes for Windows', *Tech News*, CNET.com, April 30, 2003.
58. E. Hansen, 'Microsoft Prepares Reply to iTunes', *Tech News*, CNET.com, May 23, 2003.
59. Supra note 36.
60. 'Groundbreaking Gateway Music Value by Pressplay Launches Today', December 6,

2002, at http://www.pressplay.com/pressroom/pr_20021206.html (retrieved May 18, 2003).

61. Reuters, 'Listen.com Discounts CD-copying Fee', *Tech News*, CNET.com, February 13, 2003.

62. L.M. Bowman, 'Consumer Claims Victory in CD Lawsuit', *Tech News*, CNET.com, February 22, 2002.

63. 'SunnComm Announces Peer-to-Peer Music Sharing without Piracy', MI2N.com, April 11, 2002.

64. Reuters, 'Net Music Giveaway Plays Encore', *Tech News*, CNET.com, January 20, 2003.

65. Supra note 58.

66. E. Hansen, 'Steve Jobs' Half Note', *Tech News*, CNET.com, May 21, 2003.

67. J. Borland, 'Apple Unveils Music Store', *Tech News*, CNET.com, April 28, 2003.

68. S. Scotchmer, 'Standing on the Shoulders of Giants: Cumulative Research and the Patent Law', 5 *Journal of Economic Perspectives* 29, 31–2 (1991).

69. J.K. MacKie-Mason and A.L. Jankovich, 'PEAK: Pricing Electronic Access to Knowledge', unpublished document at http://www.personal.umich.edu/~jmm/papers/PEAK (visited June 5, 2001).

70. Regarding the definition of the web interface, 'all lessons, interaction, activities, and learning resources must be accessible via the digital interface. The student must be able to use the interface, often without "hands-on" instruction in its use, and everything that the student needs – including faculty support – must be accessed via the interface' (University of Maryland University College, Comments, Promotion of Distance Education through Digital Technologies, 63 Fed. Reg. 71167, Docket No. 98-124, Washington, DC, February 5, 1999 at http://www.loc.gov/copyright/disted/comments.html (visited May 19, 2001)).

71. A provider of online databases states the benefits of price discrimination in so far as it affects small users of his content. 'If we cannot enforce [variable] access pricing ... we would not be able to charge varying amounts for different levels of access. Accordingly, we would be required to charge a single price to all institutions. This might be beneficial to the large institutions, but could make it difficult for the smallest and poorest universities, medical schools, public libraries, and smaller institutions, and the communities they serve, to be able to afford a subscription. It is precisely the ability to circumvent the access control technology which would exacerbate the digital divide' (D. Mirchin, Statement, 'Exemption Hearing', supra note 21, May 2, 2000, 5, at http://www.loc.gov/copyright/1201/hearings (visited May 19, 2001)). With limited access, resource-strapped libraries may test reader demands before committing to a full subscription and, if an item is found to be particularly popular, recover access to the historic backlog without adding a foot of shelf space. Librarians may also find that limited accessing provides a particularly useful means for navigating between contending demands for resources, and increasing the spectrum of choices.

72. Costs here should be a key concern for the best research institutions and a knowledge society that funds and benefits from them. Facing routinely high demands for service quality from members of prestigious research communities, high-quality universities can be expected to hike tuitions, increase demands on the legislature and divert resources from other uses on campus to meet budgetary needs. This presents a danger of a competitive political process that is less important in the market for consumer goods that are more subject to the spending whims of the individual user.

73. A. Odlyzko, 'Tragic Loss or Good Riddance? The Impending Demise of Traditional Scholarly Journals', *International Journal of Human Computer Studies*, 42, 71 (1995).

74. 17 U.S.C. 107(3).

75. *Campbell* v. *Acuff Rose*, 510 U.S. 569 (1994).

76. A.W. Appel and E.W. Felten, 'Initial Comments', Exemption Hearing, supra note 21, February 17, 2000 at http://www.loc.gov/copyright/1201/comments (retrieved May 19, 2001).

77. American Library Association, supra note 22, at 12.

78. Upfront costs for a digital library host service have been estimated at $100 000 for a base

of 200 digital journals (ibid., 45).

79. M.S. Bonn, W.P. Lougee, J.K. MacKie-Mason and J.F. Riveros, 'A Report on the Peak Experiment: Usage and Economic Behavior', 5 *D-LIB Magazine* 7/8, 1999, at http://www.dlib.org/dlib/july99/mackie-mason/07mackie-mason.html (retrieved June 5, 2001).

80. A.S. Okerson, 'Buy or Lease? Two Models for Scholarly Information at the End (or the Beginning) of an Era', 125 *Daedalus* 55, 73 (1996), at http://www.library.yale.edu/~okerson/daedalus.html (retrieved June 26, 2001).

81. Writes one critic: 'We access several journals online from one publisher whose password protects their site. It is set up for one user at a time. So all journals are tied up while one person looks at one, although he/she could browse all of them. They are all unavailable while that one person uses the collection' ('Initial Comments', American Library Association, supra note 22, at 22).

82. 'Basically, [persistent access controls] are designed to facilitate a metered, pay-per-use model for works in electronic form ... Usage rules will limit the number of uses or the time in which content is available ... Instead, publishers may choose a 'superdistribution' model, collecting revenues from each new user as content is redistributed ... These measures can also set time limits on review, or ensure that those who are slower to absorb information on a computer screen can be shut off from access as the time limit expires ... Access, use, and redistribution controls can – and we believe will – be built into the works, greatly restricting appropriate use of such works' ('Initial Comments', American Library Association, supra note 22, at 15–20).

83. Admittedly, blanket licenses can be 'tie in' arrangements that unduly restrict users to make inefficient 'all or nothing' choices. However, these concerns are better resolved by appropriate antitrust authorities and are not a matter for copyright administration.

84. Quoted in A. Odlyzko, 'Stronger Copyright Protection for Cyberspace: Desirable, Inevitable, and Irrelevant', at http://www.research.att.com/~amo (retrieved June 26, 2001).

85. D. Mirchin, 'Statement', Exemption Hearing, supra note 21, May 2, 2000, 3 at http://www.loc.gov/copyright/1201/hearings (retrieved May 19, 2001).

86. Ibid., 4.

87. A.R. Adler, 'Statement before the Senate Judiciary Committee Concerning S.487: The Technology, Education, and Copyright Harmonization Act of 2001', March 13, 2001, at http://www.publishers.org/home/congrpt/s487testimony.htm (retrieved May 11, 2000).

88. M.S. Bonn, W.P. Lougee, J.K. MacKie-Mason and J.F. Riveros, 'A Report on the PEAK Experiment: Content and Design', 5 *D-LIB Magazine*, 6 (1999), at http://www.dlib.org/dlib/juje99/06bonn.html (retrieved June 6, 2001).

89. Regarding the holdout problem, 'at a major university, the highly ranked cinema program recently tried to develop a distance education film course. The institution was committed to invest $600,000 in the effort. Part of the course involving the use of film clips ranging from 5 to 30 seconds. Negotiations for rights went on interminably. Permissions had to be gotten from, and payments had to be made to, copyright owners and actors. Some people never responded, others demanded a great deal of money, some simply said no. In the end, after losing a substantial amount of money, the failure to secure the rights to film clips less than a minute long shut down a promising program' (G.A. Heeger, University of Maryland University College, 'Testimony, Concerning the Technology, Education, and Copyright Harmonization Act of 2001', House Judiciary Committee, U.S. House of Representatives, Washington, DC, March 13, 2001).

90. University consortia are teams of libraries that negotiate collectively on behalf of a group of individual members. Subscribing agents are commercial agents who negotiate usage contracts on behalf of one or many licensees. Copyright collectives negotiate contracts on behalf of their rights holders, e.g., in photo-reproduction or musical performances. Rights clearance centers grant licenses based on individual terms specified by the owner. 'One-stop-shops' are a coalition of separate collective management organizations which offer a centralized source for a number of related rights, e.g. photos and music, that would be particularly useful in multimedia production (at http://www.wipo.org/about-

ip/en/about_collective_mngt.html (visited June 26, 2001)).

91. R.P. Merges, 'Contracting into Liability Rules: Intellectual Property Rights and Collective Rights Organizations', 84 *California Law Review* 1293, 1392 (1996).

92. http://www.copyright.com/News/AboutNewsReleases2001Aprl9_RL.asp (visited June 16, 2001).

93. Copyright Clearance Center, 'Comments: Promotion of Distance Education through Digital Technologies', US Copyright Office, Docket No. 98-12A, February 5, 1999.

94. http://www.rightsline.com/facts.htm (retrieved June 16, 2001).

95. V.S. Perlman, 'Reply Comments', Exemption Hearing, supra note 21.

96. http://www.info2clear.com (retrieved June 16, 2001).

97. http://www.library.yale.edu/~llicense/index.shtml (retrieved June 26, 2001).

98. D.J. Gervais, 'E-Commerce and Intellectual Property: Lock it Up or License?', at http://www.copyright.com/News/AboutArticlesIntellectualProp.asp (retrieved June 15, 2001) .

99. L.N. Gasaway, 'Values Conflict in the Digital Environment: Librarians versus Copyright Holders', 24 *Columbia Journal of Law and the Arts* 115, 134 (2000).

100. A. Okerson, 'The Transition to Electronic Content Licensing: The Institutional Context in 1997', Scholarly Communication and Technology Conference of the Andrew W. Mellon Foundation, Emory University, April 24–25, 1997, 1, at http://www.library.yale.edu/~okerson/mellon.html. Ms. Okerson continues: 'The Yale Library, for example, is now party to a number of licenses that permit substantial amounts of copying and downloading for individual learning, research, in-the-classroom learning, library reserves, coursepacks, and related activities. Interlibrary Loan and transmission of works to individual scholars are matters that still need a great deal of work. However, the licenses of 1996 and 1997 represent significant all-around improvements and surely reinforce the feeling that rapid progress is being made' (at 6).

101. At http://www.epic.org/privacy/profiling (retrieved October 18, 2002).

102. Ibid.

103. Ibid.

104. Ibid.

105. Ibid.

106. At http://www.epic.org/privacy/amazon/amasonltr10.8.02.html (retrieved October 18, 2002).

107. At http://news.bbc.co.uk/1/hi/business/914691.stm (retrieved October 19, 2002).

108. J.R. Reidenberg, 'Privacy in the Information Economy: A Fortress or Frontier for Individual Rights', 44 *Federal Communications Law Journal* 195 (1992); J.R. Reidenberg and F. Gamet-Pol, 'The Fundamental Role of Privacy and Confidence in the Network', 30 *Wake Forest Law Review* 105 (1995); J.E. Cohen, 'A Right to Read Anonymously: A Closer Look at Copyright Management in Cyberspace', 28 *Connecticut Law Review* 981 (1996). The latter writes: '[Profiling] is a well-established practice through which businesses of all types seek to learn as much as possible about customers who show interest in their products or services. For transactions that occur in "real" (as opposed to digital) space, however, the ability to profile one's customer base is limited to some extent by customers' willingness to self-report – for example, by filling out product registration cards. In contrast, profiling in the digital age holds out, for the first time, the tantalizing promise of "perfect" information, because digital communications can be structured to create detailed records of consumer purchases and reading activities' (at 988).

109. A recent study by the Conference Board found that while the percentage of Americans going online has increased from 59 to 61 percent in the last year, trust levels appear to be declining (at www.consumerinternetbarometer.us, retrieved October 18, 2002)

110. 'Business Week/Harris Poll: A Growing Threat', *Business Week Magazine*, March 2000, reported at http://www.epic.org/privacy/survey/default.html (retrieved October 19, 2002).

111. 'Privacy Concerns: Is It Time for the Government to Act?', *Wirthlin Report*, January

2001. reported at http://www.epic.org/privacy/survey/default.html (retrieved October 19, 2002).

112. The idea of information and transaction costs in a market relationship appears first in R.H. Coase, 'The Nature of the Firm', 4 *Economica* 386 (1937). *See also* Chapter 1

113. With full knowledge of customer tastes, it would be possible for, e.g., British Airways to inform likely Anglophiles of attractive tourist packages, and to skip the likely Anglophobes. Personal profiling would economize on British Airway's marketing efforts, and conceivably provide more trips and/or save dollars for tourists. Flier information can be reasonably acquired by observing how consumers visit and behave on web sites operated by, *inter alia*, the Royal Shakespeare Theatre, Windsor Castle or even other airlines.

114. R. Posner, 'The Economics of Privacy', *Papers and Proceedings*, American Economic Association, May, 1981.

115. J. Chessen, 'Information and Privacy', American Bankers Association, Washington, DC, 13 (2000)

116. Magaziner, infra note 117.

117. I. Magaziner, 'Creating a Framework for Electronic Commerce', Progress and Freedom Foundation, July, 1999, at http://www.pff.org/ira_magaziner.htm (retrieved June 4, 2002), 5–6.

118. Federal Trade Commission, 'Privacy Online: Fair Information Practices in the Electronic Marketplace: A Federal Trade Commission Report to Congress', May, 2000, at http://www.ftc.gov/opa/2001/10/privacyagenda.htm (retrieved October 19, 2002). In a 2001 speech, present Chief Commissioner Timothy Muris did not seem to express any great support for the idea of legislation (T. Muris, 'Protecting Consumers' Privacy: 2002 and Beyond', The Privacy 2001 Conference, Cleveland, Ohio, October 4, 2001, at http://www.ftc.gov/speeches/muris/privisp1002.htm (retrieved, June 4 2002).

119. Proposed legislative protection in the 107th Congress included Identity Theft Protection Act of 2001 (H.R. 220), Personal Information Privacy Act of 2001 (H.R. 1478), Social Security Number Privacy and Identity Theft Prevention Act of 2001 (H.R. 2036, S. 1014), Social Security Number Protection Act of 2002 (H. R. 4513), Social Security Number Privacy Act of 2001 (S. 324) and Social Security Number Protection Act of 2001 (S. 451). For hyperlinks, see http://www.epic.org/privacy/bill_track.html (retrieved October 18, 2002).

120. Proposed bills implicating financial and/or medical privacy included the Medical Information Protection and Research Enhancement Act of 2001 (H.R. 1215), Consumer's Right to Financial Privacy Act (H.R. 2720), National Consumer Privacy Act (H.R. 2730), Financial Information Privacy Protection Act of 2001 (S.30) and Financial Institution Privacy Protection Act of 2001 (S.450). For hyperlinks, see ibid.

121. Proposed bills include the Student Privacy Protection Act (S. 290) and the Family Privacy and Security Act of 2002 (S. 2137). For hyperlinks, see ibid.

122. The Federal Communications Commission recently issued a Notice of Proposed Rulemaking, 'Rules and Regulations Implementing the Telephone Consumer Protection Act of 1991', regarding whether to modify its present rules regarding CPNI (67 *Federal Register* 195, October 8, 2002, 62667–81).

123. Records of cable subscribers and video rentals are now protected respectively in the Cable Act and the Video Privacy Protection Act.

124. Including arrest records, bank records, cable TV, computer crime, credit, criminal justice, government data banks, employment, insurance, mailing lists, medical, miscellaneous, polygraphing, privacy statutes privileges, school records, social security numbers, tax records, telephone services, testing and wiretaps (at http://www.epic.org/privacy/consumer/states.html (retrieved October 18, 2002)).

125. Itemized concerns for Commissioner Timothy Muris included creating a national 'do-not-call' list, beefing up enforcement against spam (chain letters, pyramids, 'get-rich-quick' schemes), helping victims of ID theft, ending pretexting (fraudulently obtaining personal financial information), encouraging accuracy in credit reporting, enforcing privacy promises, increasing enforcement on children's privacy, encouraging

consumers' privacy complaints regarding fraudulent and deceptive business practices, enforcing telemarketing restraints, restricting the use of pre-acquired account information, holding workshops on new and emerging technologies, and enforcing the Gramm-Leach-Bliley Act that requires financial institutions to provide privacy notices and allows consumers to choose whether their financial institutions may share their personal information. http://www.ftc.gov/opa/2001/10/privacyagenda.htm (retrieved October 19, 2001).

126. In October, 2002, the Federal Trade Commission settled cases against American Student List and National Research Center for College and University Admissions for collecting marketing dossiers on students under the pretext of college admission and scholarship opportunities. In August, 2002, the New York Attorney General filed suit against the Student Marketing Group for much the same issue (at http://www.epic.org/privacy/profiling (retrieved October 18, 2002)).

127. Supra note 118.

128. At http://news.bbc.co.uk/1/hi/sci/tech/1653907.stm (retrieved October 19, 2002).

129. http://www.epic.org/privacy/profiling (retrieved October 18, 2002).

130. http://www.epic.org/reports/surfer-beware.html (retrieved October 18, 2002).

131. http://www.epic.org/privacy/tools.html (retrieved October 18, 2002).

132. For a discussion and criticism of P3P, see L.F. Cranor and J.R. Reidenberg, 'Can User Agents Accurately Represent Privacy Notices?' Discussion Paper 1.0, August 30, 2002, Telecommunications Policy Research Conference, Washington, DC.

133. As an example, Microsoft implemented a P3P user agent as part of its Internet Explorer 6 Browser (IE6) that permits six alternative cookie-blocking settings, customized design with additional capabilities, and a 'View Privacy Report' that directly displays an HTML translation of a complying site's policies. A previewed version of Netscape's Navigator 7 has similar capabilities, and AT&T released a public beta of an IE add-on called the Privacy Bird, which visually signals a match (or mismatch) between a site's policy and the user's expressed preferences.

134. 'A sample P3P transaction might look something like the following. Joe Surfer configures his P3P enabled web browser to say that he does not want to disclose his home address unless he is purchasing a product that will be delivered to his home. When Joe then connects to a popular news site that requires the disclosure of his home address before he can view content on the web site, Joe's P3P-enabled browser will block access to the site. If other popular news services also require home addresses, Joe's P3P-enabled browser will prevent Joe from receiving news over the Internet. Or he will have to give up his choice to keep his home address private' (Electronic Privacy Information Center, 'Pretty Poor Privacy: An Assessment of P3P and Internet Privacy', at http://www.epic.org/reports/prettypoorprivacy.html (retrieved October 19, 2002)).

135. Ibid.

136. Ibid.

137. US Copyright Office, *Report on Copyright and Digital Distance Education*, May, 1999, 144, at http://www.loc.gov/copyright/docs/de_rprt.pdf (retrieved May 19, 2001).

138. 17 U.S.C. 1201(a)(1)(C). In conducting its rulemaking, the Librarian was to consider (1) the availability for use of copyrighted works, (2) the availability for use of works for nonprofit archival, preservation, and educational purposes, (3) the impact on criticism, comment, news reporting, teaching, scholarship, or research, and (4) the effect on the market for other copyrighted works. *See also* Committee on Commerce, House of Representatives, Digital Millenium Copyright Act of 1998, H.R. Rep. No. 105-551, 37 (1998).

139. Copyright Office, Exemption to Prohibition on Circumvention of Copyright Protection Systems for Access Control Technologies: Final Rule, 68 Fed. Reg. 62011.

140. Some filtering programs unfairly block sites that do not contain undesirable material and which therefore should not be filtered. Unauthorized decryption would seem necessary to determining such errors (ibid., 64564).

141. Ibid., 64562.

142. Among others, rejected ideas appeared in 'Initial Comments' in the Exemption Hearings, supra note 21, include 'thin copyright' (J.C. Vaughan, American Association of Universities, et al., February 17, 2000), education uses (C. Collins, National Association of Independent Schools, February 10, 2000) and audio-visual archives (D.A. Francis, National Digital Library Program, February 17, 2000) (at http://www.loc/gov/copyright/1201/comments (retrieved May 19, 2001)). Similar points were supported in testimony by libraries and their users (J.G. Neal, Johns Hopkins University, May 4, 2000), and educational media centers (J.Clark and D. Vogelsong, Consortium of College and University Media Centers, May 3, 2000).

143. Exemption to Prohibition on Circumvention of Copyright Protection Systems for Access Control Technologies, 67 Fed. Reg. 199, 63578 (October 15, 2002).

144. Cohen, 'Testimony', Exemption Hearing, supra note 21, May 4, 2000, 2.

145. From an economic perspective, fair use is properly instituted in copyright law to serve as a legal escape valve when the transaction costs of a market activity are too high. Transaction costs may result from negotiation difficulties as well as third-party effects known as externalities (Wendy J. Gordon, 'Fair Use as Market Failure: A Structural and Economic Analysis of the Betamax Case and Its Predecessors', 82 *Columbia Law Review*. 1600, 1615 (1982)). ('Only where the desired transfer of resource use is unlikely to take place spontaneously, or where special circumstances such as market flaws impair the market's ordinary ability to serve as a measure of how resources should be allocated, is there an economic need for allowing nonconcensual transfer.')

146. 'Many of the concerns ... are actually related to *copy control* measures rather than *access control* measures ... The Higher Education Associations cite the frequent phenomenon of "disappearing" works – those appearing online or on disk today that may be gone tomorrow, e.g., because they may be removed from an online data base or because the library or institution has access to them only during the term of its license to use the work. ... It would appear that restrictions on *copying* are more likely to be responsible for the problem. ... It is difficult to understand how an exemption from the prohibition on circumvention of *access* controls would resolve this problem' (supra note 139, at 64572).

147. Supra note 139.

148. J.C. Vaughan, Association of American Universities, et al., 'Comments', Exemption Hearing, supra note 21, February 17, 2000, at http://www.loc.gov/copyright/1201/hearings (retrieved May 19, 2001).

149. 17 U.S.C. § 1201(d)–(j) now provisionally relaxes use restrictions in seven specified instances.

150. 17 U.S.C. § 1201(c) (1).

151. 'Defendants are not here sued for copyright infringement. They are sued for providing a technology designed to circumvent technological measures that control access to copyrighted works. ... If Congress had meant the fair use defense to apply to such actions, it would have said so. Indeed, as the legislative history demonstrates, the decision not to make fair use a defense to a claim under Section 1201(a) was quite deliberate' (82 F. Supp. 2d 211 (S.D.N.Y. 2000)).

152. Summary of bill at http://www.house.gov/boucher/docs/dmcrahandout.htm (retrieved October 31, 2002)

153. Ibid.

154. The conduct rules of conduct protection regarding access protection in Section 1201(a) contrast notably with copy protection rules of Section 1201(b), where only circumvention devices (but not the actual conduct) are proscribed.

155. http://www.house.gov/boucher/docs/dmcrahandout.htm

156. http://www.house.gov/boucher/docs/dmcrasec.htm

157. Edward Felten, 'Another DMCA Attack on Interoperation', at http://www.freedom.to.tinker.com/archives/000253.html (retrieved June 29, 2003); Declan McCullagh, 'Lexmark invokes DMCA in toner suit', CNET.com, January 8, 2003, at http://www.news.com.com/2100-1023-979791.html (retrieved June 29, 2003).

158. US Copyright Office, DMCA Section 104 Report, Washington, DC, xxviii–xxxi.

159. C.E. Lindblom, 'The Science of Muddling Through', 19 *Public Administration Review* 79 (1959).

4.   Napster and peer-to-peer

4.1   INTRODUCTION

File-sharing services provide to web users the ability to find and download files from other computer hard drives by typing an appropriate title, word or phrase. For example, a student interested in the Civil War can find and download material from other user hard drives by entering the phrase 'Abraham Lincoln'. In addition to documents, software and photographs, file-sharing can enable the unauthorized transfer and copying of copyrighted music, books and movie files that can be 'ripped' from CDs or otherwise loaded to hard drives on personal computers. The unauthorized reproduction of any copyrighted material can displace original sales and licensing opportunities and therefore presents concerns for copyright owners.

File-sharing can entail at least four topologies. In the first generation, Napster, Scour, Aimster/Madster, Audiogalaxy and iMesh routed file requests through central directories that located and accessed donor hard drives with tracks that could be copied. The Recording Industry Association of America (RIAA) successfully pursued litigation against these services and led to their eventual demise or legitimacy. In a second generation, KaZaa and Grokster use a network configuration that routes file requests through directories that are installed regionally on user computers. In a third layer of file-sharing services, smaller providers – such as Morpheus, BearShare and Limewire – use open source Gnutella programs to locate material without routing requests through any directory whatever. In a prospective fourth generation, Freenet will migrate encoded content across the web with perfect user anonymity.

Facing a rapidly growing problem, record labels, music publishers and movie studios filed copyright suits against Napster,[1] Audiogalaxy,[2] Madster[3] and KaZaa/Grokster/Morpheus.[4] As a group, file-sharing cases present an intriguing plate of issues for lawyers, technologists and economists who ponder the evolution of judicial policy in the digital era. *Ab initio*, these cases implicate the primary issue of indirect (i.e., contributory and vicarious) liability for copyright infringement; courts use indirect liability as a justification for shifting the responsibility for stopping infringement to the parties who can more efficiently deter it. As a second matter, content owners might come to control the next generation of music technology by merging, joint venturing or licensing content to a peer-to-peer (P2P) platform. As an intriguing promotional vehicle, P2P services might attract a critical network mass useful to forming an incumbent base, establishing brand loyalty, and deterring migration to infringing technologies.[5]

4.2   ECONOMIC DISPUTE RESOLUTION

Courts may generally resolve disputes involving trespass or nuisance[6] in four ways. First, the court could award an injunction or free use based on a reading of statutory or common law, or some attempt to establish all costs and benefits associated with each outcome.[7] For example, courts may sympathize with victim rights, and rule against a cattleman whose herd grazes on a farm, a factory that pollutes the adjoining baker or a prospective hospital whose ambulances endanger the lives of nearby pedestrians or drivers. Any of these decisions might actually impose greater social costs than the reverse outcome.

From a second perspective, that of Nobel Laureate R.H. Coase, the court's verdict is irrelevant if the property right can be easily transferred in the market to the more efficient outcome.[8] For if judgment were instituted inefficiently for the plaintiff, the defendant could pay the plaintiff to lift the injunction in a manner that would improve social welfare and leave both parties better off. By contrast, no such deal is possible if the starting position is efficient. However, the efficient application of the Coase Theorem generally depends on three general conditions – no excluded 'third parties', no market power and no transaction costs in negotiations between the contending parties – that are frequently absent in particular disputes.[9]

As a weaker variation of the Coase Theorem, courts might invoke liability rules to permit use with established compensation for harmed parties.[10] Infringers can efficiently internalize damages if prospective or appointed dollar awards reflect true usage costs. If costs per unit of damage can be correctly estimated, liability rules would generally deter trespass or nuisance to the efficient point of deterrence.

Finally, courts can institute specific preventive responsibilities that would limit the harm from potential infringements. Harold Demsetz makes the point; 'it would be possible for the legal system to improve the allocation of resources by placing liability on that party who in the usual situation could be expected to avoid the costly interaction most cheaply'.[11] The mandating of efficient restraints apparently found its way in 1997 to the Supreme Court, which examined statutory provisions of the Communications Decency Act of 1996 that prohibited commercial services from transmitting adult video communications via the Internet.[12]

However, there is no economic reason why courts should limit liability solely to the 'low cost' provider.[13] A multilateral resolution would be particularly compelling if different preventive methods could resolve different aspects of the same problem.[14] Courts may then require complementary practices as a cooperative solution to Prisoner's Dilemma games.[15] Indeed, failure to impose symmetric restrictions invites the moral hazard of underprotection, which can encourage more wasteful litigation as a means of resolving future conflicts.[16]

Injunctions are sometimes granted in copyright cases based on statutory and common law considerations unrelated to economic efficiency.[17] The outcome, particularly in cases that implicate innovation and new technology, may close off information channels and otherwise reduce the ability of the market to reorganize more efficiently. If other preventive methods are not explicitly considered, an injunction might then render entirely inoperable a device or service that is otherwise capable of legal and beneficial activities.

While a frictionless licensing market could reassign initial rights to make both parties better off, general transaction difficulties can be often overwhelming for markets with new technologies; contestants here particularly may have widely divergent perspectives on future values of particular property rights. The same problem can affect liability rules, as $\Delta 8$ estimated market damages necessarily implicate business models in the process of development. Accordingly, the best practical strategy that a court can often follow is to institute specific deterrents – 'electronic fences' – that impose balanced safeguards that obligate each side to act cooperatively for an indefinite period. In an open-ended knowledge system where novelty is perpetual and relevant information is slowly revealed, specific deterrence based on limited information and narrow policy goals presents a reasonable way of making key jurisprudential decisions.

4.3   ECONOMICS OF INDIRECT LIABILITY

A party can be held liable in common law for indirect infringement of copyright even if she has not directly reproduced or performed the work. This establishes a judicial platform which courts can activate for specific deterrents.

Contributory infringement results from a person 'who, with knowledge of the infringing activity, induces, causes, or materially contributes to the infringing conduct of another' and who therefore is 'equally liable with the direct infringer'.[18] Both knowledge and material contribution are implicated in a claim of contributory infringement. However, actual knowledge is not necessary; liability can also be incurred if the defendant had reason to know or was willfully blind to any form of infringing activity.[19] Indeed, merely 'providing the site and facilities for known infringing activity is sufficient to establish contributory liability'.[20]

A person may participate in vicarious infringement if he 'has the right and ability to supervise the infringing activity and also has a direct financial interest in such activities'.[21] Any party in a supervisory capacity may be guilty of vicarious infringement without any knowledge whatever of the infringing event. Moreover, it is not necessary to identify financial gain resulting from direct sale; the use of infringing material (e.g., music) to create interest and atmosphere may be sufficient.[22] However, some defendant ability to control or supervise the infringing parties is essential for a finding of vicarious infringement.[23]

Charges of contributory and vicarious infringement have often arisen in cases involving musical reproductions or performances. Courts ruled against dance halls with musical acts that made unauthorized performances,[24] a department store chain hosting a concessionaire that sold counterfeit records,[25] a store selling blank tapes for use with an on-the-premises 'Make-A-Tape' machine,[26] a retail copy service operating a cassette copying machine to reproduce sound recordings,[27] an operator of a swap meet that rented space to bootleggers,[28] a trade show operator that used music to cultivate interest and attendance,[29] bar owners who permitted unauthorized public performances of songs,[30] and a producer of specially timed audiotapes and taping equipment sold to known counterfeiters.[31]

Rules that establish indirect liability allow copyright owners to take action against, e.g., vendors of infringing technologies instead of their many users, or supervisors instead of subordinates. In so doing, indirect liability provides the incentive for superiors to heed their knowledge of, or contribution to, copyright infringements that may arise under their charge. Richard Gilbert and Michael Katz argue that indirect liability shifts the necessary costs of monitoring to the party that can presumably can bear it most efficiently.[32]

Rights owners in cyberdomains may particularly value the tools of contributory and vicarious liability when they are often unable to prosecute infringing behavior in a widely distributed user base. By contrast, network intermediaries (such as employers, colleges and Internet service providers) may have some reasonable technical ability to monitor their constituents. Courts that enforce indirect liability may then establish a financial incentive for the creation of new monitoring technologies (e.g., Audible Magic,[33] Packeteer[34]) that can better deter copyright infringement. Rights owners then appreciate the incentives as catalysts that can induce changes in business practice, market organization and enabling technology.

4.4 CONTRIBUTORY INFRINGEMENT AND THE BETAMAX CASE

A landmark decision involving contributory infringement was the 1984 Supreme Court decision, *Sony Corp.* v. *Universal City Studios*,[35] which considered the legality of Sony's videocassette recorder (VCR) that could videotape copyrighted television programs. As a reproduction technology, the VCR could be used for a wide category of purposes, ranging from time-shifting for single playback to unauthorized collection of a program library.

The District Court found the VCR to be a staple item of commerce and held for Sony;[36] the Ninth Circuit Court reversed[37] and the Supreme Court reversed again. Writing for the majority, Justice Stevens found the VCR to be a 'staple article of commerce' that could be used for significant noninfringing uses, i.e., noncommercial time-shifting of recorded programs for playback within the home.[38] Accordingly, 'the sale of copying equipment, like the sale of other articles of commerce, does not constitute contributory infringement if the product is widely used for legitimate, unobjectionable purposes. Indeed, it need merely be capable of substantial noninfringing uses.'[39] With additional testimony, the Court also found that many programmers (such as sports programmers and Mr Rogers) actually supported the home recorder, suggesting that producer harms claimed by Universal Studios and Disney were not pervasive.[40]

The Supreme Court here distinguished between commercial uses – where the likelihood of harm may be presumed – from noncommercial uses – where harm must actually be demonstrated.[41] In the latter regard, plaintiff must prove 'by a preponderance of evidence that some meaningful likelihood of future harm exists'.[42] In this respect, movie industry experts virtually disproved their own case, admitting 'at several points in the trial that the time-shifting without librarying would result in not a great deal of harm'.[43]

In the 5–4 decision, a dissenting opinion suggested considering the proportion of infringing and noninfringing uses.[44] However, the dissenting opinion offered no immediate method to determine the value of each use, nor is one apparent. Alternatively, the Supreme Court might have considered the potential for economic 'fence protection' by requiring manufacturers to redesign devices to protect against infringement. The District Court had earlier rejected this consideration, which Universal and Disney had suggested.[45]

The movie industry might not have liked the outcome of *Sony*,[46] although the VCR created the market for motion picture videos and greatly benefited Hollywood in the end. Moreover, the opinion derives its 'significant noninfringing use' criterion from an unrelated area of patent law that involved the tying of secondary products to sale of the patented good.[47] Nonetheless, the decision can be appreciated as a procedurally rational step in a policy-making process that withholds judgment so that more information can come to the table as a new technology further develops.

In *Sony*, the Supreme Court declined to make binding policy based on the little amount of information that it had. Rather, it left the game open to more information by deferring to Congress on matters of technology policy:[48] 'Congress has the constitutional authority and the institutional ability to accommodate fully the varied permutations of competing interests that are inevitably implicated by such new technology ... It is not our job to apply laws that have not yet been written.'[49] Congress would soon come to recognize some dangers and require the installation of some protective technology on digital tape recorders[50] and analog video cassette recorders.[51]

4.5   THE NAPSTER TECHNOLOGY

Napster Inc. was a startup company that distributed free-of-charge software that enabled music fans to locate and download unprotected MP3s on donor hard drives.[52] Downloading was possible without users having to pay compensation to the record labels or music publishers who owned copyrights in the affected sound recording or underlying musical composition.

The distributed user software located donor songs by accessing directory data on a central server owned and controlled by Napster. Once downloaded, MP3 files could be 'burned' on blank CDs or transferred to flash memory for use on mobile devices. As a directory service, Napster itself did not create nor copy any of the music files on its system, nor did copied music files pass through its servers. Napster software could not detect the title, content or performers of a music track, nor whether a transferred file was copyright-protected or not.[53]

New artists tended to view Napster as favorable means of promoting their material online through sampling and online chat.[54] However, major labels and performers perceived Napster as an economic threat. Accordingly, on behalf of the 18 label affiliates of the five major record companies (which together distribute 85 percent of sound recordings in the USA), the Recording Industry Association of America (RIAA) filed a complaint in December 1999 for contributory and vicarious infringement against Napster. Plaintiffs were joined a month later by Jerry Lieber, Mike Stoller and Frank Music, who acted on behalf of a class of music publishers.

On July 26, 2000, District Court Judge Marilyn Hall Patel issued a preliminary injunction against Napster,[55] which the US Court of Appeals for the Ninth Circuit vacated one day later. On February 12, the Court of Appeals for the Ninth Circuit issued a decision that affirmed in part, reversed in part, and remanded the earlier injunction, which was found to be legally valid but overly broad.[56] On remand, the District Court issued a revised preliminary injunction that enjoined Napster from copying, downloading, uploading, transmitting or distributing copyrighted sound recordings.[57]

The District Court found that Napster had both the requisite knowledge and material contribution required for contributory infringement,[58] and the supervisory capacity and financial interest required for vicarious.[59] In reaching this conclusion, the Court found that each of the four 'fair use' considerations of 17 U.S.C. § 107 held for the plaintiffs.

1. Napster was a commercial service with the intent of building a positive base to enable subscription fees or attract a corporate buyer. Napster technology enabled duplicative reproductions and was not therefore transformative.[60]
2. The act of creating a musical composition or sound recording entails creative abilities and is not rote.[61]
3. Napster's copying of music files entailed a reproduction of the entire work.[62]
4. Napster harmed the potential market for the copyrighted work by reducing CD sales and raising barriers to the label's entry into the market for digital downloading.[63]

The lower court ruled against Napster on points of law concerning sampling,[64] 'space-shifting'[65] and the authorized use of reproductions made available by particular artists.[66] The Courts also rejected the defendant's attempt to apply an exemption for space-shifting based on the Audio Home Recording Act of 1992.[67]

With respect to market harm, defendant experts argued that file-sharing may have actually stimulated the sales of CDs and concerts by enabling prospective customers to sample individual tracks, exchange information and develop a base of users and network infrastructure.[68] However, Judge Patel pointed out that the appropriate market harm test must also consider how the activity affected licensing opportunities and derivative works.[69] In this respect, plaintiffs presented credible evidence of disrupted business models and licensing plans.[70] By appropriating copyrighted material without authorization, Napster had hindered the potential for this licensing market to congeal.

The District Court found Napster to provide an ongoing network service that could be controlled over its server, and not a staple article of commerce to which the *Sony* decision might apply.[71] In contrast, the *Sony* Court saw the VCR as an appliance with a one-time purchase.[72] Through its directory,

Napster had purported knowledge of infringing behavior; consequently, the *Sony* decision was then of limited assistance.[73]

The direct knowledge of copyright infringement had been provided directly by the RIAA, which provided to Napster the names of more than 12 000 infringing files that were still available on the Napster system.[74] Citing *Religious Technology Center* v. *Netcom*,[75] 'the record supports the District Court's finding that Napster has actual knowledge that specific infringing material is available using its system, that it could block access to the system by suppliers of the infringing material, and that it failed to remove the material'.[76] With regard to *Fonovisa*,[77] Napster provides the 'site and facilities' for direct infringement and therefore materially contributes to direct infringement; 'without the support services defendant provides, Napster users could not find and download the music they want with the ease of which defendant boasts'.[78]

4.6   SPECIFIC DETERRENCE AND COPYRIGHT MISUSE

In each of the above matters, the judges of the Circuit Court came to uphold the reasoning and points of law of the lower court.[79] The courts nonetheless would differ in the way that information was to be handled and the respective role that each player must take in response to it, i.e., specific deterrence. The US District Court enjoined Napster from 'copying, downloading, uploading, transmitting, or distributing plaintiff's copyrighted compositions and recordings without express permission'.[80] The informational burden is made explicit:

> This injunction applies to all such works that plaintiffs own; it is not limited to those [identified by plaintiffs] ... [B]ecause defendant has contributed to illegal copying on a scale that is without precedent, it bears the burden of developing a means to comply with the injunction. Defendant must ensure that no work owned by plaintiffs which neither defendant nor Napster users have permission to use or distribute is uploaded or downloaded on Napster.[81]

Labels were obliged only 'to cooperate with defendant in identifying the works to which they own copyrights'.[82]

Napster would contend that the imposed information requirement was unbalanced. Defendant attorneys claimed that Napster could not discern copyrighted material because neither CD music nor MP3 files contained notices, and because plaintiffs refused to identify copyrighted works,[83] claiming that it would be burdensome to do so.[84] Rather, 'without attempting to determine the actual practicability of any potential modification of the Napster system, the District Court ordered that Napster simply had to figure out a way to prevent any and all alleged infringing uses'.[85]

The Circuit Court here concurred with the defendants, finding the resulting informational burden to be inefficient and the injunction wording to be overly broad.[86] Judge Patel failed to consider how the underlying technology could be used to protect copyrighted works and left many questions unanswered.[87] In line with its finding, the Circuit ordered the labels to provide the names of copyrighted files that must be blocked from access.[88] Consistent with the idea of specific deterrence, the court here built an efficient fence by placing liabilities upon the respective providers who were in a best position to deter damage.

On remand, the District Court ruled that Napster was preliminarily enjoined from copying, downloading, uploading, transmitting or distributing copyrighted sound recordings.[89] However, labels bore the responsibility to provide notice of the title of the copyrighted work, the name of the featured recording artist, the names of one or more files on the Napster system containing the work and a certification that plaintiffs own the claimed copyright.[90] All parties were compelled to use reasonable measures to identifying variations in the title name, including misspellings.[91] The deal left the game open for more information.

On March 27, 2001, the RIAA filed a brief that contended that Napster's system failed to filter effectively the compositions that had been identified.[92] Indeed, the plaintiff group claimed that every song in an original notice of 675000 copyrighted works remained available in the Napster system. Name-based filters were porous because certain files were misspelled or identified by idiosyncratic user mnemonics (such as pig Latin), purportedly with the assistance of Napster-provided bulletin boards that transmitted information about strategic coding.[93] The District Court ordered Napster to strengthen its protection but did not close it down.[94]

In an effort to improve monitoring, Napster purchased from Gracenote access to a vast database of song titles with common misspellings, and designed its own automated filter to look for likely misspellings.[95] Napster also licensed from Relatable audio recognition software that can take from any song a 'digital fingerprint' bearing 34 distinct audio characteristics that were measurable in the first seconds of use.[96] Fingerprinted works can be compared to data that are now available from Loudeye Technologies to check for owner permission. Napster also worked with Bertelsmann's Digital World Services to add protection layers to music files to prevent songs from being burned to CDs or transferred to portable devices.[97] Finally, Napster began distributing from its web site file-swapping software that severely restricted allowable trading.[98]

As a result of the increased security of the Napster system, the number of songs shared by the average Napster user declined from 220 in February, 2001 to 1.5 in July.[99] Napster also claimed that 99.4 percent of copyrighted works were successfully filtered.[100] As the user base dwindled from 18.7 million to

150000 people, this additional protection was not enough to satisfy plaintiffs ('The law does not tolerate any infringement') nor Judge Patel ('The standard is to get it down to zero, do you understand that?').[101] To eliminate the remaining infringement, Napster implemented a technical shutdown in July 2001 that culminated in its bankruptcy in the following year.[102]

Prior to the bankruptcy, the parties entered into a trial in October 2001 when the labels sought to extend the preliminary injunction into a summary judgment for a permanent one.[103] In its defense, Napster argued that summary judgment should be denied and discovery should proceed because the plaintiffs were engaged in copyright misuse. Sourcing *Lasercomb America* v. *Job Reynolds*[104] and *Practice Mgmt. Info. Corp.* v. *American Med. Assoc.*,[105] the court found copyright misuse to be an equitable defense against summary judgment.[106] With regard to the matter at hand, the court found that one music service, MusicNet, licensed material in a contract that disallowed Napster from transacting directly with any other individual plaintiff (including Sony and Universal, which were not part of MusicNet).[107] With the possible effect of closing off competition and raising licensing fees, this exclusive deal sufficiently concerned the court that summary judgment was not permitted: 'the evidence now shows that plaintiffs have licensed their catalogs of works for digital distribution in what could be an overreaching manner [and what could also] run afoul of the antitrust laws'.[108]

The defense of copyright or patent misuse, which may include antitrust violations, is a defense in equity that prevents plaintiffs from enforcing copyright while the misuse is taking place.[109] It does not generally suspend or invalidate intellectual property (IP) rights, nor does it award monetary damages to the parties harmfully affected. As a matter of reasonable procedure, economic fence-building would compel that no judgment can be granted until the misuse stops, as markets and negotiations cannot then move forward efficiently if one party uses copyright or patents in an abusive or anti-competitive manner. Courts then implement efficient practice by delaying action until the misuse is resolved.

4.7   THE SECOND GENERATION

The RIAA's victory over Napster – and related services Audiogalaxy[110] and Madster[111] – may yet have been Pyrrhic. As a result of the Napster shutdown, an installed base of 64 million users was released for other sharing services that came to perform more functions (i.e., videos) than had Napster. Webnoize estimated that over 3 billion files were downloaded in the month after Napster first shut down (August 2001), exceeding Napster's highest previous monthly level of 2.79 billion (February 2001).[112]

Versions of the present leading P2P service, KaZaa, have now (May 2003) been downloaded over 230 million times, exceeding Napster's 64 million by more than threefold.[113] KaZaa now claims to have 10 million unique users, in contrast to the 300 000 people who have signed up with a legitimate music service.[114] Shipments of CDs from the major labels fell by 10 percent over the past two years, which the recording industry contends is the result of unauthorized file-sharing.[115]

Three service providers – KaZaa BV (aka Consumer Empowerment), Grokster and Music City (nka Streamcast) – came to provide the new market leader, Fast Track, that KaZaa BV licensed. Without use of centralized directory, KaZaa users first access a controlled network server, which assigns to a unique name/password and provides desktop software that enables data transfer. New customers are then assigned to a regional cluster of personal computers that are oriented around a supernode, which is a selected user computer with appropriate technical characteristics that can store directory information.

Not owned or operated by the service, the supernode computer enables any party to find and download material on other hard drives in the neighborhood. Because communications between computers are encoded and anonymous, the original service provider has no way of knowing what information a user searches, downloads or shares. Service providers now give away desktop software and monetize their investments through the sales of onscreen advertising, personal data tracking, and processor and storage services made possible through distributed computing.

Twenty-nine companies in the recording and movie industries filed suit against KaZaa, Grokster, and Music City on October 2, 2001 for contributory and vicarious infringement.[116] The National Music Publishers Association joined the suit on November 19. In January, 2002, KaZaa BV sold the desktop technology, KaZaa Media Desktop, to Sharman Networks of the island Vanuatu.[117] The plaintiffs settled with KaZaa BV in May 2002.[118]

The matter against Streamcast and Grokster reached an unexpected conclusion in April 2003, when District Court Judge Stephen Wilson granted summary judgment to the defense. Invoking *Sony*,[119] 'defendants distribute and support software, the users of which can and do choose to employ it for both lawful and unlawful ends. Grokster and StreamCast are not significantly different from companies that sell home video recorders or copy machines, both of which can be and are used to infringe copyrights.'[120] While Napster played an active role in facilitating each unauthorized transaction, Streamcast and Grokster had no control over the software that they might have previously distributed: 'if either defendant closed their doors and deactivated all computers within their control, users of their products could continue sharing files with little or no interruption'.[121] A Circuit Court later upheld the verdict.

Sharman Networks

Yet outstanding is the matter of Sharman Networks, which is the market leader of the three services.

Immediately after settling with the RIAA, KaZaa BV formed a new company, called Blastoise, which continues to license Fast Track software.[122] In May, 2002, Sharman Networks and Brilliant Digital Entertainment (BDE) licensed from Blastoise usage rights for Fast Track technology that uses available storage capacity from KaZaa users to compose an edge services network to accommodate a variety of distributed computing needs.[123] This layer of distributed computing is made possible through an additional piece of software, Altnet Secureinstall, which is produced in a joint venture between BDE and software provider Blastoise. Physically connected to (but logically separate from) the KaZaa network, the size of the Altnet system greatly exceeds the base of P2P rivals, Kontiki, Centerspan and Red Swoosh.[124]

While Sharman gives away free desktop software, it monetizes its service by distributing pop-up advertising and personalization files on user computers, and providing machine capacity as computing nodes to the Altnet system.[125] Personalization files gather information on user choices and favorite words that advertising clients may subsequently access. Indeed, advertising can be made to pop up instantaneously when certain key words are typed.[126] Sharman's stealth program has led to considerable criticism by privacy groups; indeed, Altnet is now the second most complained about advertising software company on the web (behind Gator).[127]

The record industry initiated a lawsuit against Sharman in January 2003.[128] Sharman countersued on antitrust grounds, contending that the labels had cooperatively and anticompetitively refused to license material to the file-sharing service. While Sharman might alternatively have alleged that its distributed software could no longer be centrally controlled, labels and studios would apparently have disputed this.[129] The Sharman matter is now undecided.

A conceivable closure of Sharman notwithstanding, a sobering technological lesson may then be about to repeat itself. In eliminating Napster, the industry created the opportunity for more sophisticated and less controllable software to follow. While StreamCast and Grokster may now be less efficient than Sharman and their systems do not easily accommodate scaling or growth,[130] programming will not cease and entry will not stop. Also on the horizon is Freenet, an open source project that makes possible file encoding and migration to promise a wholly anonymous and untraceable way of distributing any form of content.[131]

With neither central directories nor the ability to retrieve or control distributed software, it may then be impossible to re-engineer peer-to-peer systems to retrieve old software, accommodate new software, or reject particular searches for copyrighted material. Courts furthermore might not be in a position to outlaw entirely new distributors of software. The present parties in the Sharman dispute could consider reaching a reasonable licensing or buyout arrangement.

4.8 MUSIC SERVICES AND PEER-TO-PEER

A welfare-maximizing economist might affirm with Carl Shapiro and Hal Varian, 'When managing intellectual property, your goal should be to choose the terms and conditions that maximize the value of your intellectual property, not the terms and conditions that maximize [or optimize] the protection'.[132]

Many applications of distributed computing complement the technology needs of content owners. By concentrating and utilizing available storage and process space on local PCs, distributed computing can allow cell phones, handheld devices and ordinary computers to have the same power as massive web servers.[133] Product sold through edge services network Altnet generally can be made secure, protectable by digital rights management, and monetizable through micropayments;[134] entire playlists on KaZaa can be presented and downloaded with one mouseclick.[135] Altnet now makes possible the delivery of secure entertainment product, including music-based video games from Infrogames and sound recordings from independent label 2Ksounds.[136]

Cornerband.com uses P2P technology to sell music push services to bands that can be activated when users type certain words or phrases, such as 'Chicago Blues'.[137] Microsoft used the Altnet network to distribute two promotional videos that were bundled with the company's new Windows Media 9; Microsoft now plans to add P2P applications programming interfaces to its new operating system, Windows XP, which is designed to accommodate greater applications for entertainment.[138] Sony Music now distributes content over Scour's P2P network.[139] Edge services provider Kontiki attracted investments from Time Warner[140] and Blastoise is now negotiating distribution deals with European telecom companies.[141]

There are eight compelling reasons why an integrated service between MusicNet, Pressplay and a P2P service would be attractive:

1. *Promotional instruments*: can be used as promotional devices to 'jump start' the customer base for the labels' music subscription services, which have so far had disappointing appeal among populations grown accustomed to free music. As a promotion strategy, the music services can offer a free P2P connection to new service subscribers for a limited period, say a few months. During that time, service upgrades can also be made available to any user for an additional fee. As a primary upgrade, a

new service can offer P2P service without advertisements, a key concern for many present users of KaZaa. The file-sharing service would no longer be free after the trial period.

2. *Installed base*: as more new subscribers join the music services, the installed base of shared recordings would increase, enhancing the commercial appeal of the service. This creates a 'virtuous cycle' built around positive externalities and system feedback. In a classic example of 'network tipping', the label system would gain popularity at the expense of the nonintegrated services and may culminate – 'winner take all' – in a virtual industry standard.

3. *Lock in*: after a period of introductory free service ends, a customer may wish to drop her subscription. However, migrants will lose contact with a considerable base of recordings, including those contributed by later subscribers who may yet come on the system for free. As a consequence, music fans would increasingly be discouraged from shopping for other services and might actually be willing to pay a premium to stay with a P2P system that is now established as part of a full digital service.[142]

4. *Ancillary products*: besides free introductory offers, labels may also use complementary P2P to reward loyal customers, large buyers, 'upgraders' and listeners willing to commit to multiperiod contracts that span a designated period. A larger base will facilitate the sale of more advertising, personalization data, videos, concert tickets, books, new releases, samples and high-quality recordings.

5. *Distributed computing*: the distributed computing capabilities of P2P networks offer additional supply considerations regarding scale economies and system growth. Distributed computing can accommodate caching and network storage without the buildout of additional servers. The capacity to do this actually increases as more subscribers join the system. For entertainment platforms, distributed computing can be useful to distribute recorded videos, movies, or video games without scaling up the server base. This is particularly relevant for the presentation of live concerts, where demand may surge for short intervals. Particular acts may establish a secure virtual network with firewalls that accommodate greater security.

6. *Public relations*: if complemented with P2P and distributed computing, the new music services may present a 'killer application' to a younger generation attracted more by video games, DVDs, and the Internet instead of traditional CDs. Record labels will earn a reprieve from an increasingly hostile group of fans and artists that perceives them (rightly or wrongly) to be overreaching litigants.[143] Finally, an aggressive strategy in the digital space will counter political cynics who contend that performers and

copyright owners interfere with the spread of new technology.[144]

7. *Preserving option value*: by reducing the potential market for future unfriendly software, labels also maintain more control and the option to modify or terminate the service at appropriate moments. Indeed, it may be possible to leave free subscriptions in place for a longer period if evidence shows that people eventually do graduate up to deluxe choices.

8. *Piracy*: if P2P is regarded as a temporary platform, record labels might continue other efforts to deter unauthorized takings. In this respect, labels might continue efforts to release new CDs with 'second session' protection that tethers uploaded tracks to the receiving hard drive.[145] With digital rights management, they also might find it profitable to sell digital tracks that allow no or limited copying to other hard drives.[146] Finally, trusted systems allow protected tracks to be used on a limited number of peripheral devices.[147] However, it is quite conceivable that a number of other uses should go unprotected, for permanent or temporary amounts of time, if their value can be monetized elsewhere.

The integrated entity of P2P technology can be operated as a joint venture among the major labels. The labels must apportion among one another the buyout costs necessary to obtain the software, as well as cross-payments for use of musical compositions and sound recordings.

The largest incumbent provider of P2P technology is the Fast Track system of Sharman and Grokster. With larger network size, Fast Track has considerable first-mover advantages and is the evident choice to start building a legitimate base for P2P file-sharing. It is the most user-friendly P2P system, scaling more easily and avoiding congestion more readily than decentralized systems (e.g., Gnutella).

4.9 CONCLUSION

The case of file-sharing and peer-to-peer technology exemplifies one of the most interesting issues involving Internet technology. The major record labels may continue their litigation, and may have every apparent legal precedent and may win every judgment. Nonetheless, they are finding an obstinate opponent that springs heads like hydrae. Other than ongoing litigation against individual file traders,[148] the best that labels can realistically hope for may be collective buyout or a negotiated settlement with the most attractive P2P provider, for the purpose of attracting fans from the less popular alternatives and pre-empting other entrants entirely. If done in a well-thought-out business model, buyout may indeed make considerable financial and economic sense.

NOTES

1. Infra notes 55–7 and surrounding text.
2. Infra note 110 and surrounding text.
3. Infra note 111 and surrounding text.
4. Infra note 116 and surrounding text.
5. *See* Jean Gabszewicz, Lynne Pepall and Jacques-Francoise Thisse, 'Sequential Entry with Brand Loyalty Caused by Consumer Learning by Using', 40 *Journal of Industrial Economics* 397 (1992); *see also* Gideon Parchomovsky and Peter Siegelman, 'Towards an Integrated Theory of Intellectual Property', 88 *Virginia Law Review* 1455 (2002).
6. T.W. Merrill, 'Trespass, Nuisance, and the Costs of Determining Property Rights', 14 *Journal of Legal Studies* 13, 18 (1985). Trespass applies to invasions of space by unauthorized persons and tangible objects, while nuisance applies more to indirect interferences that affect the enjoyment of that space (e.g., noise, odor, pollution). The principal distinction between trespass and nuisance is the standard of care applied to determine whether the interference is actionable; i.e., whether Marshall may enjoin and/or received damages from the action of Taney, or Taney may practice his intrusion without exclusion from Marshall. To establish an actionable trespass, Marshall must show that Taney has invaded his space.
7. C.E. Lindblom, 'The Science of Muddling Through', 19 *Public Administration Review* 79 (1959). Lindblom defines a *rational-comprehensive* policy as one that tries to consider and weigh all factors, gather all relevant information, measure all relevant quantities, and willingly jump to extreme positions as logically justified.
8. R.H. Coase, 'The Problem of Social Cost', 3 *Journal of Law and Economics* 1 (1960).
9. See Chapter 1 for a fuller overview.
10. Guido Calabresi and Douglas Melamed, 'Property Rules, Liability Rules, and Inalienability: One View of the Cathedral', 85 *Harvard Law Review* 1089, 1106–10 (1972).
11. Harold Demsetz, 'When Does the Rule of Liability Matter?', 1 *Journal of Legal Studies* 13, 27–8 (1972). For application to torts, *see* Guido Calabresi and John T. Hirschoff, 'Toward a Test for Strict Liability in Torts', 81 *Yale Law Journal* 1055, 1060 (1972); W.E. Landes and R.A. Posner, *Economic Structure of Tort Law*, ch. 1 (Cambridge, MA: Harvard University Press, 1987).
12. *Reno* v. *ACLU*, 521 U.S. 844 (1997). The Court ruled that users could more efficiently prevent exposure and disallowed the provisions. The court efficiently reassigned the responsibility of policing for adult transmissions to the party capable of providing the prevention technology at the lowest cost.
13. *See* Demsetz, supra note 11; Calabresi and Hirschoff, supra note 11; *see also* S.G. Gilles, 'Negligence, Strict Liability, and the Cheapest Cost-Avoider', 78 *Virginia Law Review* 1291 (1992).
14. Bilateral care rules applied to property disputes were suggested first by M.J. White and D. Wittman, 'Long Run versus Short Run Remedies for Spatial Externalities: Liability Rules, Pollution Rules, and Zoning', in *Essays on the Law and Economics of Local Governments* 33 (Daniel L. Rubinfeld ed., Washington, DC: Urban Institute, 1979).
15. On the other hand, if a specialized labor solution is mandated where the resources of only one player are to be mobilized, courts may reasonably prescribe compensations that could make both parties better off. See R.C. Ellickson, *Order Without Law: How Neighbors Settle Disputes* 162 (Cambridge, MA: Harvard University Press, 1991).
16. S. Shavell, 'The Fundamental Divergence between the Private and the Social Motive to Use the Legal System', 26 *Journal of Legal Studies* 575 (1997).
17. This is particularly common in infringement cases that involve 'transformative works', where innovative presentations that add new meaning to copyrighted material may be enjoined for a variety of reasons; *see also* Chapter 2.
18. *Gershwin Publ'g Corp.* v. *Columbia Artists Mgmt., Inc.*, 443 F. 2d 1159, 1162 (2d Cir. 1971); *Fonovisa, Inc.* v. *Cherry Auction, Inc.*, 76 F. 3d 259, 264 (9th Cir. 1996).
19. *Cable/Home Communication Corp.* v. *Network Productions*, 902 F. 2d 829, 846 (11th Cir.

1990); *Sega Enterprises Ltd.* v. *MAPHIA*, 948 F. Supp. 923, 933 (N.D. Cal. 1996).

20. *Fonovisa*, supra note 18, at 264, citing *Columbia Pictures Industries, Inc.* v. *Aveco, Inc.*, 800 F. 2d 59 (3rd Cir. 1986).

21. *Gershwin*, supra note 18, at 1162; *Fonovisa*, supra note 18, at 264.

22. *Polygram Int'l Pub'g, Inc.* v. *Nevada/TIG, Inc.*, 855 F. Supp. 1314, 1332 (D. Mass. 1994); *see also Famous Music Corp.* v. *Bay State Harness Horse Racing and Breeding Ass'n*, 54 F. 2d 1213, 1214 (1st Cir. 1977).

23. *Demitriades* v. *Kaufmann*, 690 F. Supp. 289, 292 (S.D.N.Y. 1988).

24. *Buck* v. *Jewell-LaSalle Realty Co.*, 283 U.S. 191 (1931); *Dreamland Ball Room, Inc.* v. *Shapiro, Bernstein & Co.*, 36 F. 2d 354 (7th Cir. 1929); *M. Witmark & Sons* v. *Tremont Society & Athletic Club*, 188 F. Supp. 787 (D. Mass. 1960); *Renmick Music Corp.* v. *Interstate Hotel Co.*, 58 F. Supp. 523 (D. Neb. 1944), aff'd, 157 F. 2d 744 (8th Cir. 1946).

25. *Shapiro, Bernstein, and Co.* v. *H.L. Green Co.* 316 F. 2d 304 (2d Cir. 1963).

26. *Elektra Records Co.* v. *Gem Elec. Distribs., Inc.*, 360 F. Supp. 821 (E.D.N.Y. 1973).

27. *RCA Records* v. *All-Fast Sys., Inc.*, 594 F. Supp. 335 (S.D.N.Y. 1984).

28. *Fonovisa*, supra note 18, at 259.

29. *Polygram*, supra note 22.

30. *Major Bob Music* v. *Stubbs*, 851 F. Supp. 475 (S.D. Ga. 1994); *Walden Music, Inc.* v. *C.H.W., Inc.*, 1996 WL 254654, at *5 (D. Kan. Apr. 19, 1996); *Broadcast Music, Inc.* v. *Hobi, Inc.*, 1993 WL 404152, at *3 (M.D. La. Jun. 24, 1993).

31. *A&M Records, Inc.* v. *General Audio Video Cassettes, Inc.*, 948 F. Supp. 1449 (C.D. Cal. 1996); *A&M Records, Inc.* v. *Abdallah*, 948 F. Supp. 1449 (C.D. Cal. 1996).

32. R.J. Gilbert and M.L. Katz, 'When Good Value Chains Go Bad: The Economics of Indirect Liability for Copyright Infringement', 52 *Hastings Law Journal* 961 (2001).

33. Audible Magic allows operators to install technology to read files transmitted over the system. With a directory of musical fingerprints, Audible Magic can be used to detect illegal transmissions of copyrighted sound recordings, which now may consume over 50 percent of a university's available bandwidth (J. Borland, 'Fingerprinting P2P pirates', CNET NEWS.com, February 20, 2003).

34. Packeteer prioritizes data flows in a manner that can detect and slow traffic that moves through a P2P network (ibid.).

35. 464 U.S. 417 (1984).

36. 480 F. Supp. 429 (C.D. Cal. 1979).

37. 659 F. 2d 963 (9th Cir. 1981).

38. Supra note 35, at 451, 453.

39. Ibid., at 442.

40. Ibid., at 444, 456.

41. Ibid., at 450.

42. Regarding empirical evidence, the court concurred with the District Court opinion that found that plaintiff evidence that demonstrated market harm was speculative, inaccurate, and worthy of dismissal (ibid., at 452–3).

43. Ibid., at 451.

44. Ibid., at 491 (Dissent).

45. 480 F. Supp. at 462. Plaintiffs Universal and Disney suggested that the infringing uses of the VCR could be addressed by removal of the tuner or introduction of a jamming signal that would stop copying of protected programs.

46. Jack Valenti, president of the Motion Picture Association of America, testified before a Congressional Committee: 'I say to you that the VCR is to the American film producer and the American public as the Boston strangler is to the woman home alone.' Valenti called the VCR an 'avalanche' and a 'tidal wave', and said it would make the film industry 'bleed and bleed and hemorrhage' ('Committee on the Judiciary House of Representative, Testimony, 97th Cong., Home Recording of Copyrighted Works', April 12, 1982).

47. Ibid., at 440 ('The Court has always recognized the critical importance of not allowing the patentee to extend his monopoly beyond the limits of his specific grant. These cases deny the patentee any right to control the distribution of unpatented articles unless they are "unsuited for any commercial noninfringing use"' (*Dawson Chemical Co.* v. *Rohm and*

Haas Co., 448 U.S. 176, 198 (1980); also citing *Henry* v. *A.B. Dick Co.*, 224 U.S. 1,48 (1912); *Motion Picture Patents Co.* v. *Universal Film Mfg. Co.*, 243 U.S. 502,517 (1917)).

48. Ibid., at 456. 'The direction of Article 1 is that Congress shall have the power to promote the progress of science and the useful arts. When, as here, the Constitution is permissive, the sign of how far Congress has chosen to go can come only from Congress [citing *Deepsouth Packing Co.* v. *Laitram Corp.*, 406 U.S. 518, 530 (1972)].'

49. Ibid., at 431, 456.

50. 17 U.S.C. § 1002

51. 17 U.S.C. § 1201(k).

52. With peripheral devices known as 'rippers', music users already had the ability to upload and compress tracks from store bought CDs for storage on hard drives using a data compression format called MP3 that reduced considerably the amount of disk space needed to contain a file. As the MP3 format lacked appropriate 'flag' bits, users could freely exchange music files in emails between friends and chat groups.

53. See R. Frackman, Napster Legal Documents; *see also* Plaintiff's Brief on 512(a) Issue; Complaint for Copyright Infringement Against Napster.

54. See Reply Brief of Appellant Napster at 15

55. *A&M Records, Inc.* v. *Napster, Inc.*, 114 F. Supp. 2d 896 (N.D. Cal. 2000).

56. *A&M Records, Inc.* v. *Napster, Inc.*, 239 F. 3d 1004 (9th Cir. 2000).

57. *A&M Records, Inc.* v. *Napster, Inc.*, No. C 99-05183 MHP, 2001 U.S. Dist. LEXIS 2186 (N.D. Cal. March 5, 2001).

58. Supra note 55, at 918–20.

59. Ibid., at 920–22.

60. Ibid., at 912.

61. Ibid., at 913.

62. Ibid.

63. Ibid.

64. Ibid, at 913–14.

65. Ibid, at 914–16.

66. Ibid., at 917.

67. Ibid., at 916.

68. Ibid., at 910.

69. Ibid., at 910–11.

70. Ibid., at 911.

71. Ibid., at 916.

72. *RCA Records* v. *All-Fast Sys., Inc.*, 594 F. Supp. 335, 339 (S.D.N.Y. 1984). (The Supreme Court 'recognized that contributory infringer status had traditionally been given to those who were "in a position to control the use of copyrighted works by others and had authorized the use without permission from the copyright owner." ... The manufacturer of the machine does not fit this definition since it has no such control once the machine is sold'.)

73. Supra note 55, at 917.

74. Ibid., at 918.

75. 'If a computer system operator learns of specific infringing material available on his system and fails to purge such material from the system, the operator knows of and contributes to direct infringement' (923 F. Supp. (N.D. Cal. 1995).

76. Supra note 55, at 918, 920–21, n. 6.

77. Supra note 18, at 264.

78. Supra note 55, at 919–20.

79. Supra note 56.

80. Ibid., at 927.

81. Ibid., at 926.

82. Ibid.

83. Napster's Motion for Stay Pending Appeal, at 8, 13–14, 51–2.

84. Appellant Napster Inc. Opening Brief, at 12.

85. Napster's Motion for Stay Pending Appeal, at 15.

86. Supra note 56. 'The district court, however, failed to recognize that the boundaries of the premises that Napster "controls and patrols" are limited. Put differently, Napster's reserved "right and ability" to police is cabined by the system's current architecture. ... The preliminary injunction ... is overbroad because it placed on Napster the entire burden of ensuring that no "copying, downloading, uploading, transmitting, or distributing" or plaintiff's works occur on the system. As stated, we place the burden on plaintiffs to provide notice to Napster of copyrighted works and files containing such works available on the Napster system before Napster has the duty to disable access to the offending content' (citations omitted).

87. Ibid.

88. Ibid.

89. Supra note 57.

90. Ibid., at part 2.

91. Ibid., at part 3.

92. Ibid., at 1.

93. Ibid., at 11–12.

94. J. Borland, 'Judge: Napster Filtering Efforts "Disgraceful"', CNET NEWS.com, Apr. 10, 2001.

95. 'The Gracenote technology inserts into the beginning of an MP3 file that was ripped with a Gracenote-enabled encoder a Track Unique Identifier (TUID). The TUID is a unique identifier that may be used to identify music tracks. Further, applications exist, and in the future could be put into the Napster client software, that would retroactively insert a TUID into MP3 files that had been ripped with a Gracenote-enabled ripper that had not previously inserted a TUID. Using this TUID, Napster could filter files based on their content rather than their name' (Plaintiffs' Report on Napster's Non-Compliance with Modified Preliminary Injunctions, at 14–15).

96. 'A recording can be analyzed for traces of unique digital characteristics, usually through the use of a proprietary or patented algorithm. As a result, a "fingerprint" of these characteristics is derived. This "fingerprint" can be used to identify specific recordings, regardless of the name placed on the file by the Napster user, the source of the recording or technical difficulties such as frequency or sampling rate' (ibid., at 14).

97. 'Napster, Bertelsmann's Digital World Services Working on Service', *Digital Media Wire*, February 16, 2001.

98. L.M. Bowman, 'Napster Orders Strict Service Upgrade', CNET NEWS.com, June 28, 2001.

99. Ibid.

100. E. Hansen and L.M. Bowman, 'Court: Napster filters must be foolproof', CNET NEWS.com (July 12, 2001).

101. Ibid.

102. J. Hu, 'Napster: Gimme shelter in Chapter 11', CNET NEWS.com, June 3, 2002.

103. In Re Napster, Inc. Copyright Litigation, No. MDL 00-1369 MHP (2002).

104. 911 F. 2d 970, 976 (4th Cir. 1990).

105. 121 F. 3d 516 (9th Cir. 1997).

106. Section II.A., supra note 103.

107. Ibid., Section II.B.1; *see also* Noll. Decl.

108. Ibid., Section II.

109. Supra note 105, at 520, n. 9 ('Copyright misuse does not invalidate a copyright, but precludes its enforcement during a period of misuse').

110. G. Mariano, 'Audiogalaxy to ask first, trade later', CNET NEWS.com, June 18, 2002.

111. J. Borland, 'Madster told to pull the plug', CNET NEWS.com, December 3, 2002.

112. J. Borland, 'Suit Hits Popular Post-Napster Network', CNET NEWS.com, October 3, 2001.

113. Reuters, 'KaZaa Nears Download Record', CNET NEWS.com, May 22, 2003.

114. J. Weaver, 'Compact disc sales slid in 2002', MSNBC.NEWS.com, February 29, 2003.

115. Ibid. Other experts blame high CD prices, radio consolidation, and an industry focus on hit-oriented artists of limited or nonexistent talent.

116. Plaintiff's Complaint for Damages and Injunctive Relief for Copyright Infringement, *Metro Goldwyn Mayer et al.* v. *Grokster et al.*, C.D. Ca., No. 01-CV-8541 SVW, 2001; Class Action Complaint for Copyright Infringement, C.D. Ca., No. 01-09923 GAF, 2001.
117. J. Hu, 'KaZaa picks up the speed with update', CNET NEWS.com, February 11, 2002.
118. D. McCullagh, 'Judge: KaZaa can be sued in U.S.', CNET NEWS.com, January 10, 2003.
119. Supra notes 35–51 and surrounding text.
120. Quoted in J. Borland, 'File-swapping tools are legal', CNET NEWS.com, April 25, 2003.
121. Ibid.
122. J. Borland, 'KaZaa, Morpheus legal case collapsing', CNET NEWS.com, May 22, 2002.
123. J. Borland, 'Stealth P2P Network Hides Inside KaZaa', CNET NEWS.com, April 1, 2002.
124. Ibid.
125. J. Borland, 'The brains behind KaZaa', CNET NEWS.com, December 29, 2002.
126. J. Borland, 'New KaZaa likely to raise labels' ire', CNET NEWS.com, September 22, 2002.
127. J. Borland, 'Spike in "Spyware" accelerates arms race', CNET NEWS.com, February 24, 2003.
128. Ibid.
129. Re Grokster and StreamCast, supra notes 119–21 and surrounding text.
130. G. Mariano, 'Rival Services Prepare for Napster Onslaught', CNET NEWS.com, March 1, 2001.
131. 'This is the first [release] where we can confidently encourage people to go download the software and comfortably expect it to work for them.' J. Borland, 'Freenet keeps file-trading flame burning', CNET NEWS.com, October 28, 2002. See 'Protecting Free Expression Online with Freenet', IEEE Internet Computing 6(1), 40–49 (2002). (Currently the most up-to-date explanation of Freenet, including details of innovations in Freenet's security architecture since Ian Clarke's original design.) The original unpublished paper upon which the Freenet architecture is based in I. Clarke, 'A distributed decentralized information storage and retrieval system' (MS thesis, Division of Informatics, University of Edinburgh, 1999). For the first publication, see I. Clarke, O. Sandberg, B. Wiley and T.W. Hong, 'Freenet: A Distributed Anonymous Information Storage and Retrieval System', *ADAISARS in Designing Privacy Enhancing Technologies: International Workshop on Design Issues in Anonymity and Unobservability*, LNCS 2009 (ed. H. Federrath, New York: Springer, 2001). *See also* J. Borland, 'Networks promise unfettered file swapping', CNET NEWS.com, June 19, 2001.
132. C. Shapiro and H.R. Varian, *Information Rules* (Boston, MA: Harvard Business School Press, 1999) 5.
133. J. Borland, 'Sun's Joy Rapturous over Jxta', CNET NEWS.com, June 6, 2001.
134. J.V. Douglas, 'Altnet Tops 2 Million downloads', CNET NEWS.com, July 2, 2002.
135. J. Healey, 'Microsoft using KaZaa as a Marketing Portal', *L.A. Times*, September 22, 2002.
136. J. Borland, 'Paid content comes to KaZaa', CNET NEWS.com, May 19, 2002.
137. J. Borland, 'Bands to buy KaZaa search results', CNET NEWS.com, August 22, 2002.
138. M. La Monica, 'Microsoft makes P2P play', CNET NEWS.com, February 26, 2003. The company also has purchased Xdegrees and invested in Groove Networks as part of an integrative P2P strategy designed to promote application software. S. Junnarkar, 'P2P boost for Microsoft's .Net?', CNET NEWS.com, September 16, 2002.
139. J. Borland, 'Paid Content comes to KaZaa', CNET NEWS.com, May 19, 2002.
140. J. Borland, 'Freenet founder launches P2P product', CNET NEWS.com, April 30, 2002.
141. J. Borland, 'The brains behind KaZaa', CNET NEWS.com, December 29, 2002.
142. From an economic perspective, customers who forego the digital services for any of these alternatives actually suffer switching costs resulting from an interior P2P selection.
143. The RIAA is the first trade association to have attracted organized boycotts of its members, replete with appropriate apparel, housewares, auto goods, cards, prints and tote bags. See http://www.boycott-riaa.com.
144. Giovanna Fessenden identifies six. Musicians in 1877 boycotted the phonograph that would displace live music, music publishers in 1909 sought to prevent the distribution of the piano roll that would displace sheet music, songwriters in 1920 opposed broadcast

music for fear that it would reduce performance royalties, the music industry in 1982 lobbied Congress to require manufacturers of tape recorders to pay royalties, the movie industry in 1983 opposed the VCR and brought action against Sony, and the RIAA in 1997 sought to enjoin the Rio portable music player (G. Fessenden, 'Peer-to-Peer Technology: Analysis of Contributory Infringement and Fair Use', 42 *Idea* 391 (2002)).

145. J. Wilcox, 'Microsoft protecting rights – or Windows?', CNET NEWS.com, February 3, 2003.
146. J. Wilcox, 'Microsoft expands rights management tool', CNET NEWS.com, February 21, 2003.
147. Ibid.

5.   Digital music and the anti-commons[*]

5.1   INTRODUCTION

The American copyright system now separately protects the sounds in musical recordings and the words and melodies in the underlying compositions upon which they are based. Separate rights are defined for the reproduction and performance of each. Some of these component rights are under the exclusive control of one owner, while other rights can be under the exclusive or regulated control of a second. Moreover, different licensing and monitoring organizations operate in contrasting procedural manners and practice differing techniques for monitoring use and collecting revenue.

The consequences of diffuse copyright are now pronounced in the digital era, where digital distribution has produced a breakdown of legal categories that had some basis in analog applications. Through the channels of the Internet, digital music can be accessed through *downloading* and *streaming*.[1] Depending on whether the choice of a particular song is exercised at user or provider discretion, streaming further can be *interactive* or *non-interactive*.[2] Complicating both downloading and streaming, there is also a wide spectrum of temporary downloads made available in music subscription services that incorporate variations in length of ownership, as well as interactivity, portability and listening quality.[3]

With digital technology, the same transmission of a recording or composition may implicate the distinct rights of temporary reproductions[4] and wired performances;[5] one copyright authority famously termed the outcome an example of 'double dipping'.[6] The two categories of reproductions and performances implicate the collecting and administrative interests of overlapping agencies that have no consistent procedure for pricing related rights, i.e., unrelated arbitration bodies now set rates for performance rights in sound recordings and music compositions using historical methods and benchmarks that have little relation to one another.[7] Consequently, copyright fragmentation may lead to an anti-commons, with duplicate regulation and negotiation, license overgrowth and rent-seeking.

This chapter uses economic analysis to suggest a more rationalized copyright system. First, an economically efficient licensing scheme should ensure that the copyright system favors no one delivery method over a substitute by imposing upon one a higher percentage charge that distorts relative prices. Second, transaction costs can be reasonably economized by 'one-stop' rights that avoid duplicate negotiation or administration, e.g., users of statutory (or compulsory) licenses for purposes of noninteractive streaming should be able to get performance rights for sound recordings and compositions simultaneously. Third, the system should convey necessary usage rights through a minimum of administrative or regulatory layers; two or more different arbitrating bodies should not perform the same work that one might do as well.

This chapter will advocate a number of reforms for streamlining the American copyright system to protect the people who create music, the marketers who promote it and the consumers who buy it. The suggested outcome implicates two distinct concepts. First, an integrated 'making available' right, which is now protected respectively for creators and performers by the WIPO Copyright Treaty[8] and the WIPO Performances and Phonograms Treaty,[9] would cover the rights of songwriters and composers to receive payment for musical works made available through digital transmissions at a time and place selected interactively by· an individual listener. Second, an integrated equitable remunerative performance right for noninteractive uses that are covered by statutory licenses would tie payments for the sound recording and underlying musical composition in some determined proportion to one another.[10] The fee-setting structure for these statutory licenses would be assigned to one administrative body, the US Copyright Office, and collected by one appointed agent.

5.2   MUSICAL COMPOSITIONS

Copyright in musical compositions and sound recordings is now protected by the Copyright Act of 1976, the principal provisions of which became effective in January, 1978 and encoded in Title 17 of the US Code.[11] Per statute, each track of recorded music implicates separate copyrights in the sound recording and the underlying composition. For example, when Bing Crosby recorded Irving Berlin's 'White Christmas' on disk, the record label owned rights in the sound recording, while the writer owned rights in the song.

In more detail, Section 106 of the Copyright Act grants four exclusive rights to composers of musical compositions or the publishers to whom they pass copyright.[12] These four rights include:

1.   The right to reproduce the copyrighted work in copies or phonorecords.
2.   The right to prepare derivative works based on the copyrighted work.

3. The right to distribute copies or phonorecords of the copyrighted work to the public by sale or other transfer of ownership, or by rental, lease, or lending.
4. The right to perform the copyrighted work publicly.

Mechanical Rights

The three related rights to reproduce copyrighted works, prepare derivatives, and distribute copies are commonly called the *mechanical right*.[13] Music publishers collect mechanical royalties for compositions through the services of mechanical rights organizations (MROs), most prominently the Harry Fox Agency (HFA).[14] Due royalties are generally based on the number of physical imprints made of the protected work. After deducting a small percentage for administrative expenses, the MROs return collected moneys to publishers, who pay writers their contracted share. Publishers may compete for writers by offering high royalty shares, and particularly successful writers may self-publish so as to keep more royalties.

The publisher of a copyrighted song has exclusive authority to license first-time reproductions of the work. After an authorized phonorecord[15] of a composition is publicly distributed, subsequent performers may legally record the same work without public permission, subject to a statutory (or compulsory) license. By making it possible for secondary users to access works without negotiation, statutory licensing presumably reduces bargaining costs between label and publisher. This license requires compliance with certain procedural requirements and payment of a fee established by a Copyright Arbitration Royalty Panel under 17 U.S.C. § 115.

The rate-setting process involves two steps. First, voluntary, industry-wide negotiations to set rates to be adopted by the Copyright Office are encouraged. If these negotiations falter, any interested party can petition the Copyright Office to convene an arbitration proceeding to establish the fees.

At present, the statutory mechanical royalty fee is the larger of 8.0 cents per song (cps) or 1.55 cents per minute (cpm); increases are scheduled for 2004 (8.5 cps, 1.65 cpm) and 2006 (9.1 cps, 1.75 cpm).[16] Instead of choosing the statutory option, record companies often obtain from the HFA mechanical form licenses for cover recordings that are derived from the statutory license.

Reproduction rights for musical compositions now are implicated both in downloads, where compositions are captured on hard drives for indefinite storage, and in streaming, where the receiving device temporarily stores a few seconds of transmitted data in random access memory (RAM).[17] A number of parties suggest that such temporary reproductions can safely be made exempt from copyright.[18] One conflict in the digital music arena arises regarding the proper legal handling of appropriate rights for these digital reproductions, as the mechanical rights organizations assert that all permanent and temporary reproductions implicate mechanical copyright.[19]

Performance Rights

As a fourth assigned right, song publishers receive compensation for public performances of their works. Under 17 U.S.C. §101, to 'perform' a musical composition (outside audiovisual applications) is to 'recite, render, play, dance, or act it, either directly or by means of any device or process.'[20] To perform ... a work 'publicly' means:

> (1) to perform ... it at a place open to the public or at any place where a substantial number of persons outside of a normal circle of a family and its social acquaintances is gathered; or
> (2) to transmit or otherwise communicate a performance ... of the work to a place specified by clause (1) or to the public, by means of any device or process, whether the members of the public capable of receiving the performance ... receive it in the same place or in separate places and at the same time or at different times.[21]

The second part of the definition of a performance is particularly significant for digital transmissions, where streaming or downloading to a listener in a private location may legally constitute a public performance.[22]

Public performance rights for compositions that are used in audio, non-dramatic presentations are almost universally conveyed through licenses granted by the nation's three performing rights organizations (PROs) – the American Society of Composers, Authors, and Publishers (ASCAP), Broadcast Music, Inc. (BMI) and SESAC[23] – which license musical works registered in their respective catalogs,[24] after deducting operating expenses of 15–18 percent.[25] Virtually all music publishers and songwriters are members of or affiliated with one of the three societies; dual membership is not possible. Each PRO now generally issues blanket licenses that enable most licensees to perform all of its catalogued works during any contract run.[26]

License fees for individual or groups of licenses at all three organizations are established in a sequence of negotiations with broadcasters, webcasters, general users or their appointed agents. If the parties are unable to agree on a fee within 60 days of receipt of the initial application at ASCAP or BMI, any party may request an administrative hearing at the federal court for the Southern District of New York. These independent magistrate hearings (called Rate Courts) enforce the terms of two antitrust Consent Decrees that ASCAP and BMI negotiated separately with the US Department of Justice.[27] The Rate Court administration then represents a separate regulatory substrate that operates independently of the Copyright Office.

Recognized by the Supreme Court, the same performing rights organizations generally license music through blanket licenses that economize on negotiation costs and monitor for infringement by avoiding the need for direct licenses between composers and licensees.[28] However, the Court also recognized that the prevailing monitoring process implicated analog technology and, quite presciently, 'changes brought about by new technology or new marketing techniques might also undercut the justification for the practice'.[29] More recently, the US Justice Department in 2000 affirmed the same point: '[T]echnologies that allow rights holders and music users to easily and inexpensively monitor and track music usage are evolving rapidly and may erode many of the justifications for collective licensing of performance rights.'[30]

Also problematic is the legal structure of the Consent Decree. Because Consent Decrees may be amended only with the consent of the signing parties, full legal standing to propose changes redounds only to the collecting society and the Justice Department.[31] Under American law, only the Department or the signing rights organization may petition for an interpretation of the Consent Decree. Ironically, the writers, publishers, and licensees who create, market and use the copyrighted music have standing in court only within the narrow definition of the specific Consent Decree. In particular, they cannot appeal any term that the Department and the signing organization might have negotiated beforehand.[32]

5.3   SOUND RECORDINGS

In addition to the song melodies and lyrics of underlying music compositions, the Copyright Act extends copyright protection to the sound recordings that imprint the work on disks, tapes, or other phonorecords.[33] As originally enacted, the protection of sound recordings was limited to mechanical rights. Consequently, stations that played recorded music paid copyright royalties to writers and publishers, but not to the artists and labels that actually recorded the track.[34]

For several decades, record labels unsuccessfully petitioned Congress to grant a public performance right in sound recordings.[35] Finally, Congress passed the Digital Performance Rights in Sound Recordings Act of 1995 (DPRSRA),[36] which amended section 106 of the Copyright Act to include the right 'to perform the copyrighted [recording] publicly by means of a digital audio transmission'.[37] The DPRSRA also amended 17 U.S.C. § 114 to exempt certain digital uses from this performance right.[38] In 1998, Congress passed the Digital Millenium Copyright Act (DMCA), which further amended sections 17 U.S.C. § 114.[39] As a result, record labels may now be compensated for non-exempt public performances[40] on music subscription services, satellite radio, webcasters and Internet music providers that offer online music services.[41]

Performance Licenses for Sound Recordings

Section 114(d) of the Copyright Act establishes a three-tier structure for governing digital audio transmissions through exemptions, statutory licenses, and exclusive performance rights. For digital audio transmissions, the US Congress considered the possibility that wired transmissions might more readily displace music sales. Accordingly, the differential treatment of kinds of users with respect to sound recording performance liability – exemption, eligibility for compulsory license, full liability – reflects a judgment about the probable adverse effects of each on sales of sound recordings.[42] We now describe each of these tiers.

Under 17 U.S.C. § 114(d)(1), radio stations continue to maintain a performance exemption for digital over-the-air broadcasts. Statutory exemptions are now limited to nonsubscription broadcast transmissions and, to a degree, their retransmissions.[43] To be exempt, the transmission must be noninteractive and must be broadcast to the general non-paying public rather than to individual subscribers. Performances of sound recordings made on simultaneous webcasts of over-the-air broadcasts are not exempt from performance royalties and are governed instead by statutory licenses described below.[44]

Under 17 U.S.C. § 114(d)(2), noninteractive streaming (i.e., webcasting) of a sound recording is eligible for a statutory license if a number of additional eligibility requirements are met.[45] These conditions seek to limit the license to those transmissions seen as least likely to substitute for record sale.[46] If a prospective user and a copyright owner cannot agree on a negotiated license rate, any interested party may petition the matter to a Copyright Arbitration Royalty Panel (CARP).[47] Arbitrated rates and terms should reflect benchmarks that were actually or could be expectedly negotiated between a willing buyer and seller in a competitive marketplace, and whether the service may substitute for or enhance phonorecord sales.[48] A coincidental fee administered through the CARP is the affected royalty that is implicated by the ephemeral server reproduction of the track.[49]

Under 17 U.S.C. § 114(d)(3), record labels retain exclusive authority for licensing of all remaining (i.e., downloaded, interactively streamed and non-eligible noninteractively streamed) digital audio transmissions that are more likely to displace record sales.[50] While the act grants copyright owners full rights to negotiate licenses, exclusive licenses cannot bind for more than one year until the owner has granted at least five such licenses.[51] This limitation recognizes the need for markets to congeal so to establish reasonable competitive benchmarks.[52]

Statutory Mechanical Licenses

In addition to performance rights for sound recordings in digital audio transmissions, the DPRSRA extended statutory mechanical licenses for secondary reproductions of musical compositions that are imprinted in digital phonorecord deliveries (DPDs).[53] As with physical reproductions, statutory licenses for a work can be activated only after a legitimate recording of the composition is distributed to the public.[54] For digital deliveries made on or after January 1, 1998, the royalty rate payable with respect to each work in the phonorecord shall equal the rate applied to physical reproductions (i.e., 'Physical Rate').[55]

Since downloads and physical sales of music are economic substitutes for one another, economists would generally suggest that optimal copyright charges not distort the price ratio. That is, both types of tracks should be increased by the same percentage (e.g., 8 percent[56]) to recover royalties for mechanical copyright. For if percentage-of-revenues royalties of, e.g., 5 and 10 percent were hypothetically placed on two substitute goods, the asymmetric system would create listener incentives to substitute inefficiently to the less burdened product. This would interfere with the capacity of the market to allocate demand efficiently between two competing goods based on their respective price ratios

This is the efficiency of a non-distorting sales tax. From an ideal economic perspective, the equal unit charges imposed on digital and physical products are not theoretically perfect. However, the practice maintains a reasonably efficient relationship between the relative prices of the two products and can reasonably be defended as a streamlined procedure to set all mechanical fees in a reasonable balance.

5.4   DOWNLOADS AND SUBSTITUTION

Like downloads, interactive streaming enables digital users to choose music tracks in 'jukebox' play that involves personal choice without storage.[57] With interactivity, streaming can be an effective substitute for downloading, which requires storage in computer memory. Also implicated here are temporary downloads, which may be stored on a hard drive for a period of time before a specified expiration date, at which time the user may have an option to buy. Access terms for both interactive streams and temporary downloads may vary by a number of factors, including permitted plays, duration of access, and number of devices on which the work may be played.

As distinguished from permanent downloads, both interactive streams and temporary downloads are generally sold in music subscription services that charge buyers a flat subscription rates for a fixed number of specified uses in a month or year.[58] As a matter of economic efficiency and fairness, it would not be appropriate to affix the same per unit royalty charge on streams and temporaries as are affixed upon permanents. Rather, in judging the potential for sales displacement among permanent downloads and the music subscription services that offer streaming and a certain number of reproductions, policy-makers would best avoid distorting relative prices by feeing the revenues collected from each with the same percentage markup. These balanced copyright fees may then be conceived a 'making available right'; however, since the 'making available right' should be cued off of the mechanical right, the charges could also be conceived as a mechanical right.

The Copyright Office Report

If a 'making available' right is imposed on streams and downloads, it would be economically inefficient to affix additional fees on any one group of delivery services. Nonetheless, the potential for this distortion now exists, as a current question is whether downloads also constitute a public performance that is subject to copyright liability.[59] Attempting to resolve this issue, the Copyright Office issued a report in the year 2001 in connection with its statutory responsibilities under section 104 of the DMCA.[60]

Regarding permanent downloads, the report urged that digital phonorecord deliveries be exempt from the performance right:

> To the extent that such a download can be considered a public performance, the performance is merely a technical by-product of the transmission process that has no value separate from the value of the download ... Demanding a separate payment for the copies that are an inevitable by-product of that activity appears to be double-dipping and is not a sound equitable basis for resisting the invocation of the fair use doctrine.'[61]

This would suggest that physical and digital downloads can be appropriately cued to one another.

Turning to interactive streams, the Copyright Office then recommended that Congress enact legislation that would amend the Copyright Act to preclude any reproduction right liability with respect to temporary buffer copies that are used during any digital transmission, included those used in interactive streaming.[62]

> Buffer copies have no independent economic significance. They are made solely to

enable the performance ... The same copyright owners [i.e., publishers and songwriters] appear to be seeking a second compensation for the same activity merely because of the happenstance that the transmission technology implicates the reproduction right, and the reproduction right of songwriters and music publishers is administered by a different collective than the public performance right.[63]

By exempting interactive streams from mechanical copyright, the Copyright Office would instead place the stream under exclusive domain of performance rights. The Copyright Office's recommendations mirrored provisions from a European Union Directive, which now exempts transient copies from the reach of the reproduction right.[64]

If the report were adapted, the strategy would put the 'making available rights' of downloading and streaming under two different administrative regimes. This would reduce considerably any real possibility of coordinating the related rights and would invite asymmetric price effects.

5.5   NONINTERACTIVE STREAMING

As a final matter, we now consider noninteractive streaming services (i.e., 'webcasting') that qualify for a statutory license.[65] 'Webcasting' provides 'broadcast-like' services that may greatly expand the scope of music delivery to new audiences, regions and countries. Though it is uncertain what business models will prove most viable, advertising revenues, e-commerce and the sales of market data can be expected to figure prominently.

Though webcasting is noninteractive, it is more likely than traditional broadcasting to displace the sales of CDs and legitimate music services for a number of reasons. First, broadcast radio is listened to often during rush hour and at work, and therefore occurs at a time when people generally do not use CDs for entertainment. By contrast, listeners tune in to webcasts while operating home personal computers, possibly displacing consumer demand for interactive services or CD accompaniment.[66] Second, webcast users may accommodate better selection with automatic search software that can designate and capture preferred artists or tracks;[67] analog broadcasting now offers no such comparable capacity.[68] Third, prospective displacement may increase yet more as local area networking builds out and audiences transmit music from receiving devices throughout the house. The Copyright Office accordingly states:

The terms and conditions of a statutory license must then compensate record companies for the increased risk that a listener may make a high-quality unauthorized reproduction of a sound recording directly from the transmission instead of purchasing a legitimate copy in the marketplace, a risk that is clearly greater when the recipient is receiving the transmission on a computer, which can instantly replicate and retransmit the transmission.[69]

The question then remains how to fee the musical compositions that are used in noninteractive webcast performances. Licensing procedures at ASCAP and BMI recognize that music is a support service that attracts listeners to broadcast advertising messages. Accordingly, songwriters are generally compensated through blanket licenses that are fixed, usually in direct proportion to adjusted advertising revenues.[70] Such licensing models contrast with performance royalties now established for sound recordings, which are based instead on the number of listener streams of a particular record track.[71]

Because streaming is more likely to displace purchases of tracks and compositions, and because it is difficult to suggest a fee model for related sales of data and e-commerce, performance rights for musical compositions can similarly be licensed on a per unit basis in a proportional manner that would ensure congruency with the sound recording rights. This would establish an American equivalent of a 'single equitable remuneration' for composers and performers that appears in the EU Directive 92/100/EEC.[72]

For example, the Copyright Office recently re-established that the appropriate rate for an eligible nonsubscription transmission of a sound recording should be set at 0.07 cents per performance, per listener, for commercial performances on webcast and radio simulcast services.[73] In a previous rule-making on the Audio Home Recording Act,[74] the Copyright Office set forth that equipment levies gathered on the sale of digital tape recording equipment should be apportioned roughly in a '2 to 1' ratio for sound recordings to compositions.[75] Adopting *arguendo* the same proportion, public performances of musical compositions should then be priced at 0.035 cents per performance per listener. Per rule-making, an additional 8.8 percent of revenue can be added to both sound recordings and compositions to cover the copyright for the ephemeral reproduction of the recording on the server.[76]

For digital transmissions, Rate Courts do not yet have a common set of rate-making procedures that are congruent with performance rights in sound recordings that are now administered by the Copyright Office. Accordingly, more congruence and administrative transparency can be had if digital performance royalties were reassigned to the Copyright Office. Under its present governance structure, the Copyright Office can issue Notices of Inquiry and Proposed Rulemaking that would invite comments from all affected parties and can grant equal legal standing to any. This change would particularly address the legal concerns of publishers and writers, who now often lack legal standing on some issues in the Rate Courts.[77] While the performing rights organizations may be free to testify, there is no need for them to monitor use or collect money. Rather, such monitoring can be done by an independent party, such as Sound Exchange[78] or Music Reports Inc.,[79] that administers collections for sound recordings or other performance licenses.

5.6 DISTANCE EDUCATION

On November 2, 2002, President Bush signed into law the Technology, Education and Copyright Harmonization Act (the TEACH Act), as part of the larger 21st Century Department of Justice Appropriations Authorization Act.[80] The TEACH Act modified 17 U.S. C. § 110(2) to redefine the terms and conditions on which accredited, nonprofit educational institutions may use copyrighted materials for distance education on web sites and through digital transmissions. As a major modification of the pre-existing law, the new law exempted from the public performance and display right nearly all works transmitted to enrolled students at specified classroom periods during mediated instruction, so long as copyright information and proper notice regarding unauthorized reuse is given. The scope of the new legislation now concerns the content industries, which argue that a broad exemption would cut into new licensing opportunities in a fast-growing market. Moreover, classroom uses of first-run movies and classics may displace box office sales.

As argued in Chapter 6, there are general economic reasons to enforce copyright for digital uses in a diligent manner and to allow markets time to congeal, i.e., digital technology in many instances actually reduce transactions costs, prices may signal the incentives for future efforts and rights owners are entitled to just deserts for their contribution to value. However, the particular legislation at hand may yet prove to deal properly with the immediate right to public performance and display for digital transmissions, at least in so far as nondramatic uses of musical compositions and recordings are concerned.

In the first place, the law does not relax the related reproduction right for compositions and recordings, which the Copyright Office advocated.[81] Both rights are necessarily implicated whenever a track or movie is uploaded to a server. Digital transmission differs here from analog radio transmission, which does not implicate any corresponding reproduction right. With digital technology, content owners may then recover revenues through innovative contracts put in place for server reproduction, which can comprise both a flat-fee and unit price, as was established for musical works in 2000 in a deal involving the Harry Fox Agency and MP3.com.[82]

The performance 'royalty' can then be recovered through a use-based reproduction right. Accordingly, even if performance rights are not collected for copyrighted tracks, rights owners can be made whole for lost revenue through ongoing mechanical licenses based on volume of use. That said, it is unclear what benefits an additional performance right would provide, but for contributing to the coffers of collecting organizations that excise some fraction of license revenues for salaries, retirement plans and 'business development'. The duplicate burden of collection for performance royalties would be administratively burdensome and economically useless.

From an economic standpoint, the matter is similar to an earlier case, *Alden Rochelle* v. *ASCAP*, that disallowed ASCAP from collecting on behalf of its members a disjoint performance fee for cinema performances of movies.[83] As a result of *Alden Rochelle*, ASCAP composers came to license simultaneously the synchronization and performance rights for movie soundtracks. The practice in the industry became universal, although the decision did not legally implicate the practices of BMI and SESAC. In bundling two rights that are necessarily tied to one another in a movie, the *Alden Rochelle* decision greatly improved administrative efficiency, i.e., except for the music performed in their lobbies, cinemas were made free from visits from PROs. In a low-margin industry such as movie exhibition, the difference could have had a considerable effect upon market buildout.

However, *Alden Rochelle* did not eviscerate entirely the performance right. Rather, it simply required its bundled collection with the synchronization. In deference to the legal concerns of rights owners, the TEACH Act might have been more symmetric. It could have maintained the performance right, but mandated rights bundling in manner of *Alden Rochelle*.

As mentioned, the advocated position is more conservative than that of the Copyright Office, which advocated that corresponding mechanical rights for compositions and sound recordings be also vacated.[84] The Copyright Office here may have aimed to establish a correspondence with the previous exemption for classroom use of broadcast performances of nondramatic musical and literary works, which did not implicate any reproduction right at the broadcast station. However, broadcast performances are generally noninteractive, while digital performances can be chosen interactively by the instructor. The interactive digital use is more valuable to the instructor, more readily displaces the institutional purchase of the underlying recording, and is more conducive to unauthorized capture and redistribution. It is not then clear whether the reproduction right itself should be entirely vacated.

5.7 CONCLUSION

In summary, the administration of digital rights for musical compositions can be simplified in three key respects. First, download services may compensate copyright owners for unit reproductions based on mechanical fees that are now in effect for CDs. Music subscription services with downloads and interactive streams may pay a royalty for 'making available' royalties that can be fixed in the same percentage-of-revenue as the download amount. Webcasters may compensate songwriters in the manner by which they pay for sound recordings. By not reforming the administration of copyright, policy-makers then indeed promulgate distorted prices, extra negotiations and redundant administrative layers.

From a political science perspective, a fear with deregulation is that the regulatory body gets captured by the regulated entity, and that reform cannot be expected. In fact, the past 25 years have dislodged this premise. The Civil Aeronautics Board has entirely deregulated the airlines, the Interstate Commerce Commission has deregulated trucking and railroads, and telephone and energy regulators have forced telephone, electricity and natural gas monopolies to compete. An assertive measure in copyright can similarly streamline redundant operations that burden the creative community and its marketers, and interferes with the buildout of an information superhighway that enables the convenient delivery of music content.

NOTES

* This chapter was co-written with Lewis Kurlantzick.
1. In downloading, a copy of the audio file is transmitted and stored for a period of time on the hard drive of the receiving machine. By contrast, streaming users receive content and play it immediately with a few seconds delay.
2. An 'interactive' stream is 'one that enables a member of the public to receive ... a transmission of a particular sound recording ... which is selected by or on behalf of the recipient' (17 U.S.C. § 114(j)(7) (2000)).
3. See Chapter 3, section 2
4. Infra note 17 and surrounding text.
5. Infra notes 20–22 and surrounding text.
6. R. Kohn, 'A Primer on the Law of Webcasting and Digital Music Delivery', *Entertainment Law Reporter*, September 1998, at 4, 9, 11, 12.
7. *See* J.C. Ginsburg, 'Can Copyright Become User-Friendly? Essay Review of Jessica Litman', 25 *Columbia Journal of Law and the Arts* 71 (2002).
8. World Intellectual Property Organization, Copyright Treaty, Art. 8.
9. World Intellectual Property Organization, Performances and Phonograms Treaty, Art. 10, 14.
10. Infra note 72 and surrounding text.
11. 17 U.S.C. § 101–1332 (2000).
12. 17 U.S.C. § 106 (2000).
13. The term *mechanical right* is historically derived from the time when records were mechanically and not electronically reproduced. The right to license the reproduction of music on television, video and motion picture soundtracks is termed the *synchronization right*.
14. The HFA is the music publishing industry's principal clearinghouse for the administration of licences for mechanical rights. Unlike the performing rights societies, the HFA is only a collection agency and does not negotiate individual contracts. It files petitions and appears in arbitration hearings before the Copyright Office that involve compulsory mechanical royalties.

15. 17 U.S.C. § 101 (2000): ('"Phonorecords" are material objects in which sounds ... are fixed by any method now known or later developed, and from which the sounds can be perceived, reproduced, or otherwise communicated, either directly or with the aid of a machine or device. The term "phonorecords" includes the material object in which the sounds are first fixed.')

16. 37 C.F.R. § 255.3 (2001).

17. The receiving device collects in its RAM buffer a few seconds of data to guard against interruptions or delays due to line congestion or slow Internet connections. The data cannot be accessed for other purposes within the receiving device. Once performed, the transmitted data leave the buffer permanently and cannot otherwise be stored. If the user wants to hear the streamed recording again, he must once more contact the web site and request that it transmit the file again.

18. Infra notes 59–64 and surrounding text. *See also* R.A. Reese, 'The Public Display Right: The Copyright Act's Neglected Solution to the Controversy over RAM "Copies"', *University of Illinios Law Review* 83 (2001) 138–46.

19. *See,* e.g., Joint Reply Comments on Copyright Industry Organizations, Report to Congress Pursuant to Section 104 of the Digital Millennium Copyright Act 8–13 (September 5, 2000).

20. 17 U.S.C. § 101 (2000).

21. Ibid.

22. Ibid.

23. The acronym is no longer meaningful.

24. To this end, the societies sell licenses, collect fees, monitor users, bring infringement action, sample music for frequency of use and distribute revenues to rights owners.

25. At http://www.ascap.com/press/meeting-020800.html (visited January 5, 2001); http://www.bmi.com/iama/media/faq/money.asp (visited May 1, 2000; links no longer active).

26. Another option for radio and television stations includes licensing of individual programs ('per program license'), complemented by an add-on license to cover the ambient commercial and lead-in music.

27. *United States* v. *Am. Soc'y of Composers, Authors and Publishers*, 1950 Trade Cas. (CCH), ¶ 62,595 (S.D.N.Y. 1950); *United States* v. *Am. Soc'y of Composers, Authors and Publishers*, Second Amended Final Judgment, 2001 WL 1589999, 2001–2 TRADE CAS. ¶ 73,474 (S.D.N.Y. 2001); *United States* v. *Broadcast Music Inc.*, 1966 TRADE CAS. (CCH), ¶ 71,941 (S.D.N.Y. 1966).

28. *BMI* v. *CBS*, 441 U.S. 1, 22 (1977), (Stevens, J., dissenting).

29. Ibid. at n. 34.

30. The Department also noted that it is 'continuing to investigate the extent to which the growth of [digital] technologies warrants additional changes to the [Consent Decrees], including the possibility that the [performing rights organizations] should be prohibited from collectively licensing certain types of users or performances' (Memorandum of the United States in Support of the Joint Motion to Enter Second Amended Final Judgment, at note 10, *United States* v. *Am. Soc'y of Composers, Authors and Publishers* (S.D.N.Y. 2001) (Civ. No. 41–1395)).

31. Consent Decrees must be interpreted within their plain meaning, are not modifiable by the Court, and are adjusted only with the bilateral consent of the signing parties. *See United States* v. *Atl. Refining Co.* 360 U.S. 19 (1959); *Suarez* v. *Ward*, 896 F. 2d 28 (2nd Cir. 1990); *Berger* v. *Heckler*, 771 F. 2d 1556 (2nd Cir. 1985).

32. Licensee standing was denied in *United States* v. *Am. Soc'y of Composers, Authors and Publishers*, 208 F. Supp. 896 (S.D.N.Y. 1962), aff'd, 331 F. 2d 117 (2nd Cir. 1964); *United States* v. *Am. Soc'y of Composers, Authors and Publishers*, 708 F. Supp. 95 (S.D.N.Y. 1989). Writer standing was denied in *United States* v. *Am. Soc'y of Composers, Authors and Publishers*, 708 F. Supp. 95 (S.D.N.Y. 1989); *United States* v. *Am. Soc'y of Composers, Authors and Publishers*, 739 F. Supp. 177 (S.D.N.Y. 1990); *United States* v. *Am. Soc'y of Composers, Authors and Publishers*, 914 F. Supp. 52 (S.D.N.Y. 1996).

33. The Copyright Act defines 'sound recording' as a work that results 'from the fixation of a series of musical, spoken, or other wounds ... regardless of the nature of the material

subjects, such as disks, tapes, or other phono records, in which they are embodied' (17 U.S.C. § 101 (2000)).

34. Presumably, broadcast performances promote record sales that otherwise would not take place. *See*, e.g., S. Rep. No. 104–28, at 14–15 (1995).

35. Ibid., at 1–4.

36. Pub. L. No. 104–39, 109 Stat. 336 (1995). For a comprehensive account of the legislative history of the Act and a highly detailed description of its terms, see E.D. Leach, 'Everything You Always Wanted to Know about Digital Performance Rights but were Afraid to Ask', 48 *Journal of the Copyright Society* 191 (2000).

37. 17 U.S.C. § 106(6) (2000).

38. 17 U.S.C. § 114, 115 (2000).

39. Pub. L. No. 105–304, 112 Stat. 2860 (1998). For criticism of the complexity of this licensing framework, see D. Nimmer, 'Ignoring the Public, Part I: On the Absurd Complexity of the Digital Audio Transmission Right', 7 *UCLA Entertainment Law Review* 189 (2000).

40. 17 U.S.C. § 114(d)(1)–(3) (2000).

41. Supra note 3.

42. H.R. Rep. No. 104–274 (1995).

43. 17 U.S.C. § 114(d)(1)(A)–(B) (2000).

44. Public Performance of Sound Recordings: Definition of a Service, 65 *Federal Register* 77292 (2000), upheld in *Bonneville Int'l Corp.* v. *Peters*, 153 F. Supp. 2d 763 (E.D. Pa. 2001).

45. 17 U.S.C. § 114(d)(2)(A)(i) (2000) An 'eligible nonsubscription transmission' is a non-interactive nonsubscription digital audio transmission that is not exempt and that is part of a service that provides audio programming consisting of performances of sound recordings. (17 U.S.C. § 114(j)(6) (2000)).

46. 17 U.S.C. § 114(d)(2)(A),(C) (2000).

47. 17 U.S.C. § 114(f)(2)(B) (2000).

48. Ibid.

49. 17 U.S.C. § 112(e).

50. 17 U.S.C. § 114(b),(d)(3) (2000).

51. 17 U.S.C. § 114(d)(3)(A),(B) (2000).

52. The Copyright Office rejected in the year 2000 a petition that sought a clarifying amendment to the definition of 'interactive' in the Copyright Office's regulations (Public Performance of Sound Recordings: Definitions of a Service, 65 *Federal Register* 77330 (2000)). The Copyright Office decided that 'a service does not become interactive merely because consumers may have some influence on the music programming offered by the service' (at 77332). While recognizing that uncertainty existed over 'how much influence a consumer can have on the programming offered by a transmitting entity before that activity must be characterized as interactive' (at 77332*)*, the Copyright Office concluded that it was neither necessary, desirable, nor feasible to try to resolve the uncertainty via regulation at the present time.

53. 17 U.S.C. § 115 (2000). A 'digital phonorecord delivery' is each individual delivery of a phonorecord by digital transmission of a sound recording which results in a specifically identifiable reproduction by or for any transmission recipient of a phonorecord of that sound recording (17 U.S.C. § 115(d) (2000)).

54. 17 U.S.C. § 115(a)(1) (2000).

55. 17 U.S.C. § 115(c)(3)(A)(ii) (2000).

56. This is a rough number obtained by dividing a mechanical royalty payment of 8 cents by an overall sales price of $1.00.

57. The phrase 'celestial jukebox' appeared in P. Goldstein, *Copyright's Highway: From Gutenberg to the Celestial Jukebox* (Palo Alto, CA: Stanford University Press, 1996) to represent the capacity of a computer to deliver streamed music at customer request at a moment's notice.

58. Supra note 3.

59. *See*, e.g., ASCAP, 'Frequently Asked Questions about Internet Licensing', at http://www.ascap.com/weblicense/webfaq.html (retrieved December 13, 2001 ('every

Internet transmission of a musical work constitutes a public performance of that work').

60. US Copyright Office, DMCA Section 104 Report (2001). Section 104 of the DMCA directed the Register of Copyrights and the Assistant Secretary for Communications and Information of the Department of Commerce to jointly evaluate: '(1) the effects of the amendments made by this title and the development of electronic commerce and associated technology on the operation of sections 109 and 117 of Title 17, United States Code; and (2) the relationship between existing and emergent technology and the operations of sections 109 and 117 of Title 17, United States Code' (Pub. L. No. 105–304, 112 Stat. 2860 (1998)).

61. Ibid., 146–8, xxvii–xxviii.

62. Ibid., xxiii–xxvii, 132–46.

63. Ibid., 143.

64. Directive 2001/29/EC of the European Parliament and of the Council of 22 May 2001 on the harmonization of certain aspects of copyright and related rights in the information society, 2001 O.J. (L167) 10, par. 33, Art. 5(1). *See also* ibid. at Art. 5(2)(d) (preservation of ephemeral recordings made by broadcasters permitted). Member states must implement the Directive in their national laws by December 22, 2002 (ibid. at Art. 13(1)).

65. 17 U.S.C. § 114(d)(2) (2000). Eligible licensees may choose to negotiate other alternative arrangements with individual content owners.

66. B. Rose and L. Rosin, 'Internet V: Startling New Insights about the Internet and Streaming', New York: Arbitron/Edison Media Research, 13. Indeed, more than 80 percent of webcast listeners confirm that they multitask on the computer at the same time (at 12). The incidence of multitasking is higher for webcasts than any other form of entertainment; 55 percent listen to music from CDs and tapes, 49 percent listen to radio, 36 percent talk on the telephone and 32 percent watch television.

67. Griffin, J. (2000), 'Statement, The Future of Digital Music: Is there an Upside to Digital Downloading?', Senate Judiciary Committee, Washington, DC, July 11, 2000.

68. Copyright Office, Public Performance of Sound Recordings: Definition of a Service, 37 CFR Part 201, Docket No. RM 2000-3B, 65 *Federal Register*, 77292, 77301.

69. Digital transmissions pose an 'increased risk that a listener may make a high-quality unauthorized reproduction of a sound recording directly from the transmission instead of purchasing a legitimate copy in the marketplace, a risk that is clearly greater when the recipient is receiving the transmission on a computer, which can instantly replicate and retransmit the transmission' (ibid. at 77294).

70. For example, blanket fees for radio broadcast uses at ASCAP are set at 1.615 percent of station advertising revenues less reasonable deductions ASCAP, Local Station Blanket Radio License, at 8(A)(2), available at http://www.ascap.com/licensing/radio/Blanket_Radio_License.pdf (last visited May 3, 2003).

71. Determination of Reasonable Rates and Terms for the Digital Performance of Sound Recordings and Ephemeral Recordings; Final Rule; 67 *Federal Register*, 45239 (2002).

72. Council Directive 92/100/EEC, Rental Right and Lending Right and on Certain Rights Related to Copyright in the Field of Intellectual Property, Art. 8.2 (1992). ('Member States shall provide a right in order to ensure that a single equitable remuneration is paid by the user, if a phonogram published for commercial purposes, or a reproduction of such phonogram, is used for broadcasting by wireless means or for any communication to the public, and to ensure that this remuneration is shared between the relevant performers and phonogram producers.') *See also SENA* v. *NOS*, Case C-245/00, European Court of Justice (2003).

73. Supra note 71, 45255.

74. Pub. L. No. 102–563, 106 Stat. 4237. codified at 17 U.S.C. 1001–8.

75. Code of Federal Regulations, Title 37, Volume 1, 460–61.

76. Supra note 73, 45261–2.

77. Supra notes 31–2 and surrounding text.

78. Sound Exchange is the monitoring authority of the recording labels.

79. Music Reports Inc. is an independent monitoring authority that now collects music use data on broadcast radio and television.

80. Pub. L. 107–273; Division C, Title III, Subtitle C, Section 13301; 116 STAT. 1758.

81. Infra note 84.
82. Under the royalty terms of the agreement, MP3.com paid one quarter cent for each song that was streamed by a user as well as a one-time fee per user-stored track. Claire Saliba, 'MP3.com Inks Tentative Licensing Pact', *Wireless News Factor*, October 18, 2000, at http://www.wirelessnewsfactor.com/perl/story/4575.html (retrieved June 1, 2003).
83. 80 F. Supp. 888, 894 (S.D.N.Y. 1948). In 1948, 164 cinema owners sued ASCAP for violations of Sections 1 and 2 of the Sherman Act regarding its requirement that movie producers contract only with theaters that purchased ASCAP licenses. In the District Court decision, ASCAP was found to be a combination in restraint of trade because all members were required to license works at pooled rates and could not therefore compete against one another in marketing their performance rights. The District Court issued an injunction against the practice, and disallowed ASCAP from licensing unbundled performance rights to cinemas
84. US Copyright Office, *Report on Copyright in Digital Distance Education*, xvi–xvii, 146–7 (1999): 'Because the exemption in its current form permits only acts of performance and display, digital transmission over computer networks would not be excused. We therefore recommend expanding the scope of the rights covered, in order to add those needed to accomplish this type of transmission. The rights of reproduction and/or distribution should [be added] only to the extent technologically requires in order to transmit the performance or display authorized by the exemption.'

6. Publicity rights and consumer rights

6.1 INTRODUCTION

The right of publicity is the right of every human being to control the unauthorized use of her name, likeness or other index of personal identity for purposes of trade.[1] Distinguishable from privacy rights that implicate the unauthorized disclosure of information on personal matters, publicity rights commonly appear in law when celebrities bring action for liability or damage against producers or advertisers for distributing commercial products or advertising messages that bear some representation of their public image. Publicity rights then implicate two deeply held but countervailing beliefs in American society. First, people must be able to use cultural images to communicate thoughts and concepts freely to one another. Second, individuals must be protected from actions that diminish their ability to invest money and effort in advancing in their chosen professions.

Regarding the first point, both adaptive culture and efficient economy demand clear communications, which explains why dictionaries grow and why trademarks are necessary. The truth is that images in audio, video or text are compact and nuanced symbols that can be used to represent combinations of complex qualities. For example, particular buyers are grateful for the trademark Volvo instead of having to explain to spouses that they must search 'customized auto lots for a seller of dependable Swedish cars for $40000 that are not ostentatious but are status symbols nonetheless'. Moreover, by having the ability to identify itself as the manufacturer of such cars, Volvo has greater incentive to invest and improve all of its automotive products.[2]

Celebrity images bear many of the same communications efficiencies as trademarks. Such images accommodate complex representations of attributes made possible by people who form an important part of our cultural landscape. Jimmy Stewart, Gregory Peck and John Wayne convey similar images of good citizenry, personal honesty and healthy masculinity that differ nonetheless. A movie set designer for a suburban bedroom may immediately conjure audience mindfulness about the inner life of a teenage boy by locating a wall poster of Lou Gehrig, Elvis Presley, James Dean, Allan Ginsburg or Judy Garland. The interaction of nuanced characters in cinema and theater enables the presentation of complex themes, as in the Academy Award-winning movie *Chariots of Fire*, where cultural alienation and integration are conveyed by a presentation of two Olympic runners who commanded national attention in the UK. Michael Frayn's *Copenhagen* used the personae of Niels Bohr and Werner Heisenberg to represent moral and scientific ambiguity, while Steve Martin achieved comedic synergy by introducing Pablo Picasso to Albert Einstein at the Lapin Agile.

As a second dimension, artists and athletes are economic agents who invest money and effort to acquire and hone skills to succeed in crowded professions where stardom is rare. While some commentators have suggested that all fame is a social construction related more to luck than ability, this postmodern narrative has little nuance and is intellectually indefensible.[3] For all the Vanna Whites and Ed McMahons who are long on luck, the skills of accomplished actors, musicians and athletes implicate considerable technical abilities, and often deep understandings of human psychology and wider culture. Principals in art and entertainment must make initiating and ongoing investments in skill and image, and rational players may consider financial rewards and job security in launching and steering professional careers.

However, there is a distinction between a primary investment that responds to incentives and a subsequent spinoff activity designed simply to garner rents with no increase anywhere in production; it is indeed arguable whether all publicity rights escape the second. For example, it is difficult to believe that the financial incentives to train for and play major league baseball could be improved by assuring to baseball players exclusive licensing rights for a line of sports merchandise.[4] Rather, publicity enforcements may be *ex post* undertakings that can extract consideration for uses of bottleneck positions that have some value to the user, but impose zero actual cost upon anyone.

Moving beyond incentives to invest, R.H. Coase made the point that publicity rights to any figure would ideally be acquired through a private market that necessarily compensates each 'victim' for psychic and economic harms of unauthorized taking.[5] Related to this is Landes and Posner's contention that a market in copyrighted works may be necessary to eliminate congestion resulting from overuse.[6] Mark Grady more directly extends the concept to publicity rights and therefore compares the problem to fishing, where excessive harvesting exploits the commons and diminishes the value of the fishery in the long run.[7] Grady contends that publicity rights prevent the premature exhaustion of the celebrity's name or likeness.[8]

Overuse of celebrity personae certainly is a viable economic concern if celebrities are displaced from performing their primary professions through digital clones or impersonators, or assigned to roles that would damage their image or create confusion. Grady himself provides a particularly good example regarding the unauthorized impersonation of singer Tom Waits in a television advertisement.[9] However, it is by no means clear that a more general 'overuse' of a public persona (e.g,. Dustin Hoffman's 'Tootsie') presents comparable congestion, as in the physical world of fisheries, highways, and cow pastures to which celebrity status is imperfectly analogized. Public images are not immediately destroyed or diminished, but are extended to yet a greater degree. Moreover, existing images are continually replaced by new ones with fresher meanings.

Accordingly, Posner's concept of congestion related to the use of cultural icons in signs and speech seems speculative. Particularly in view of the Supreme Court's landmark ruling in *Moseley* v. *Victoria's Secret Catalogue*,[10] supporters of the congestion theory are called upon more carefully to demonstrate its practical occurrence, perhaps using observations from states or countries (e.g., Canada) where publicity rights are not protected. Indeed, while endorsing the idea, the only evidence that Landes and Posner can cite of purported overuse is the *Mona Lisa*, the opening of Beethoven's *Fifth Symphony* and some of van Gogh's paintings.[11] These writers apparently feel we have saturated ourselves with too much of each and compare social use of these immortal images unfavorably with the mercenary use of Disney characters.[12] Moreover, they seem to suggest that we would be better off if rights to these masterpieces were controlled by private rights owners, as they advocate indefinitely renewable copyright that would permit just that.[13]

Rejecting extreme arguments, I am more inclined to think that courts may assign some exchanges to the market by enforcing strong property rights, while elsewhere granting to users rights to approximate the outcome of hypothetical negotiations aimed at maximizing social surplus. As a motivating procedure, I would establish categories of uses.[14] Related to protected uses are responsibilities for self-help and bilateral cooperation, which aim to protect against social harm in the most effective manner.[15]

6.2 THE NATURE OF THE RIGHT

The publicity right was created in common law in 1953, when the Second Circuit adjudicated a dispute between two baseball card manufacturers that contested whether one had legally signed a player to an exclusive contract.[16] In upholding the contract, the Court ruled that 'a man has a right in the publicity value of his photograph; i.e., the right to grant the exclusive privilege of publishing his picture'.[17] Following the decision, Melville Nimmer defined the publicity right as the right to reap the commercial value of one's identity for advertising and other commercial purposes, and the related right to stop others from exploiting the same.[18] William Prosser subsequently suggested a four part distinction for privacy and publicity rights that was eventually incorporated into the Restatement (Second) on Torts in 1977 (652A–652I).[19] In contrast to privacy, publicity takings implicate acts unrelated to name or public image that may be both psychically and financially harmful.[20]

By contrast, a publicity rights claim generally subsumes the unauthorized use of the plaintiff's name or public image. With no federal statute, about 36 states recognize some statutory or common law variant of the publicity right, which 19 now apply posthumously.[21] In the statutes of California, any person who knowingly uses another's 'name, voice, signature, photograph, or likeness, in any manner, on or in products, merchandise or goods, or for purposes of [advertising, selling, or soliciting purchases]' is liable for damages to the injured party.[22] A similar use of the persona of a deceased personality is similarly handled, but such protection is explicitly denied to artistic, historic, political or newsworthy works (such as books, play, programs).

6.3   THE PERFORMANCE RIGHT

The only Supreme Court decision in publicity rights implicates takings that may displace demand for the original celebrity act.[23] A local television station broadcast an entire 15-second human cannonball act that was performed at the Ohio state fair. The performer, Hugo Zacchini, contended that the station unlawfully broadcast the film without his consent. The court agreed and found that much of the economic value of Zacchini's performance lay in the right of exclusive control over its publicity; if it were available over broadcast television, fewer people would be willing to attend the fair to see Zacchini perform.[24] The Court here explicitly considered precedents in patent and copyright law which invested intellectual property with Constitutional and economic imperatives to promote the arts and sciences.[25]

The *Zacchini* case implicates a performance right, which concerns not the appropriation of a reputation or image, but rather the displacement of the very activity by which an entertainer acquired the reputation in the first place.[26] However, publicity rights for performances were enforced long before *Zacchini*. The California Court of Appeals enjoined in 1928 the imitative performances of actor Charles Amador, who appeared in movies as 'Charlie Aplin' and imitated Chaplin's style and costume.[27] The court reasoned that Amador would deceive the public into believing that he was the real Chaplin. More likely, Chaplin's unique marketability was reduced since he was now implicitly competitive with a theatrical clone who could substitute in many roles.

A well-established performance right is now necessary in the digital era. Evidenced by the appearance of John F. Kennedy in *Forrest Gump*, film producers now may use digital technology to adopt sequences and morph images to accommodate full-movie presentations of any individual.[28] With digital clones, a great actor may act in fewer roles, or suffer in contract negotiations for particular movies, because he can be replaced by a clone that can substitute for his recognizable role.

Clones present a second economic difficulty. In addition to displacing roles that actors might otherwise perform, clones may put actors in spots they would never accept. The same image may appear in one month as a corporal, a drag queen and an ax murderer, and collect nothing for the trifecta. Since public image affects future casting, the artful choices of professional performances is a key consideration in entertainment; bad identifications harm careers. For example, Margaret Hamilton and Bela Lugosi hurt themselves with historical performances as the Wicked Witch and Count Dracula that defined their celluloid images. By contrast, John Wayne and Humphrey Bogart benefited from their typecast roles, while Anthony Hopkins and Dustin Hoffman distinguished themselves by extreme diversification.

Also displacing a primary profession would be doctored photographs that borrow the likeness of fashion models, or human or computer impersonations of professional singing voices.[29] A New York State Court recognized that a suit involving a photograph likeness of model Christie Brinkley was cognizable under New York law regarding publicity.[30] Both Bette Midler[31] and Tom Waits[32] won damages against impersonating advertisements that they had first refused. Each of these performances would implicate primary abilities of the celebrities and may conceivably 'down market' their recognized professional talent.

The performance right would then extend to protect all living people, particularly celebrities, from unauthorized representations or impersonations that perform a significant number of their personal behaviors of their primary profession. The performance right would include, *inter alia*, live, broadcast and wired performances, as well as sound or video reproductions. Exempt from the performance right would be professional impersonators, who conjure a remembrance of the celebrity without really displacing their professional performance!

Posthumous Rights

Courts have often extended performance rights past death to posthumous cases. A District Court in New York ruled that the estates of Laurel and Hardy could stop two movie actors from using their mannerisms.[33] Rights owners to the Marx Brothers similarly prevailed in New York against an unauthorized production where actors simulated the appearance and style of the original quartet.[34] Apple Corp. ('The Beatles') collected damages in California against *Beatlemania*, which featured imitators who interwove Beatles music with video fare from the 1960s.[35]

However, a District Court in Washington permitted a posthumous Janis Joplin impersonation to continue since it was part of a larger play about the deceased, and therefore coverable by the First Amendment.[36] A District Court in New Jersey allowed an unauthorized Presley impersonator to continue so long as the producers did not sell commercial material and advertised the production as an imitation of the deceased (so to eliminate consumer confusion regarding sponsorship).[37] A Tennessee District Court held that a band of Beatles impersonators could not be restricted from performing but could be restricted from advertising.[38]

Each of the above acts implicates new entertainment product that illustrates the comedic and acting abilities of impersonators and permits comment on historic individuals and culture. It is difficult to know where one ends and the other begins. For example, the Marx Brothers play implicated a hypothetical rewrite of Anton Chekhov's *The Bear*, as acted by the comedy quartet, and *Beatlemania* was apparently a top-flight multimedia show that astounded its audiences.[39] The cultural loss may be great if estates can close down unpopular acts that have offending material that is not consistent with a public image, as almost happened when Elizabeth Taylor tried to stop an unauthorized biographical movie.[40] If performance rights are to be extended at all after death, some considerable exemption must be allowed immediately for artistic, political and historical works, as California explicitly recognized.[41]

6.4   PRODUCT NAMES

A deeply personal taking is the name of a celebrity for a product or cause that she may detest. In this context, Birmingham protestor Rosa Parks brought a suit against a record label for manufacturing and distributing a CD with a popular track entitled 'Rosa Parks'.[42] The track celebrated the countercultural joys (re profanity, racial slurs and sexist language) of urban teens 'hanging out' in the back of a bus. The District Court recognized that the use of Mrs Parks's name was metaphoric and symbolic: 'any purported vulgarity or profanity was irrelevant to a form of expression deserving of substantial freedom as entertainment and social and literary criticism'.[43] The outcome here is similar to *Rogers* v. *Grimaldi*,[44] where the Second Circuit ruled that Ginger Rogers's right of publicity in a movie entitled *Ginger and Fred* must 'bow to the superior interest in allowing her name to be used as a symbol to communicate ideas',[45] as it was entirely suitable for the application.[46] Both decisions seem wise, the borrowing is related to public image, and there is no implied endorsement of content that may confuse buyers.

Distinct from the above artistic product, certain merchandise may have market appeal if it bears a celebrity's name in its title, e.g., individuals may consider trying, at least once, Paul Newman's Own Salad Dressing or George Foreman's Lean Mean Grilling Machine, even if the namesake does not himself appear at the dinner table. Not an easy phenomenon to understand, more rational fans might regard Newman and Foreman as likely arbiters of good culinary taste and personal health, while the simpler folks may just feel an emotional need to behave like their hero.

However, unauthorized takings may be harmful in two key respects. First, they may associate popular games with low-quality product and therefore harm public goodwill. Second, they may create buyer confusion that is often rectifiable with a forthright disclaimer on the container,[47] i.e., many products (e.g., foods and clothes) are often referred to by name when the disclaimer label is not immediate. To avoid both dangers, celebrity names must be protected from unauthorized attachment to the title of any product. Furthermore, celebrities cannot be depicted using any product without permission.

To avoid consumer confusion, protection should be extended to public nicknames; otherwise, 'Mark Twain', 'Ike' and 'Buzz' (Aldrin) would have been fair game for new products. Indeed, football great Elroy 'Crazy Legs' Hirsch prevailed against a producer of women's leg cream that used his nickname to label its product. The court held that the jury needed to decide whether 'Crazy Legs' was indicative of the plaintiff's occupation and whether there was a likelihood of confusion.[48]

However, a wider level of protection beyond an occupational connection may be appropriate. Without a copyright license, a restaurant owner chose to name his business 'Spanky McFarland' after the Little Rascal character of the same name.[49] The establishment attracted suit by surviving actor George McFarland, who never owned any restaurant but did have something of an ongoing celebrity reputation. Holding for the plaintiff, the Third Circuit held that an actor may legally claim a publicity right in the character he played if the character and actor are, in effect, equivalent.[50]

As an economic matter, the *McFarland* decision seems appropriate. Despite the fact that McFarland himself was no professional restaurant owner, a prospective patron could reasonably assume that was connected in some fashion with the establishment. Moreover, the owner of the restaurant could have maintained his 'Little Rascals' theme in the interior with a different recognizable name, such as 'Our Gang'. As it were, the defendant claimed to have gotten the name from his son's nickname 'Spanky', and the need to choose something that sounded Irish.[51] If this blarney is more than baloney, he could rename the restaurant Spanky Maloney.[52]

Regarding phrases, the Sixth Circuit ruled that Johnny Carson stated a proper cause of action against a manufacturer of portable toilets for its advertising use of *The Tonight Show*'s famous introductory phrase, 'Here's Johnny'.[53] Carson apparently had been able to license the phrase beforehand.

Regardless of whether Carson's name was used, 'a celebrity's legal right of publicity is invaded *whenever* [emphasis mine] his identity is intentionally appropriated for commercial purposes'.[54] The Carson decision drew a dissent from Justice Kennedy: 'I do not believe that the common law right of publicity may be extended ... to include phrases or other things which are merely associated with the individual [e.g.], "Here's Johnny". To do otherwise would remove common phrases from the public domain.'[55]

As an economic matter, Carson's licensing operations of 'Here's Johnny' admittedly appear to be spinoffs that impose transaction costs on speech; evidently, his license provided no additional incentive for his production of the television show. However, the key economic issue here is the implied endorsement, and resulting buyer confusion under the Lanham Act. The issue would seem resolvable by factual evidence, e.g, a survey that could show what fraction of the population actually believed that Carson actually endorsed the product. The court could have also considered whether self-help protection would have been appropriate, i.e., could Carson have trademarked the phrase?

Domain names frequently implicate celebrity names and therefore present an area for conflict between publicity rights and the need to establish URLs with good recall names. However, domain names are different than product names, since it is possible to post immediately an electronic disclaimer that disassociates the named person and the content of the site.[56] A number of other specific legal protections now exist: the Anticybersquatting Consumer Protection Act,[57] specific domains (.TLDs) that indicate individual meaning,[58] trademark protection for people with names that have secondary meanings[59] and actions for defamation of character.[60] The further enforcement of publicity rights in domain names may have a chilling effect upon fan club activity, and therefore interfere with personal communications among a particular group of citizens.

Also not reasonably protected would be the use of names used in the operation of the product. For example, a number of retired baseball players and their estates asserted that software manufacturer Accolade violated their publicity right by putting them as characters in the game.[61] The takings of names here are not here related to the actual title, and therefore do not create consumer confusion. Rather, the names here are best viewed as public images that can be modified for enjoyment in a commercial product, in a manner analogous to a fictionalized sports story that included all the players as characters.

6.5   PUBLIC IMAGES IN ADVERTISING

More than a vehicle for crude persuasion and want creation, advertising provides information to a wide base of consumers. As competitive players in the market for attention, advertisers use public images to attract viewers. Though the content often has nothing to do with the advertisement, such tactics nonetheless focus audience attention and therefore economize on time and effort needed for effective communication. By relying upon the recognized symbols and themes of the wider culture, advertisers conjure mindfulness.

However, the unauthorized use of an individual's persona for advertising purposes is prohibited by all state right of publicity laws.[62] Jacqueline Onassis obtained an injunction against Christian Dior for using a look-alike in an advertisement photographed to appear as a real-life New York social gathering.[63] The Ninth Circuit held in 1998 that baseball great Don Newcombe could state a claim against Coors Brewing for using a photograph of his 'high kick' windup to promote its 'high-kick' beer.[64] Legendary car racer Lothart Motschenbacher prevailed against R.J. Reynolds for depicting one of his track cars with a Winston banner,[65] and Vanna White recovered damages against Samsung for using a faceless and mindless robot that accurately depicted her appearance in the 'Wheel of Fortune'.[66]

While none of these takings represents a performance of primary profession by a digital clone or impersonation, each of these uses of celebrity images presents the economic problem of implied endorsement. Per Section 43(a) of the Lanham Act,[67] commercial speech is subject to requirements of accuracy and truthfulness, and deliberate confusion is unlawful. In this connection, a New York District Court held that an advertisement would violate the Lanham Act by using a Woody Allen impersonator unless the advertisement was accompanied by a disclaimer of Allen's endorsement.[68] This would seem the most efficient means to provide acceptable boundaries on commercial takings of image that do not qualify as performances. For commercial misappropriation (including negligent labeling), an enforced publicity right may additionally award punitive damages for the celebrity.

However, the right of publicity now is a broader right that does not require any showing of likelihood of confusion,[69] i.e., advertising presumably represents a 'commercial exploitation' of a celebrity image. Moreover, in contrast to protection against imitations or clones that can displace performances, nowhere is it seriously suggested that wider publicity rights stimulate primary investment. Accordingly, this wider extension seems economically unnecessary.

With the suggested guidelines, appliance-maker Salton would be free to sell 'George Foreman's Grilling Machine' as the Champion Grilling Machine, with a picture on the carton of boxer Foreman in action; they also may not show Foreman using the equipment and must include appropriate disclaimers disavowing any necessary endorsement. Similarly, Hanes and Nike may use athletic pictures of Joe Namath and Michael Jordan in connection with underwear and sports apparel, but must similarly disavow any implied use or endorsement. In each case, it would seem that producers would be better off paying Foreman, Namath, and Jordan for endorsements and 'full use' of their personalities.[70]

More generally, the statutory and judicial bias against commercial use of public images stems from a legal precedent that sees commercial speech as exploitative. The Supreme Court in 1942 ruled that commercial speech aptly receives no First Amendment protection,[71] but reversed itself in 1976.[72] The court modified its position again in 1980, when it established a four-part test for judicial scrutiny.[73] In 1996, four justices openly advocated full First Amendment protection for nonmisleading commercial speech: 'advertising has been a part of our culture throughout our history. Even in colonial days, the public relied on commercial speech for vital information about the market'.[74] Speech is as much an economic matter as a First Amendment concern, and the four judges established an economically efficient position. Moreover, it is sometimes difficult as a practical matter to distinguish commercial and non-commercial speech; a voice or image impersonation on an advertisement that sells cars may be deemed commercial, but the same impression on a television program that sells the advertising might not be.[75]

6.6   IMAGES IN ART AND MERCHANDISE

The most celebrated battles involving publicity rights entail the use of celebrity video image in art and merchandise

Products and Profits

While no celebrity ever attempted to enforce publicity rights against Andy Warhol, other artists were less fortunate. Golfer Tiger Woods sought to enjoin the merchandising of a limited edition of artist prints entitled 'The Masters of Augusta', which depicted as a central element the famous golfer in a swinging pose.[76] Granting summary judgment, the court found defendant Rick Rush ('America's Sporting Artist – Painting America through Sports') to be a serious art professional. His paintings and drawings were protected by the First Amendment, and subsequent activities for sale and financial gain were of no legal bearing.[77] The Circuit Court upheld.

A contrasting balance of market and art occurred in 1982, when the estate of Martin Luther King enforced publicity rights to stop the manufacture and sale of a plastic bust with King's head, as well as a booklet that describes his life.[78] The court was especially concerned that others may profit unfairly from King and held for the estate. The right to publicity for the deceased here was inheritable and devisable, even if King did not exercise such rights during his life.[79]

As evidenced by the contrasts of *Woods* and *King*, the law often begins by considering whether the work is artistic or commercial. Economic analysis, by contrast, begins by ignoring the distinction, as implicated goods are bundles of attributes that may simultaneously be artistic, utilitarian and commercial. This economic insight is exemplified best by Norman Rockwell's artistic illustrations (including those of Bob Hope and Jack Benny), which commanded an all-museum show at New York's Guggenheim Museum but were created originally for mass distribution on the covers of the *Saturday Evening Post*. Well argued in a dissent in *King*, biases against profit may chill production and new expression.[80]

However, it is not just profits and remuneration that must be vindicated. What the *haute culture* analysis fails to appreciate is that the most important forms of expression often do not inhere in fine art, but rather the everyday goods that people buy and display: 'the utilitarian function of such objects does not change the nature or expressiveness of the images or text printed on them'.[81] As clearly evidenced in *King*, mass-produced items have great communicative value between common citizens who might not hang limited editions in their sports den, or visit an art gallery, or even tour the Georgia State Capital where King's portrait is hung.[82] The capacity to enforce publicity rights in commercial articles amounts in the end to restrictions on expression and speech.

Transformation and Speech

An important legal distinction in California now features the concept of transformativeness. In *Comedy III* v. *Saderup*,[83] right holders in the Three Stooges estate attempted to enjoin the production of T-shirts that bore a sketch of the comedy trio, with the caption 'I'm No Stooge'. The California Supreme Court reached outside the state's publicity statute to import parts of the fair use doctrine from the federal Copyright Act, which had been written without reference to any publicity right.[84] Per the Court's consideration of the first condition of fair use, the sketch made no significant transformative or creative contribution.[85] By contrast, Andy Warhol 'conveyed a message that went beyond commercial exploitation ... to become] a form of ironic social comment'.[86] The court then held for the Stooges.

Once admitted in common law in California, the transformative use would return in June 2003, when rock musicians Johnny and Edgar Winter brought an action against D.C. Comics for taking their personal features (i.e., clothing

and albinism) to compose fictitious images of Johnny and Edgar Autumn –
'villainous half worm half man characters' who scrounged the earth, to be
killed by comic hero Jonah Hex. Accommodating the Stooges precedent, the
California Supreme Court held that the comic use was transformative; takings
were for purposes of lampoon, parody or caricature.[87] However, the overruled
Court of Appeals had been less accommodative, finding no parody attributes
to appellants or their music.[88] Reminiscent of the Eleventh Circuit in
SunTrust[89] the courts conflicted over the definition of an appropriate parody.
The ambiguity in their definition of 'transformative' is considerable.[90]

Ignoring such ambiguities, the right of free expression is granted to the artist
in *Winters*, but denied to wider members of the general public in *Saderup*.
Wearing a Three Stooges T-shirt obviously is a means of communicating
something about aesthetic tastes and general personality, and invites some
level of social interaction. Moreover, the commercial use of the image is a
spinoff; it does not affect disincentives for career investments that an actor
might make. The *Saderup* decision ignores an aspect of communication as a
public good.

The distinction here between artist rights and public wrongs hearkens back
to *Cardtoons* v. *Major League Baseball Players*, where the court did not
enjoin production of comic-style cards that featured player parodies.[91] This
outcome contrasted with *Haelen*, which ruled that a baseball player had
exclusive publicity rights in his image.[92] The *Cardtoon* court found that
parodies poked fun at baseball players, 'an important form of entertainment
and social commentary' about the American pastime.[93] Apparently less
deserving of exemption would be non-parodying pictures of the same players
in action. Yet such takings would enable considerably more communication
and social interaction among the majority of sports fans who enjoy baseball
'straight up'. Like T-shirts, baseball cards are spinoff products that do not
provide incentives to career development.

By advocating that the publicity right be somewhat limited for mass
merchandise, we do not void the role of market intermediaries, such as Global
Images,[94] from matching commercial uses and celebrity images in a
constructive manner to improve social communication through signs.
However, licensing of publicity rights is not necessary to perform this
service. Rather, the particular matching skills that many licensing agencies
now perform can be practiced by the same people as consultants and hired
staffers at advertising agencies.

6.7   PUBLICITY RIGHTS AND COPYRIGHT

Performers who assert publicity rights in images in film, record, and text may bump against federal law regarding copyright. For example, the Three Stooges estate unsuccessfully brought a publicity rights claim against New Line Cinema,[95] which integrated a Three Stooges film clip now in the public domain into the background of the movie, *The Long Kiss Goodnight*. As a matter of legality, Section 301 of the Copyright Act now stipulates when the work should fall into the public domain; Section 301(a) pre-empts any state law 'legal or equitable rights that are equivalent to any of the exclusive rights within the general scope of copyright'.

Publicity rights seemed to prevail over copyright in *Wendt v. Host International, Inc.*, where the court enjoined the use in a chain of airport restaurants of robotic figures 'Norm' and 'Cliff' that conjured a mental connection to characters in the television series *Cheers*.[96] The dummies bore no physical resemblace to the real celebrities George Wendt and John Ratzenberger,[97] but were identified solely from their clothes and physical location behind the bar. The chain properly licensed the characters from the television series, but the actors did not transfer their rights of publicity in their respective contracts. The court held for the plaintiffs, holding that the actors themselves had contributed to the commercial value of the models and retained the relevant rights.[98] The outcome noticeably differs from *Toney v. L'Oreal*, where the court ruled that a model conveyed her publicity rights to a copyright owner through a valid contract.[99]

The US Supreme Court upheld – without comment – the Circuit's recognition in *Wendt* of publicity rights that went beyond copyright, apparently confirming non-equivalence of publicity rights and copyright under Section 301.[100] The outcome here is troubling from an economic perspective.[101] Split rights are economically inefficient, as they interfere with the right of copyright holders to license the particular material in which they invested; an anti-commons results when too many parties have a potential veto.[102] Some groundrules then are necessary to break possible deadlocks.

Regardless of copyright ownership, publicity uses that violate rights of privacy or consumer confusion should be presumptively under the control of the celebrity. To prevail, a copyright owner must then contract for permission to make such uses.

More intriguing is the issue of capture of a celebrity image, by video or audio means, in a manner that could substitute for a professional performance. Here, a starting approach is to view whether a contract has been, or could have been, negotiated beforehand, or whether the taking in any way involved intrusive or fraudulent activity (as may result from paparazzi). If so, the performance right should presumptively remain with the celebrity.

However, if there is no practical opportunity to negotiate contracts beforehand (e.g., as may result in an impromptu news clip of social interest in which a celebrity appears or performs with other recognizable parties), rights are inherently split. Moreover, split rights will create frequent log jams *ex post* that may chill the abilities of media companies from integrating and distributing their content. As a practical matter, the imposed transactions cost and potential loss to media companies that could result from split rights seems likely to dominate the decreased incentives that may result from displaced performances. Consequently, copyright should prevail over publicity rights in bona fide takings of performing events where no contracting was not practicable.

If these standards were applied in *Cheers*, the Host restaurant chain might have won, as the taking did not displace a professional performance. However, the restaurants might have been required to post notice that the use of any recognizable image does not necessarily imply an endorsement by the implicated actor. By contrast, the Supreme Court's decision in *Zacchini* seems appropriate.[103] Despite the fact that the television reporter had been explicitly asked not to film the event; he returned the next day and videotaped the entire act. A contract with Zacchini could have been established beforehand, and the photographer's copyright must fall.

Finally, we consider *Baltimore Orioles, Inc. v. Major League Baseball Players Association*,[104] in which baseball players sought rights to control their electronic performances on television broadcasts in which their publicity rights were not transferred beforehand. The Circuit Court held for the Orioles, contending that the publicity right was a state doctrine equivalent to federal copyright, and thereby subsumed under Section 301.[105] This now seems incorrect in view of *Wendt v. Host*,[106] in which the Supreme Court seemed to uphold non-equivalence. Accordingly, publicity rights here seem enforceable for the players, as the Association and the team could have bargained for rights in the off-season.

6.8   CONCLUSION

A number of organizations, including the American Bar Association, have called for federal legislation to establish a uniform right of publicity.[107] Given the patchwork of state doctrine and the presence of nationally and electronically distributed products and advertisements, federal coordination would seem to be an economically efficient proposition. Based on our analysis, some reasonable considerations for a federal statute might be as follows:

1. In violations of personal privacy, publicity rights can be extended during lifetimes to protect against economic damages that the victim has suffered above and beyond mental suffering.

2. No live celebrity may be portrayed without consent in any representation or impersonation that performs a significant number of the behaviors in their primary occupation. This would include live, broadcast and wired performances, as well as sound or video reproductions on any media.

3. No product or service may be titled with the recognized name or nickname of a celebrity without their explicit endorsement.

4. Advertisements may use celebrity public images that do not displace primary performances. The advertisement must carry an immediately discernible notice of non-attribution that disclaims implied endorsement.

5. Web domains may use the celebrity names. However, the web site must post an immediately discernible notice of non-attribution that disclaims any professional or personal connection.

6. Commercial merchandise may use the public images of a celebrity, so long as it does not displace a primary performance.

7. Celebrities may recover punitive and monetary damages under publicity rights for failure to disclose, or improper disclosure, of a non-attribution notice.

8. Celebrities retain relevant publicity rights in copyrighted works whenever the use violates privacy or creates consumer confusion.

9. Celebrities retain performance rights in copyrighted material unless the taking was an impromptu use in which rights could not have practically been negotiated beforehand.

NOTES

1. Restatement (Third) on Unfair Competition, § 46.
2. See also W.M. Landes and R.A. Posner, 'Trademark Law: An Economic Perspective', 30 *Journal of Law and Economics* 265, 269–70 (1987).
3. M. Madow, 'Private Ownership of the Public Image: Popular Culture and Publicity Rights', 81 *California Law Review* 125, 139 (1993); R.J. Coombe, 'Authorizing the Celebrity: Publicity Rights, Postmodern Politics, and Unauthorized Genders', 10 *Cardozo Arts and Entertainment Law Journal* 365, 370–73 (1992).
4. Infra notes 65–7 and surrounding text.
5. R.H. Coase, 'The Problem of Social Costs', 3 *Journal of Law and Economics* 1, 12–13 (1960).
6. W.M. Landes and R.A. Posner, 'Indefinitely Renewable Copyright', at http://www.ssrn.com (retrieved June 23, 2003).
7. M.F. Grady, 'A Positive Economic Theory of the Right of Publicity', 1 *UCLA Entertainment Law Review* 97 (1994).
8. Ibid., 103, 126.
9. Ibid., 104–5.
10. Docket No. 01-1015 (U.S. Mar. 4, 2003). The Court held that a Kentucky sex shop named Victor's Little Secret did not infringe upon the Victoria's Secret trademark as VS could not demonstrate that the use actually lessened the capacity of their mark to identify and distinguish goods and services. See also *Ringling Bros.-Barnum & Bailey Combined Shows, Inc.* v. *Utah Division of Travel Development*, 170 F. 3d 449, 453 (4th Cir. 1999)

(requiring famous trademark owners to show actual economic harm resulting from use).

11. Supra note 6, 15.
12. Ibid., 13.
13. Ibid., 41.
14. See Chapter 2.
15. V.M. de Grandpre, 'Understanding the Market for Celebrity: An Economic Analysis of the Right of Publicity', 12 *Fordham Intellectual Property, Media and Entertainment Law Journal* 73, 114 (2001). *See also* R. Cooter, 'Unity in Tort, Contract, and Property: The Model of Precaution', 73 *California Law Review* 1 (1985).
16. *Haelan Labs, Inc.* v. *Topps Chewing Gum, Inc.* 202 F. 2d 866, 867 (2d Cir. 1953)
17. Ibid., 868.
18. M.B. Nimmer, 'The Right of Publicity', 19 *Law and Contemporary Problems* 203, 215–18 (1954).
19. W.L. Prosser, 'Privacy, 48 *California Law Review* 383, 389 (1954). In addition to the publicity right, three privacy rights are intrusion into physical solitude or seclusion, public disclosure of private facts, and publicity which places a person in a false light in the public eye.
20. In a recent matter involving publicity and personal privacy, the court found credible plaintiff claims of irreparable injury that would have resulted to years of investment in career development (*Bret Michaels* v. *Internet Entertainment Group, Inc.*, 5 F. Supp. 2d 823 (C.D. Ca. 1998)).
21. M.S. Lee, 'Agents of Chaos: Judicial Confusion in Defining the Right of Publicity-Free Speech Interface', 23 *Loyola of Los Angeles Entertainment Law Journal* 471, 478 (2003).
22. California Code, Civil Code, Section 3344 (2003).
23. *Zacchini* v. *Scripps-Howard Broadcasting, Co.*, 433 US 564 (1977).
24. Ibid., 575–6. This point seems very arguable in the particular instance at hand.
25. Ibid., 576–7.
26. Beard, infra note 28, 1201–2.
27. *Chaplin* v. *Amador*, 93 Cal. App. 358 (1928).
28. For a description of technology for making video clones, see E. Giacoppo, 'Avoiding the Tragedy of Frankenstein: The Application of the Right of Publicity to the Use of Digitally Reproduced Actors in Film', 48 *Hastings Law Journal* 601, 604–8 (1997); J.J. Beard, 'Clones, Bones, and Twilight Zones: Protecting the Digital Persona of the Quick, the Dead, and the Imaginary', 16 *Berkeley Technology Law Journal* 1165, 1171–6, 1186–90 (2001). For matters regarding to facial animation, see Beard, 1193–7.
29. For a description of technology, see Beard, ibid., 1190–92.
30. *Brinkley* v. *Casablancas*, 438 N.Y.S. 2d 1004, 1012 (App. Div. 1981).
31. *Midler* v. *Ford Motor Co.*, 849 F. 2d 460, 7 U.S.P.Q. 2d 1398 (9th Cir. 1988).
32. *Waits* v. *Frito Lay*, 978 F. 2d 1093 (9th Cir. 1992).
33. *Price* v. *Hal Roach Studios, Inc.*, 400 F. Supp. 836 (S.D.N.Y. 1975).
34. *Groucho Marx Productions, Inc.* v. *Day & Night Co.*, 523 F. Supp. 485 (S.D.N.Y. 1981).
35. *Apple Corps. Limited* v. *Leber, et al.*, 229 U.S.P.Q. 1015 (1986).
36. *Joplin Enterprises* v. *Anderson*, 795 F. Supp. 349 (W.D. Wash. 1992).
37. *Estate of Elvis Presley* v. *Russen*, 513 F. Supp. 1339 (D.N.J. 1981).
38. *Apple Corps. Ltd.* v. *A.D.P.R., Inc.*, 843 F. Supp. 342 (M.D. Tenn. 1993).
39. Supra note 34, at 1018.
40. *Taylor* v. *NBC*, 1994 WL 762226, at 6 (Cal. Supp. 1994).
41. California Code, Civil Code, Section 3344.1 (2003).
42. *Parks* v. *LaFace Records*, 76 F. Supp. 2d 775 (1999).
43. Ibid., 780–81.
44. 875 F. 2d 994, 999 (2nd Cir. 1989)).
45. Ibid., 1004–5.
46. Ibid.
47. Infra note 67 and surrounding text.
48. *Hirsch* v. *S.C. Johnson & Son, Inc.*, 205 U.S.P.Q 920 (Wis. Sup. Ct. 1979).
49. *McFarland* v. *Miller*, 14 F. 3d 912 (3d Cir. 1994).

50. Ibid., 916.
51. Ibid.
52. But not Spanky Mahoney, which borrows from puppet Jerry Mahoney, implicating publicity rights for his ventriloquist Paul Winchell.
53. *John W. Carson* v. *Here's Johnny Portable Toilets*, 698 F. 2d 831 (1983).
54. Ibid., 837.
55. Ibid., J. Kennedy dissent, at 842.
56. Supra note 67 and surrounding text.
57. 15 U.S.C. 1125(d) (2000): 'Any person who registers a domain name that consists of the name of another living person, or a name substantively and confusingly similar thereto, without that person's consent, with the specific intent to profit from such name by selling the domain name for financial gain to that person or third party, shall be liable in a civil action by such person.'
58. ICANN, New TLD Program, at http://www.ican.org.tlds (retrieved June 16, 2003).
59. *Bihari* v. *Gross*, 119 F. Supp. 2d 309, 317 (S.D.N.Y. 2000).
60. See generally T. Belczyk, 'Domain Names: The Special Case of Personal Names', 82 *Boston University Law Review* 485 (2002).
61. *Newcombe et al.* v. *Accolade, Inc.*, B.C. 164847 (1998).
62. Beard, supra note 28, at 1198.
63. The court held that while imitators can take from a celebrity image in non-commercial settings, 'no one is free to trade on another's name or appearance, and claim immunity because what he is using is similar to but not identical with the original' (*Jacqueline Onassis* v. *Christian Dior*, 472 N.Y.S. 2d 254 (Sup. Ct. Spec. Term 1984)).
64. *Donald Newcombe* v. *Adolf Coors Company*, 157 F. 3d 686 (9th Cir. 1998).
65. *Lothar Motschenbacher* v. *R.J. Reynolds, Inc.*, 498 F. 2d 821 (9th Cir. 1974).
66. *White* v. *Samsung*, 971 F. 2d 1395 (9th Cir. 1992).
67. 15 U.S.C. 22.
68. In *Allen* v. *Men's World Outlet, Inc.*, 679 F. Supp. 360 (S.D.N.Y. 1988); *see also Allen* v. *National Video, Inc.*, 610 F. Supp. 612 (S.D.N.Y. 1985) (holding that a look-alike created a likelihood of confusion regarding endorsement).
69. Beard, supra note 27, at n. 213 and surrounding text.
70. Supra notes 63–7 and surrounding text.
71. *Valentine* v. *Christensen* 316 U.S. 42, 47 (1942).
72. *Virginia State Board of Pharmacy* v. *Virginia Citizens Consumer Council, Inc.* 425 U.S. 748, 772 (1976).
73. *Central Hudson Gas & Electric Corp.* v. *Public Service Commission*, 447 U.S. 557, 564 (1980).
74. *44 Liquormart, Inc.* v. *Rhode Island*, 517 U.S. 484, 116 S. Ct. 1495, 1515–20 (1996).
75. Supra note 66, at 1399 (Kozinski, J., dissenting). Clearly, the dealer ad may contain important information for car buyers regarding locations and lot prices that exploits no one.
76. *ETW Corp.* v. *Jireh Publ'g, Inc.* 99 F. Supp. 2d 829 (N.D. Ohio 2000).
77. Ibid., 835.
78. *Martin Luther King Center* v. *American Heritage Prods.* 296 S.E. 2d 697 (Ga. 1982).
79. King was a public figure who 'could have exploited his name and likeness during his lifetime. That this opportunity was not appealing to him does not mean that others have the right to use his name and likeness in ways he himself chose not to do' nor that his family should be denied posthumous control of the same (ibid., 147).
80. Ibid. 150–51 (J. Weltner dissenting) 'When our Constitution declares that anyone "may speak, write and publish his sentiments on all subjects", it does not confine that freedom exclusively to verbal expression ... Are not [Confederate statues, busts of Chief Justices, or portraits of Dr. King in the Georgia Capitol] expressions of sentiment.' The dissent also understands the importance of money; the majority says that 'our right of new publicity is violated in cases involving financial gain. Did the sculptors of our Confederate soldiers, and of our Chief Justices, labor without gain? Was Dr. King's portraitist unpaid for his work?'
81. Infra note 82, at 300.

82. D.L. Zimmerman, 'Competing Perspectives and Divergent Analyses: Fitting Publicity Rights into Intellectual Property and Free Speech Theory', 10 *Journal of Art and Entertainment Law* 283, 301–2 (2000).
83. 21 P. 3d 797 (Cal. 2001).
84. Ibid., 801–2.
85. Ibid.
86. Ibid.
87. *Edgar Winter et al.* v. *DC Comics et al.*, Case No. S108751 (2003).
88. Ct. App. Case No. B121021 (2002).
89. *See* Chapter 2, notes 1–6 and surrounding text.
90. E. Volokh, 'Freedom of Speech and Intellectual Property after Eldred: 44 Liquormart, Saderup, and Bartnicki', forthcoming, *Houston Law Review* at IV.C.2 (2003).
91. *Cardtoons* v. *Major League Baseball Players* 95 F. 3d 959 (10th Cir. 1996).
92. Supra note 15.
93. Supra note 91, at 965.
94. At http://www.globalicons.com/aboutus/main-overview.html (retrieved June 16, 2003). Global Icons now licenses publicity rights for 'Buzz' Aldrin, the Three Stooges, Marlene Dietrich, Greta Garbo, Charlie Chaplin and Bing Crosby.
95. *Comedy III Productions, Inc.* v. *New Line Cinema*, 200 F.3d 593 (9th Cir. 2000).
96. *Wendt* v. *Host International*, 125 F.3d 806 (1997).
97. Ibid., 809.
98. Ibid., 810.
99. *Toney* v. *L'Oreal USA, Inc.*, 64 U.S.P.Q. 2d 1857 (N.D. ILL. 2002).
100. 'Supreme Court says Norm and Cliff can sue over robots', at http://www.cnn.com/2000/LAW/scotus/10/02/scotus.cheers.ap/ (retrieved June 16, 2003).
101. Supra note 65, at 1399 (J. Kozinski, dissenting).
102. J.M. Buchanan and Y.J. Yoon, 'Symmetric Tragedies: Commons and Anti-Commons', 43 *Journal of Law and Economics* 1 (2000).
103. Supra note 22.
104. *Baltimore Orioles, Inc.* v. *Major League Baseball Players Association*, 805 F. 2d 663, 667 (7th Cir. 1986).
105. 17 U.S.C. 301 (2000).
106. Supra note 96 and surrounding text.
107. O.Y. Lewis, Jr., 'Personality, Persona, and Publicity Rights', at http://www.hllaw.com/a_personality.html (retrieved June 16, 2003).

7. Software, search and data

7.1 INTRODUCTION

The domain of intellectual property (IP) is of primary importance in the areas
of information and software, where consumers can easily access great amounts
of data, crawl the web and deploy sophisticated programs to create, calculate
and organize new information. Any of these undertakings implicates a wide
range of human efforts related to great intellectual creativity and 'sweat of the
brow', and everything between. Moreover, creative efforts face the
considerable problem that the risk of unauthorized taking increases
substantially with digital technology, and producer incentives can be gravely
harmed if law is not duly protective. However, an overly restrictive regime for
intellectual property may overly discourage secondary uses, promulgating a
long-run loss in social wealth and intelligence that can be both considerable
and nonquantifiable.

This chapter will gauge the economic rationality of a number of recent IP
cases that involve topics in software interoperability, copyright misuse,
antitrust, data protection and search. We judge outcomes by four economic
criteria:

1. The market may have the capacity to accommodate the use through
    licensing or market exchange, reducing the need for courts to take a hand.
    However, when licensing difficulties are expected, court interference may
    be necessary to secure rights and enable exchange.
2. The market may have reduced ability to provide for licensing, but may
    nonetheless compel actors to behave innovatively to 'win the field' from
    competing rivals. Forced exchange or cooperation may appropriate just
    rewards, and actually dampen the incentive to innovate and improve
    products.
3. Particularly with regard to tying and refusal to deal, antitrust or misuse
    claims can harm reasonable business models for intellectual property that
    may actually lower prices, benefit consumers, hasten penetration of new
    products and increase producer incentives.
4. Courts may sometimes expedite transfer in frail markets by establishing a
    fair price at which exchange may take place, and relying upon parties to
    reach a mutually accommodative offer. At other times, courts may

reasonably suggest that the plaintiff rely upon self-help.

7.2   SOFTWARE AND INTEROPERABILITY

Software has two key attributes that complicate a textbook model of market competition. First, as intellectual property, software is costly to develop but inexpensive to copy. As such, early efforts in research and development can be appropriated by later copyists who can take the exact code or clone the technical know-how directly from viewing a facial interface. Without protection, copying and cloning reduce incentives for small but highly competitive providers of new works.[1] Second, all embedded program code to some degree builds on previous program efforts; little really is invented from scratch.[2] Overly restrictive IP law then can actually retard further interoperability among programs and devices,[3] and the development of products that do not yet exist.[4]

Reverse Engineering

Related to both cloning and interoperability in software programs is reverse engineering, which is the process of extracting applied know-how from a human-made artifact that embodies technical knowledge contributed by others.[5] Among other applications, reverse engineers can use gained knowledge to make simple clones or imperfect versions of the original, and to learn the structure of the applications interface in order to design compatible products. They do this without paying a license fee for access to the original information, thereby 'free riding'[6] on previous investments. Reverse engineering is sometimes practiced in order to produce a product that directly competes with those of the original IP owner.

At present, reverse engineering can be treated under widely disparate legal categories. Reverse engineering is permitted in common law in order to take trade secrets,[7] statutorily permitted with restrictions for computer chips,[8] often permitted under copyright law,[9] and illegal under patent protection (where disclosure of know-how is otherwise required).[10] The Federal Circuit ruled in 2002 that a current 'shrinkwrap' license may legitimately enjoin the act of reverse engineering.[11] The legal ability to stop reverse engineering can then be a key consideration for firms that consider whether to initiate contracts or to patent software.[12]

However, negotiation and licensing is often the best means of determining what is efficient, and what property rights should be enforced in a responsive market. From a Coasean perspective, negotiated resolution should be avoided only if some operating or signaling efficiency is missing;[13] i.e., transactions costs are unappreciated, externalities redound to excluded third parties, or one party has market power. It is then unclear why 'free-riding' should be permitted in well functioning markets, regardless of whether original work is copyrighted or patented.

In *Sega Enterprises Ltd.* v. *Accolade, Inc.*,[14] the Ninth Circuit heard a case that implicated reverse engineering pursued for software interoperability. Sega developed and marketed a video console (Genesis III) and compatible games, while Accolade independently manufactured competing game cartridges. While Sega had licensed access to its code to provide interoperability for independent game developers, Accolade ended negotiations because Sega insisted upon being exclusive manufacturer.[15] Rather, Accolade decompiled object code in Sega's console and so reconfigured the games that it had made previously to operate with other consoles.[16] The District Court issued a preliminary injunction for Sega, finding that Accolade's disassembly was for a commercial purpose, Sega lost game sales, and other alternatives to disassembly were available.[17]

On appeal, the Circuit Court found that Accolade's unauthorized infringements[18] were affirmatively defensible by fair use.[19] While Accolade's copying aimed to 'modify existing games and make them usable with the Genesis console',[20] 'the commercial aspect of its use can best be described as of minimal significance'.[21] The court also ruled that Accolade avoided no creative work or customarily paid fee, and that no other method of obtaining information was available.[22] Turning to the fourth factor, the court found that copies that allowed Accolade to enter the market did not usurp previous Sega's demands,[23] Accolade expanded user choice in a nonexclusive manner that did not hurt Sega[24] and Sega apparently attempted to monopolize the market (*sic*) by making it impossible for others to compete.[25]

From an economic perspective, these considerations appear incongruous. Accolade in fact accessed no disembodied fact, expression, or idea, but highly functional intellectual property in which a considerable investment had been made. Thanks to its licensing systems, Sega had partially recouped its development from game sales and licenses that other game producers paid. Even if Accolade were to have stimulated demand for Genesis III, the potential for alternative technologies or products to increase sales does not detract from market harm resulting from lost licensing opportunity.[26] Game manufacturers who got access to Sega's platform 'on the cheap' then were free-riding[27] on primary development costs and undercutting Sega's game prices, reducing in the process Sega's ability to recover the initial costs of research and development (R&D).

The court acknowledged that Sega had reached licensing arrangements with some game producers, but Accolade had insisted upon manufacturing the games itself.[28] Sega's business rationale seems compelling; manufacturing exclusivity is related to quality control, where a reputation for bad performance could compromise future sales. While potential buyers of Genesis III might have lost the network benefit of a wider selection of games that already had been made available to competitors, there is no apparent reason why negotiations were inadequate for the purpose of providing a license to enable interoperability.

More generally, the 'no-harm' decision ignores the nature of complex business models often used in high-tech markets. Quite commonly, a platform developer will willingly lower price – possibly below production cost[29] – in order to attract more buyers for subsequent applications.[30] It is then quite conceivable that Sega might have reduced console prices as part of this strategy. Under such circumstances, unit production costs may actually have decreased as more Sega platforms were sold.

In the later but closely related *Sony Computer Entertainment, Inc.* v. *Connectix Corporation*,[31] the Ninth Circuit upheld Connectix's right to copy into memory Sony's copyrighted basic input output system (BIOS) as well as three game cartridges. Although Connectix engineers admitted that other engineering and licensing solutions were possible,[32] the court held that the defendant had adopted a unique method of learning the interface.[33] The economic difficulties here are similar to Sega, upon which the decision was based. In a competitive market, it would have been in Sony's economic interest to license the Connectix emulators. The court identified no potential source of market failure that could have interfered with such a transaction.

In addition to matters of liability, the resulting damages that now may result are from contract obligations[34] or patent protection.[35] Both contracts and patents can be used more directly to protect the underlying functions in a computer program and therefore affect considerations for reverse engineering. In such matters, economic experts in any software litigation where liability is established should then consider the entire market value of the infringement, including both competitive substitution of the original program and the harm resulting from commercial displacement of collateral programs and services.[36] This would reasonably require experts to establish the prices in each related market that would prevail 'but for' the infringement.[37] Analysis of the 'but for' world requires an understanding of producer capacity, ease of entry, demand substitutability, price elasticity and the likelihood of licensing.[38]

Quite a different matter of interoperability appeared in *Lewis Galoob Toys* v. *Nintendo of America*.[39] Nintendo manufactured a home video game system that include both cartridges and consoles. Lewis Galoob manufactured a device, the Game Genie, that a user could insert between the cartridge and the console that allowed players to alter up to three features of the Nintendo game.[40] The device operated mechanically by replacing the value of a single data byte sent from the game cartridge to the central processing unit (CPU),[41] and therefore enhanced the audiovisual displays that originated in Nintendo's cartridges.[42] Nintendo contended that the resulting work was a derivative work and sued for copyright infringement. Both the District Court and Circuit Court held for Galoob.

While Nintendo argued that Game Genie users were supplanting its own right to make and sell derivative works, the court held that the use was for private home enjoyment and therefore presumptively fair.[43] After the District Court concluded that Nintendo failed to show any present or foreseeable future harm in game sales,[44] Nintendo contended on appeal that a potential market for future works was usurped. However, the Circuit Court ruled further that Nintendo failed to show the reasonable likelihood of such a market or the likely profitable development of expert or junior versions of the same game.[45]

From an economic perspective, the case differed from Sega in a key respect; there is little reason to believe that a licensing market for game users would have evolved or been transactionally efficient. From an economic perspective, there is a careful distinction to be drawn between software uses that could reasonably have been licensed, and those that might not; fair use is granted efficiently in the latter case.[46]

Program Interfaces

A different matter of compatibility involving the ability to switch platforms emerged in *Lotus Dev. Corp.* v. *Borland Int'l. Inc.*[47] Lotus's market-leading spreadsheet, Lotus 1-2-3, allowed users to perform accounting functions electronically on a computer. Among Lotus's impressive functionalities were the abilities to write 'macros' – a series of command choices in a menu tree that a user could activate with a single keystroke.[48] As part of a new and improved spreadsheet (named Quattro Pro), Borland included the Lotus Emulation Interface, which was a virtually identical copy of the Lotus menu tree,[49] and Key Reader, which was a translation program that executed macros written previously for Lotus 1-2-3. Without copying Lotus code, Borland adopted the appearance of its interface from information published in Lotus operating manuals.

Reflecting its own previous opinion in a related cloning of the Lotus spreadsheet,[50] the District Court held that Borland's Emulation Interface and Key Reader both infringed on Lotus's copyright.[51] The Circuit Court reversed, finding that Lotus's menu tree was a method of operation properly exempted from copyright protection.[52] Moreover, users with a large installed base of macro programs, which were personal works, would face considerable difficulty if they lacked the ability to reuse the Lotus menu list.[53] In a concurring opinion, Judge Boudin stressed the economics more directly: 'it is hard to see why customers who have learned the Lotus menu and devised macros for it should remain captives of Lotus because of an investment in learning made by the users and not by Lotus'.[54] The Supreme Court upheld the opinion in a 4–4 split decision.[55]

The decision is quite problematic as an economic matter,[56] since Borland spreadsheets directly competed with Lotus. The user interface design is a key determinant of program success and very costly to develop; indeed, half of the costs of a program design are optimally devoted to interface development.[57] While no code was literally copied, unrestrained competition in taking key factors from a successful interface may reduce both profits and incentives to the original creator.[58] Moreover, if a free taking of an interface is to be permitted, it would be difficult to distinguish a break point between a clone that replicates all functionality of a copyrighted work, and a partial clone that duplicates a number of valuable elements.[59] Accordingly, 'it becomes apparent that plaintiffs in user interface cases are really trying to stop competitors from selling a functionally indistinguishable product, not just protecting a display of command terms'.[60]

While market leader Lotus may have had lesser incentives to license its interface to Borland, such short-run competitive concerns fail to consider gains made possible when two parties compete to establish or replace a market standard. For if switch costs are high and lock-in is greatly profitable, competitors will 'compete for the field'[61] in early rounds to attract a large base of customers.[62] They will do this by aggressively promoting product, adding features and lowering prices.[63] In the race to be first, competitive producers accordingly may dissipate later profits through early investments designed to capture market share.[64] It is not evident that winners are efficiently expropriated at the end through compatibility requirements that dissipate further profits.

Furthermore, it is also quite possible that one standard can overtake another. That is, competing suppliers who lack access to a popular platform product may actually devise their own platform, improving product quality and variety in the process.[65] Rather than evolving to one final standard, markets may evolve in which 'firms compete through innovation for temporary market dominance, from which they may be displaced by the next wave or product advancements'.[66] Just this creative destruction occurred in the spreadsheet market, where Lotus overcame the market leader Visicalc, and Excel overcame Lotus, without cloning the interfaces of the previous incumbent.[67] This illustrates the importance of design competition and weakens the lock-in hypothesis.

Europe faced a similar case involving interface access in *NDC Health* v. *IMS Health*.[68] IMS Health was an American pharmaceutical company that did business in Germany, where it developed a copyrighted format (termed the

'1860 brick structure') for collecting and distributing data on pharmacy sales. The format became the de facto industry standard and contributed to a market-leading position for its provider. NDC Germany was a rival provider that sold data using a similar format that IMS contended was infringing. After IMS refused a license, NDC filed the complaint before the European Commission. NDC contended that IMS abused a dominant market position[69] and asked the court for a compulsory license.

Concurring with the plaintiff in an interim decision, the Commission concluded that the 1860 structure was indispensable to its existence, and serious and irreparable harm could result if relief were not forthcoming. The Court of First Instance (CFI) suspended the interim decision in 2001, and the European Court of Justice upheld the CFI in April 2002. The ECJ expressed doubts as to the Commission's interpretation of the 'exceptional circumstances' test previously expressed in *Magill*,[70] which had allowed the plaintiff access to copyrighted program listing from two television stations. The matter must now go before a full hearing.[71] In *Getmapping PLC* v. *Ordnance Survey*,[72] a UK court similarly rejected a plea from a plaintiff that Ordnance Survey allow it to access proprietary map interfaces so as to produce an integrated online mapping service; it was not *per se* anticompetitive for a dominant producer in one market to use his financial muscle to enter a new market and enjoy a commercial advantage over others.[73]

7.3   COPYRIGHT MISUSE AND ANTITRUST

A related issue to interoperability and interfaces is copyright misuse, which often includes antitrust concerns.[74] Court scrutiny for misuse began with turn-of-the-century patent litigation that concerned inventions that owners tied to staple inputs beyond the scope of the grant.[75] In three landmark decisions, the Supreme Court reversed its own precedent,[76] found misuse to be distinct from antitrust liability[77] and found the presence of copyright to be a per se indication of market power.[78]

When compared to antitrust, misuse is generally easier to prove and more inclusive.[79] The misuse claim is available as an affirmative defense against infringement,[80] but involves no compensation for court costs[81] or financial damages.[82] However, if misuse can be demonstrated, the courts will withhold infringement remedies, even against those parties not harmed by the abusive practice.[83] Misuse permits wider standing[84] and therefore allows greater judicial scrutiny than antitrust claims, where plaintiffs must demonstrate actual damages.[85]

As a key matter, misuse may implicate a wider domain of policy areas than antitrust. When divorced from economic reasoning, Judge Posner points out that such claims can be quite incorrect.[86] For example, 'misusing' actions that require licensees to make payments beyond expiration,[87] or measure royalties for sales of unpatented end products,[88] would necessarily implicate lower prices upfront.[89] The Congress would follow Posner's judicial lead by modifying Title 35 to make patent misuse with regard to tying of patented goods substantively identical to antitrust behavior.[90]

Though frequently instructive, Posner's analysis may ignore the possibility that patented or copyrighted works sometimes nonetheless implicate blocks of embedded information that can be useful beyond any discernible antitrust market. The societal acquisition of such information is the justification for public revelation in patent law.[91] Accordingly, parties to a license negotiation regarding copyrighted software may fail to appreciate the imposed costs of continued lockup of embdedded information. If cabined by a careful understanding of the underlying economic issues, copyright misuse in some instances can then serve a wider public purpose than antitrust analysis.[92] However, this extension should not be entered into cavalierly, and must full understand the nuances of information exchange, revelation, and 'impactedness'.[93]

Copyright misuse was formally applied in *Lasercomb America* v. *Job Reynolds*,[94] where the plaintiff licensed a competitive software program for die-making. As part of the licensing contract, Reynolds agreed not to manufacture competing die-making software. Apparently dissatisfied with the arrangement, the defendants circumvented the protective shield and made infringing copies of the original program. Acknowledging infringement, the defendants claimed Lasercomb's licensing clause implicated copyright misuse. The Circuit Court concurred with Reynolds.[95]

From an economic perspective, the decision ignores a conceivable rationale for Lasercomb's business practice. Lasercomb was concerned about protecting its market-leading product from being cloned or otherwise knocked off in a short amount of time, and therefore understood that product life for software is short.[96] Lasercomb's agreement then protected embedded know-how against misappropriation in a competitive downstream market and did not economically misuse its copyright. There is evidently no compelling rationale to require a producer to sell product or license information to would-be competitors.

In *Alcatel U.S.A., Inc.* v. *DGI Technologies, Inc.*[97] Alcatel (aka DSC) designed and sold telecommunication switches and cards that expanded switch capacity. A customer, DGI disassembled the software and worked out a number of design processes that allowed them to be a competitive provider of cards.[98] DSC alleged trade secret misappropriation, unfair competition, and copyright infringement.[99] DGI counterclaimed for antitrust, tortious interference, and unfair competition through copyright misuse.[100] In affirming and reversing parts of a complex District Court decision, the Circuit Court dismissed the antitrust claim,[101] pre-empted the state misappropriation claim through the Copyright Act[102] and held that Alcatel's behavior implicated copyright misuse to control the sale of unpatented cards.[103]

From a matter of law, the court relied upon a definition of per se patent misuse[104] that failed to recognize the statutory modification of 1988,[105] which conditioned misuse upon demonstrated market power in a 'rule of reason'.[106] From an economic perspective, Alcatel was a nondominant switch provider and each buyer contractually consented before purchase to the tying arrangement between switches and cards. By recovering revenues from tied sales of switches and cards, Alcatel could better defray development costs, lower switch prices and compete more effectively with larger players. As in Lasercomb, there was no embedded information in Alcatel's switches that deserved any particular public dispensation.

In *Practice Mgmt. Info. Corp. (PMIC)* v. *American Medical Association*,[107] PMIC published without authorization medical procedure code copyrighted by the American Medical Association. In its defense, PMIC pointed out that the AMA adopted a previous coding system (Current Procedural Terminology – CPT) on behalf of the Health Care Financing Administration (HCFA) under a non-exclusive, royalty-free and irrevocable license for copying, publishing and distributing the code. In exchange, HCFA agreed not to use any other system of nomenclature and required use of the CPT in programs administered by the HCFA. Finding a copyright misuse, the court ruled that

> what offends the copyright misuse doctrine is not HCFA's decision to use the AMA's coding system exclusively, but the limitation imposed by the AMA licensing agreement on HCFA's rights to decide whether or not to use other forms as well ... conditioning the license on HCFA's promise not to use competitors' products constituted a misuse of the copyright by the AMA.[108]

The AMA's actions indeed had the potential to foreclose entirely the use of a different system; the behavior seems anti-competitive and the court's ruling here seems a proper use of the misuse doctrine.

7.4   ANTITRUST AND COPYRIGHT

While courts have generally recognized that patent and copyright owners may exclude others,[109] 'contractual tying of a patented or copyrighted good can give rise to antitrust liability if a "seller exploits his dominant position in one market to expand his empire into the next"'.[110] Contractual tying[111] then is a potential anticompetitive act under Section 1 of the Sherman Act and Section 3 of the Clayton Act, and may additionally implicate actual or attempted monopolization under Sherman Section 2.[112] These business practices should then be distinguished from technological integration of two products that have operational synergies, which is generally allowed unless the integration had been undertaken primarily to foreclose competition.[113]

While early cases held that patent or copyright indicated that market power[114] and contractual tying was per se illegal,[115] more recent courts limited the former notion,[116] and considerably modified per se scrutiny.[117] Contractual tying in antitrust litigation now is per se unlawful when four criteria are met.[118] First, tying and tied products are two distinct products with separate market demands. Second, there is an agreement or condition, express or implied, that establishes a tie between the two goods. Third, the entity accused of tying has sufficient power in the market for the tying product to distort consumers' choices with respect to the tied product. Fourth, the tie forecloses a substantial amount of commerce in the market for the tied product. Quite problematically, per se cases do not allow room for competitive justification, presenting here a compelling case for an alternative rule of reason that would be more admissive of economic evidence in a defense.[119]

The two pivotal elements of the present per se test are the existence of two separate product markets and the presence of sufficient market power[120] in the tying good. The separate product test depends on demonstrable historic demands for the purchase of two nonintegrated products.[121] However, tying into separate product markets may actually be economically efficient. For if bottleneck and competitive goods are used in fixed proportions (e.g., operating system [OS], personal computer [PC]) the bottleneck producer (OS) has incentives to tie into the competitive market (PC) only if the combination is more efficient.[122]

By contrast, tying with 'variable proportions'[123] assigns to purchasers of bottleneck goods (e.g., cameras) payments that are based to some degree on their purchase levels of tied goods (e.g., film) that vary among different users. With a presumably higher profit level as a result of the tie, such tying is an attractive way of monetizing the costs of developing a patented product. Moreover, 'since ... there is no principle that patent owners may not engage in price discrimination [e.g., usage charges or regional differences],[124] it is unclear why one form of discrimination, the tie-in, alone is forbidden'.[125]

The determination of 'sufficient economic power' – once defined as the presence of market power, a patent or copyright, or a unique product – is equally problematic for products with embedded intellectual property.[126] As traditionally represented in microeconomic theory, market power reflects a producer's ability to set price above marginal cost. The direct linkage of market power to price margin is particularly problematic for tying products where production entails upfront investments and each new product carries a potential failure rate that must be implicitly compensated. Quite often, new product introductions are priced at premium levels, but followed by rapid price declines as production economies develop.[127] Finally, tying producers will lower prices of access goods, sometimes below marginal cost, in order to promote a platform to sell tied products. The above considerations then make the price–cost margin at any time an ambiguous measure of true market power.

If a direct price–cost comparison is ambiguous, power conceivably can be judged by indicators – market share,[128] demand elasticity,[129] the existence of economic substitutes,[130] relative production costs,[131] and barriers to entry[132] – as set forth in the Joint Horizontal Merger Guidelines,[133] or the Supreme Court's *Brown Shoe* decision of 1962.[134] Each of these tests poses real practical problems for high-tech industries with divergent production costs, uncertain product substitution, inestimable demand parameters, scarce data, unpredictable entry and nonquantifiable quality differences. As a result of innovation and entry by new platforms, 'high technology' markets may undergo paradigm shifts that lead to technological discontinuities and the emergence of new platforms (personal computers overtaking mainframes). Indeed, it is not clear that a market for many products can be reasonably defined within the traditional definition.

With regard to patent/copyright or uniqueness, economists now strongly criticize the notion that a patent, copyright, or unique characteristic by itself bestows market power upon its owner:

> A patented product may well be unique. It may, however, face a lot of substitutes, perhaps equally unique, and, as a result of this extensive availability of substitutes, confer very little, if any monopoly power. Statistical studies suggest that the vast majority of all patents confer very little monopoly power – at least, they are not very profitable.[135]

The Department of Justice now agrees that patents do not necessarily confer market power,[136] and courts now concur that the *Loews'* doctrine[137] is very simplistic.[138]

Section 1 claims for anticompetitive tying died with a conspicuous whimper in *U.S.* v. *Microsoft*,[139] when the DC Circuit Court remanded a District Court opinion that held that Microsoft's bundling of Explorer and Windows was per se unlawful.[140] While not disputing the potential demand for separate browsers, the Court found that the separate markets test was backward-looking and inappropriate for judging technological efficiencies made possible by integration;[141] the conventional four-part test might then have ignored welfare-enhancing efficiencies and therefore reduced consumer surplus.[142] The District Court was directed to review the case under a rule of reason that considered the possible efficiencies of technological bundling.[143] The case settled before retrial.

The nature of the high-tech operating system did not, to any great degree, confound the Department's monopolization claims regarding Section 2.[144] The Circuit Court found demonstrable proof that Microsoft had a monopoly in desktop operating systems, and held that the defendant levered its position through exclusive licensing restrictions against competing middleware from Netscape and Sun Microsystems.[145] Microsoft's primary copyright argument, which contended that an owner had the right to place unrestricted licensing terms on its product, was found to border upon the frivolous.[146] Evidently, the court concluded that exclusive licensing rights in one market did not extend to actions designed to preserve monopolies through behavior in others.

As a course, courts should judge contractual tying arrangements by a rule of reason that considers prevailing economic circumstances,[147] particularly when the defendant is attempting to recover development costs for its intellectual property. Furthermore, it might be wise for the Antitrust Division simply to relax enforcement of Section 1 and not challenge contractual tying of high-tech goods unless such behavior demonstrably maintains[148] or attempts[149] monopolization in an identifiable market. While identification of a relevant market for a high-tech product can be daunting, it is the absence of structural competition, characterized by monopolization and entry barriers, which is the primary retardant of long-run technological change.[150] Tying, in and of itself, is not inherently anticompetitive and can actually be a means of creating more efficient business models and stimulating more invention.

However, for matters such as monopolization of an operating system, the court might also reasonably consider the role of copyright misuse. Unlike the switching costs that are implicated by an individual's use of his macros and spreadsheets, operating systems implicate network externalities that users bestow upon each other.[151] That is, one operating system tends toward dominance because the utility derived from consumption of the product increases with the number of other application programs, which depends upon the number of potential users in the network base.[152] A dominant platform then may confer monopoly power in the present product markets, as well as additional leverage with regard to products that have not yet emerged. Anticompetitive activities designed to foreclose entry at the platform and application level then present the considerable danger of closing off entry by new applications that are not now part of any reasonable antitrust market.

Refusal to Deal

A flipside issue to tying, refusal to deal implicates behavior of vertically integrated firms that restricts access to bottleneck goods, often patented or copyrighted, for non-integrated rivals. By denying to rivals particular components or services, producers implicitly tie their goods to related competitive products that they themselves produce

American law now is quite forbearing of owner rights when all refused parts are protected by patent or copyright. Once a fierce litigant against strong IP rights, the Justice Department noted in 1995 that 'market power [does not] impose on the intellectual property owner an obligation to license the use of that property to others'.[153] In response to a claim that it had infringed a copyright in a diagnostic software program used in computer service, Grumman contended that Data General engaged in restraints of trade and illegal monopolization by unilaterally refusing to license the copyrighted program.[154] Noting the contrast between the competitive process of antitrust laws and the protective incentives of IP monopolies,[155] the Circuit Court ruled that a legal patent or copyright grants to the owner exclusive rights that trump antitrust concerns that may otherwise arise from monopoly power in the immediate product market: 'even if it is clear that exclusive use of a copyright can have anti-competitive consequences, some type of presumption may nonetheless be appropriate as a matter of either antitrust law or copyright law'.[156]

With a valid copyright the key difference, the court rejected a Supreme Court precedent in *Aspen Skiing*[157] that 'a monopolist may be guilty of monopolization if it refuses to cooperate with a competitor in circumstances where some cooperation is indispensable to effective competition'. In the later case of *CSU* v. *Xerox*, a District Court similarly upheld Xerox's right to refuse to sell patented parts and copyrighted software to independent service organizations; the key distinction from *Kodak*[158] was the limiting condition to the patent.[159] The court again rejected the relevance of *Aspen Skiing* because it did not implicate IP rights.[160]

The legal matter becomes more complex when refused components include nonproprietary items. Strongly resembling an earlier case that involved the refusal to deal of diagnostic software and related maintenance services,[161] the landmark case of *Eastman Kodak Co.* v. *Image Technical Services* saw eighteen independent maintenance providers bring antitrust action for tying (Section 1) and monopolization (Section 2) against Kodak for refusing to deal to them any replacement parts (both patented and not) for its copiers.[162] After the Supreme Court first ruled that the matter could survive Kodak's motion for summary judgment because Kodak's replacement parts represented a separate 'aftermarket' segment that was substantively disjoint from photocopiers themselves,[163] the Ninth Circuit Court held that Kodak's action lacked legitimate business justification and was a violation under Section 2.[164]

Unmentioned by the Circuit Court was the Justice Department's amicus brief to the Supreme Court. The Department argued that Kodak's behavior in the parts market implicated a 'marketing strategy of spreading over time the total cost to the buyer of Kodak equipment'.[165] Regardless of whether replacement parts were patented or not, Kodak's strategy would then represent a reasonable business model for any producer of a large durable, particularly a competitive platform product with embedded intellectual property. The Supreme Court had earlier ruled that preventing the ISOs from 'exploiting the investment Kodak has made in product development, manufacturing, and equipment sales' does not suffice as business justification.[166] As explained above, the Court here ignores the reasonable economic considerations in a complex business model with variable proportions.

European courts have at times adopted a contrasting position regarding the exclusive rights, at least in so far as the product represents an essential facility for a prospective competitor in a neighboring market. Data protection was tested in the *Magill* case.[167] Radio Telefis Eireann (RTE) and Independent Television (ITV) were two major broadcasters of television content in Ireland. Both RTE and ITV published weekly television guides of their respective listings; each company also provided listing to daily newspapers free of charge on condition that no advance listing be made. Seeking to consolidate buyers, Magill TV Guide attempted to publish a comprehensive weekly listing of the same programs, but was enjoined from doing so. Magill then lodged a complaint in 1986 with the European Commission that sought a declaration that the stations were abusing their dominant position in the market by refusing to grant licenses.[168] The Commission concurred and ordered the stations to supply advance information non-discriminatorily in order to enable publication of competing weeklies.[169]

Both the Court of First Instance[170] and the European Court of Justice[171] upheld the decision due to the 'exceptional circumstances' of the data. Because there were no market substitutes for the weekly guides and the appellants were the only sources of the basic information, the refusal therefore denied the creation of a new integrated product without justification.[172] Consequently, the appellants 'reserved to themselves the secondary market of weekly television guides by excluding all competition on the market ... since they denied access to the basic information which is the raw material indispensable for the completion of such a guide'.[173] However, in the contrasting case of *Tierce Ladbroke* v. *European Commission*,[174] the Court of Justice rejected a plea by owners of betting shops to compel copyright owners of films to grant performance rights because the contended exclusive behavior did not implicate essentiality.[175]

The European position on exclusive licensing then hinges on whether or not the contested good or service is an essential facility for competitors. While IP protection may be reasonably relaxed for spinoffs of databases that implicate no incremental amount of dedicated investment, the *Magill* decision focuses instead on dominant position and therefore ignores entirely the related costs of producing the IP component. By failing to consider the offsetting financial harm and conceivable lost incentives to a would-be innovator, the European essential facilities doctrine as applied to IP may compromise the intended purpose of a patent or copyright.

7.5 DATA: COLLECTION AND SEARCH

Proper protection of data in cyberspace implicates an appreciation of both the considerable costs of assembling a database and the ability for digital technology to put great amounts of new data at the disposal of a wide population. The discussion can then be divided into considerations regarding collection and presentation, and subsequent concerns regarding search.

Facts and Economic Reality

The US Supreme Court heard the landmark case of *Feist Publications, Inc.* v. *Rural Telephone Service Company, Inc.* in 1991.[176] As required by state regulation, Rural Telephone Service Company – a Kansas public utility – published and updated a telephone directory with *White* and *Yellow Pages*. The books were freely distributed to all customers, but advertising space was sold in the *Yellow Pages* to defray production costs. To compose a wider regional listing, Feist collected telephone listings and sold advertisements for a book that subsumed eleven service areas, including Rural's. When Rural refused to license directory information, Feist extracted and published the needed listings. Rural sued for copyright infringement, which both the District Court and Circuit Court upheld.[177]

In a unanimous Supreme Court judgment, Justice O'Connor found that Rural's *White Pages* contained only facts with no originality. Since originality is a constitutional requirement for copyright,[178] the facts in the directory were not subject to protection.[179] And while compilations of facts – in which the author displays some skill in inclusion and arrangement – may at times qualify for copyright protection,[180] Rural's simple alphabetizing lacked the requisite creativity and therefore did not.[181] The ruling dismissed[182] the earlier court doctrine of 'sweat of the brow' or 'industrious collection', which had held that 'copyright was a reward for hard work that went into compiling facts',[183] even if related to timely news reporting.[184] Simply put, 'while it may seem unfair that much of the fruit of the compiler's labor may be used by others without compensation ... this is ... the essence of copyright and [therefore] a constitutional requirement'.[185]

The Supreme Court's decision, which was legally grounded in the

Constitutional idea of copyright and terms of the Copyright Act of 1976,[186] begs the question of an economic incentive for collection, preparation and presentation of data in analog or digital services. From an economic perspective it admittedly would be transactionally difficult to impose copyright protection for raw facts and ideas, i.e., requiring users to license facts and ideas would raise the cost of research and reporting, create needless duplication of efforts, increase administrative costs and create a land rush to develop commercial 'ideas' primarily for the purpose of exploiting their copyrights.[187] However, the duplication of an entire telephone directory appropriates rewards needed to monetize the expense of collecting and organizing facts into accessible listings, however mundane the process.

The Supreme Court in *Feist* could safely ignore production costs because Rural, a public utility, was compelled by state regulation to produce the *White Pages*.[188] However, if the directory were produced instead as a discretionary market activity, a general legal allowance for uncompensated takings of facts in works of 'low authorship' (e.g., directories, databases, maps) may reduce or eliminate just rewards and incentives to produce such highly useful works.[189] The insistence on a Constitutional standard might also eliminate the capacity to protect 'low authorship' through misappropriation statutes,[190] but may provide incentives for 'low authors' to limit access through bilateral contrasts.[191]

Such contractual protection would have its moment in *Pro CD* v. *Zeidenberg*.[192] At great expense, Pro CD compiled phone number information from more than 3000 telephone directories into an online database that telemarketers could access for a subscription fee. A smaller version of the data collection was also encoded on a pack of five CDs that were sold to individual users at a lesser price. Lacking copyright protection due to *Feist*, Pro CD encoded on each CD a 'shrinkwrap license' that appeared on the computer screen at each use to inform the reader that her continued use implicated consent to a contract that disallowed commercial reproduction.[193] Unwilling individuals were invited to return the product to their purchaser. Disregarding the terms, defendant Zeidenberg instituted a commercial taking to provide data for a competing online service.

The District Court held for the defendant, agreeing that Zeidenberg did not have a chance to bargain for the contract and therefore did not voluntarily assent to it. ProCD's contract also improperly pre-empted the exemption for facts and ideas in *Feist*.[194] The Circuit Court reversed and remanded, pointing out that Zeidenberg had the opportunity to read the contract at leisure, and had been free to return the CD if displeased.[195] Moreover, parties to a private transaction are free to consent to different terms than traditional copyright.[196]

The Circuit Court's decision grasps the economic reality behind Pro CD's business practices.[197] Much like any IP producer, Pro CD had to cover its fixed costs of composing the database. If individual 'low-price' users/arbitrageurs could resell data, they would reduce or eliminate Pro CD's capacity to monetize expenses from 'high-price' services. If it lacked a sustainable high-end service, Pro CD would necessarily increase the price of CDs to 'low-price' buyers, conceivably to a level that would discourage a great number of purchases. By contracting to eliminate arbitrage, Pro CD then retained its ability to price discriminate profitably. The process then simultaneously provided a desirable economic option and increased overall revenues.

European Initiatives

Though two legislative proposals in the USA have called for some *sui generis* protection of databases, Congress has not yet acted. However, the European Parliament enacted in 1996 a Directive that established a 'right for a maker of any database which shows that there has been qualitatively and/or quantitatively a substantial investment in either the obtaining, verification, or presentation of the contents to prevent extraction and/or re-utilization of the whole or of a substantial part'.[198] Granted rights would include temporary or permanent reproduction, alteration, distribution, performance, or display.[199] Member states may grant limitations for uses that implicate private reproductions of non-electronic databases, scientific research, public security, and issues of traditional national law.[200] Moreover, content owners may not prevent a lawful user from extracting and/or re-utilizing insubstantial parts of its contents for any purposes whatsoever.[201] The term of protection is 15 years from the date of completion of the database.[202]

The nature of the Directive invites economic considerations for (1) spinoffs that do not involve substantial investments, and (2) databases where the owner maintains a dominant position. An economically astute approach to the former issue has emerged in the Netherlands, which transposed the Directive in 1999.[203] During legislation, the Dutch Minister of Justice agreed with Members of Parliament that products such as restaurant listings, broadcast data, and a list of stars in a new galaxy fell short of the substantial investment test.[204] With an eye toward legislative intent, subsequent Dutch courts denied protection to spinoffs of ancillary data gathered for discretely different primary uses, including compilations of newspaper headlines[205] and broadcast program listings.[206] However, the Dutch Supreme Court also overruled an Appeals Court ruling after finding that the specialized collection of real estate data implicated investments made directly to compose a primary base:[207] 'if a data base is used for a variety of uses, the Database Directive does not require that a substantial investment be made for each of these uses'.[208]

The economic reasoning of the Dutch courts is quite nuanced. The courts protect joint uses of data where those uses can reasonably be expected to provide additional incentive for upfront investments in collection and preparation. So protected, secondary uses may encourage more investments and drive down prices charged for other uses of the same data. However, Dutch courts do not protect *post hoc* investments that attempt simply to bootstrap on other efforts (such as the compilation of newspaper headlines) that gather data as a residual byproduct. The implicit recognition is that the data would have been gathered regardless of database rights, and that any additional protection therefore is rent-seeking without providing any offsetting social gain.[209] 'There would appear to be no reason to grant sui generis protection to data compilations that are generated quasi "automatically" as by-products of other activities.'[210]

Database protection was also tested in *Magill*.[211] As explained, plaintiffs prevailed because defendants had a dominant position with regard to an essential facility. Had *Magill* been tried as a spinoff, courts might reasonably have concurred that the program directories did not qualify as primary investments under the Database Directive.

7.6   SEARCH AND DESTROY?

'Spiders', 'metacrawlers' or 'bots' are automated Internet search tools that scan web sites in search-and-retrieve missions that can enact thousands of processing instructions per minute.[212] They are particularly useful for portals, information aggregators, and shopping services, which may extract information on product prices and other related data across the web. Evidently supportive of consumer choice and market efficiency,[213] 'crawler' use nonetheless should not be permitted to harm the business interests of the visited web site. Economic insights are useful in these cases where consumer and producer interests seem at particular odds.

Trespass to Chattels

In a decision characterized by one reporter as 'the most liberal use of a preliminary injunction ever applied to a traditional cause of action adapted to the Internet',[214] the US District Court in the Northern District of California decided *eBay Inc* v. *Bidder's Edge* (BE) in May, 2000.[215] eBay was a market-leading internet-based auction site that allowed buyers to search and bid for goods in over 2500 product categories. Bidder's Edge was an information aggregator that offered online buyers the ability to search for items across a number of different auction sites without having to visit each individually.

Approximately 69 percent of the auction items in the BE database were from eBay.[216]

eBay had been willing to allow automatic searches of its site if queried directly by BE at the moment of use. However, to expedite searches, BE instead chose to deploy 'crawlers' to automatically and recursively visit eBay's site up to 100000 times per day to compile its own database.[217] Bidder's Edge's searches consumed a fraction (1–2 percent)[218] of eBay's processing and storage capacity and thereby rendered a portion of the system unavailable to other users. Bidder's Edge also deliberately circumvented 'electronic fences' that eBay had put in place for the purpose of blocking unauthorized robotic searches; other search engines – such as Yahoo, Google, Excite and AltaVista – respected these exclusion standards.[219] In suing BE for trespass to chattels,[220] the plaintiff suggested to the court a prorataed access price that would have allocated to BE a share of capacity costs based on its respective proportion of usage of the eBay site.

The court held that eBay's monetary assignment overestimated the incremental costs that BE actually imposed.[221] Nonetheless, the court ruled that if BE's trespass were to continue unchecked, 'it would encourage other auction aggregators to engage in similar recursive searching of the eBay system such that eBay would suffer irreparable harm from reduced system performance, system unavailability, or data losses'.[222] Finding that BE had engaged in trespass to chattels,[223] the court granted an injunction that foreclosed robot access to eBay's server entirely.[224] However, eBay's right to exclude BE from its server was found not to be equivalent to copyright.[225]

From an economic perspective, the court would have been better off taking eBay's price offer that would have accommodated BE's searches. If agreeable to all parties, a liability rule can be the first step in a negotiation process that leads to mutually beneficial solution.[226] Since initial negotiating positions are more equitably established if access is obtainable at a finite price (rather than enjoined entirely), eBay's prorataed fees, though higher than the economically efficient solution of incremental cost,[227] might have immediately enabled some usage.

Indeed, a modifiable liability rule might also have led to a preferable alternative; the parties in time might have negotiated to a two-part arrangement where BE paid a blanket license fee to search the eBay system in an unrestricted manner during moments of low demand, and a limited number of times otherwise. The permitted amount could have varied in real time with the number of searches simultaneously performed by other crawlers. The contract could also have been supplemented with additional surcharges that would have enabled BE (and others) to purchase priority access during congested periods.

Deep Linking

Yet a different solution would have been possible in *Ticketmaster (TM)* v. *Tickets.com (T.com)*,[228] which the court decided in August 2000. As the nation's largest vendor for entertainment and sports events, TM's web site included a home page directory and separate 'event' pages for each ticketed item sold through its service; the company earned online revenues from ticket commissions and advertising payments based on the number of viewer hits on the home page. Similar to Bidders' Edge, T.com was an online ticket clearinghouse that pulled relevant event, price and URL information from web pages of other ticket services. The most frequently visited host site for event and price information was TM.

Fearing that 'deep linkers' would avoid hitting home pages that carried advertisements, TM sought to enjoin T.com's searches, arguing that T.com infringed its copyright because, *inter alia*, the clearinghouse made copies of TM's material into random access memory. Ticketmaster also alleged breach of contract, misappropriation, and trespass. The District Court held that T.com's copies into random access memory of extracted facts were not copyrightable.[229] However, the copyright claim survived because T.com had made thousands of copies of TM's interior web pages for data extraction.[230]

Although the court found the eBay decision to be a convincing discussion of trespass to chattels,[231] TM failed to demonstrate economic harm, obstruction of access to business operations, or further likelihood of additional 'parasites joining the fray, the cumulative total of which could affect the operation of TM's business'.[232] Tickets.com was found not to compete with TM, and consumers benefited from the provided referrals.[233] Regarding market harm, ads were avoided but more tickets possibly were sold.[234]

From an economic perspective, the argument whether T.com imposed market harm upon TM was not relevant to a larger consideration of how the matter might have been resolved. Ticketmaster had the 'self-help' power to undo advertising losses from T.com's unwanted visits by setting ticket commissions differently to viewers who avoided its home page. That is, TM could have affixed a premium to 'deep linkers'. Moreover, all incoming ticket buyers could have been informed that discounts were available for people willing to 'click through' to view advertisements on TM's home page.

Price differentiation here would have allowed each site visitor the direct option of viewing TM's advertisements, or paying for the convenience of avoiding them. Had TM done this, T.com itself could have agreed to route users through TM's home pages or buy down the commissions by compensating TM for advertising dollars lost through 'deep links'.

Ticketmaster would have been made whole for its advertising losses and T.com's references would have been unalloyed boons. No court injunction could have benefited TM any more than unilateral self-help, and it would have been economic for the court to have required it.

Framing

Online intermediaries may also use crawlers to search the web and collect images related to a particular theme. An evident gain results for any end-user who might not be capable of locating related material herself. However, the searching intermediary may nonetheless be taking copyrighted material from other websites, and reframing the content by removing advertising, e-commerce icons and related commercial periphery. If the fair use defense is to be invoked, its application should be appropriately limited through efficient fence-protection, as happened in *Kelly* v. *Arriba Soft Corp.*[235]

The plaintiff was a professional photographer who maintained two web sites that displayed photos he had taken of scenes in California's 'gold rush country'. Arriba (later Ditto) operated an innovative search engine that allowed viewers to retrieve photographic images from other web sites. In response to any viewer request, the Arriba engine produced a display of related 'thumbnail' photographs that were gleaned by a crawler.[236] By clicking on a particular 'thumbnail', a user could view a full-size image, a description of its dimensions and an originating web address.

Kelly claimed that he was denied an opportunity to license his material and that Arriba's viewers avoided his home page advertisements. The District Court ruled that Arriba's thumbnail directory qualified for 'fair use' because its application was transformative and of a 'somewhat more incidental and less exploitative nature than more traditional types of commercial use'.[237] The court saw greater difficulties in Arriba's images attributes page, which displayed and framed a full-size image separated from Kelly's originating web page.[238] Nonetheless, it conflated the two uses and ruled that Arriba's takings on the whole were significantly transformative to qualify for 'fair use'.[239]

The Circuit Court reversed in part. While Arriba's thumbnail reproductions that expedited web searching might have qualified for fair use, the reframed full-size reproductions deprived Kelly of advertising dollars and an expectable licensing opportunity. The court then appropriately categorized Arriba's takings into 'fair use' and 'licensable' components, and disallowed Arriba's free taking of the latter. From an economic perspective, the Circuit Court practiced efficient deterrence. If fair use rights are to be granted to a defendant without compensating rights owners, it is imperative that takings be narrowly limited to specific uses that cannot otherwise be reasonably licensed.

7.7   CONCLUSION

We conclude with a number of summary points:

1. Licensing of IP defrays investment costs and should be encouraged as a means of making access available. Legal readings of copyright statute and Constitutional intent do not avoid the reality that a discernible investment can be at stake. The same is true for rulings that hold 'reverse engineering' to be creative work, while ignoring the avoidance of a licensing market.
2. Fair use remains a reasonable economic option to protect consumer rights for uses that cannot be expectedly licensed in any discernible market.
3. If licensing is not certain due to the presence of market power, courts must yet consider the potential that free takings or compulsory licensing of intellectual property may interfere with incentives to undertake primary investment.
4. Copyright misuse may have a compelling economic justification in a number of instances where new goods may lack access to necessary platform products. At other times, copyright misuse has been used in a manner that ignores important economic considerations.
5. Contractual tying arrangements, which may appear as unfair and anti-competitive, may accommodate efficient business models and provide greater incentives for their development and introduction of new products.
6. Tying arrangements, at least for intellectual property, should be viewed through 'rule of reason' that admits more nuances for economic contingencies.
7. Particularly with regard to databases, the spinoff rule seems to introduce more properly the appropriate nuances to determine whether a free taking of facts is acceptable.
8. For trespassing actions, courts may encourage parties to adopt liability rules or self-help tactics that lead to efficient resolutions without injunction or fair use.

NOTES

1. J.H. Reichman, 'Computer Programs as Applied Scientific Know-How: Implications of Copyright Protection for Commercialized University Research', 42 *Vanderbilt Law Review* 639, 650 (1989). ('[T]oday's most productive and refined technical innovations are among the easiest of all forms of industrial know-how to duplicate. Because each product of the new technologies tends to bear its know-how on its face, like an artistic work, each is exposed to instant predation when successful and is likely to enjoy zero lead time after being launched on the market.')
2. S. Scotchmer, 'Standing on the Shoulders of Giants: Cumulative Research and the Patent

Law', 5 *Journal of Economic Perspectives* 29 (1991).

3. R. Nelson and R. Merges, 'On Complex Economics of Patent Scope', 90 *Columbia Law Review* 839, 975. ('Property rights that are too narrow will not provide enough incentive to develop the asset, while overly broad rights will preempt too many competitive developments.') The article contrasts with Edmund Kitch's prospect theory that contends that coordination economies result when all rights are concentrated with one owner (E. Kitch, 'The Nature and Function of the Patent System', 20 *Journal of Law and Economics* 265 (1977)).

4. US Department of Justice and Federal Trade Commission, *Antitrust Guidelines for the Licensing of Intellectual Property*, § 3.2.3 (Washington, DC: Government Printing Office, 1995).

5. P. Samuelson and S. Scotchmer, 'The Law and Economics of Reverse Engineering', *Yale Law Journal* (2002). The more technical legal definition is 'starting with the known product and working backwards to divine the process which aided in its development or manufacture'. *Kewanee Oil Co.* v. *Bicron Corp.*, 416 U.S. 470, 476 (1974). *See also* A. Johnson-Laird, 'Software Reverse Engineering in the Real World', 19 *University of Dayton Law Review* 843, 845–6 (1994).

6. With regard to reverse engineering, see *Triad Systems Corporation* v. *Southeastern Express Company*, 64 F. 3d 1330, 1337 (9th Cir. 1995).

7. *Kewanee Oil*, supra note 5, at 481–2. See also *Videotronics Inc.* v. *Bend Electronics*, 564 F. Supp. 1471, 1475–6 (D. Nev. 1983) (trade secrecy alone provides no protection to mass-marketed software products).

8. 17 U.S.C. § 906.

9. Infra notes 14–33 and surrounding text.

10. 35 U.S.C. § 112 (2003).

11. Nos 01-1108 and 01-1109 (Fed. Cir. Aug. 20, 2002).

12. *Diamond* v. *Diehr*, 450 U.S. 175, 182, 67 L. Ed. 2d 155, 101 S. Ct. 1048 (1981). *See also State Street Bank & Trust Co.*, v. *Signature Financial Group*, 149 F. 3d 1368 (Fed. Cir. 1998).

13. See Chapter 1.2.

14. 977 F. 2d 1510 (9th Cir. 1993). *See also Atari Games Corp.* v. *Nintendo of America, Inc.*, 975 F. 2d 832, 836 (Fed. Cir. 1992).

15. Ibid., 1514.

16. Ibid., 1516.

17. 785 F. Supp. 1392. *See also Apple Computer, Inc.* v. *Franklin Computer Corp.*, 714 F. 2d 1240, 1246–8 (3rd Cir. 1983), *cert. dismissed* 464 U.S. 1033, 79 L. Ed. 2d 158, 104 S. Ct. 690 (1984). *Digital Communications Assoc.* v. *Softklone Distrib. Corp.*, 659 F. Supp. 449, 462–3 (N.D. Ga. 1987).

18. The court rejected three arguments that Accolade did not copy. First, intermediate copying is infringing (supra note 14, at 1518, citing *Walker* v. *University Books*, 602 F. 2d 859, 864 (9th Cir.); see also *Walt Disney Productions* v. *Filmation Associates*, 628 F. Supp. 871, 876 (C.D.Cal. 1986)). Second, the disassembly of object code is lawfully protected as a taking of unprotected ideas and functional concepts per 17 U.S.C. § 102(b) (at 1519, *Johnson Controls, Inc.* v. *Phoenix Control Sys., Inc.*, 886 F. 2d 1173, 1175 (9th Cir. 1989), *Apple Computer, Inc.* v. *Formula Int'l Inc.*, 725 F. 2d 521, 524–5 (9th Cir., 1984)). Third, the court favorably cited the CONTU Report (National Commission on New Technological Uses of Copyrighted Works, Final Report, 1978) and the Computer Software Copyright Act of 1980 (December 12, 1980, Pub. L. No. 96-517, 94 Stat. 3015, 3028 (1980), amending 17 U.S.C., § 101, 117), that Accolade's copying into random access memory is a reproduction not exempted by 17 U.S.C. § 117 (at 1520).

19. Ibid., 1518–20. (In summation, 'where there is good reason for studying or examining the unprotected aspect of a copyrighted computer program, disassembly for purposes of such study of examination constitutes a fair use'.)

20. Ibid., 1522.

21. Ibid., 1523.

22. Ibid., 1520–28.

23. Ibid., 1523.
24. 'By facilitating the entry of a new competitor ... Accolade's disassembly of Sega's software undoubtedly "affected" the market ... in an indirect fashion. We note, however, that ... video game users typically purchase more than one game. There is no basis for assuming that Accolade's "Ishido" has significantly affected the market for Sega's "Altered Beast", since a consumer might easily purchase both; nor does it seem unlikely that a consumer particularly interested in sports might purchase both Accolade's "Mike Ditka Power Football" and Sega's "Joe Montana Football", particularly if the games are, as Accolade contends, not substantially similar' (ibid., 1523).
25. Ibid., 1524.
26. From the bench of copyright scholar Judge Pierre Leval, the present defining case would seem to be *On Davis* v. *The Gap, Inc.*, 246 F. 3d 152 (2nd Cir. 2001) (upholding the idea that plaintiff's distinctive eyewear was a properly licensed item in the clothing advertisements in which it facilitated a visual draw).
27. Supra note 6.
28. Supra note 14, at 1522.
29. Richard Schmalensee, 'Monopolistic Two-Part Pricing Arrangements', 11 *Bell Journal of Economics*, 445 (1981).
30. For example, Microsoft now sells Windows near cost in order to sell applications software (e.g., Excel and Word) (Lemley and McGowan, infra note 151, at 78). Intuit discounts its software platform in order to sell related services for checking and bill paying (supra note 59, manifesto).
31. 203 F. 3d 596 (2000).
32. Ibid., 604.
33. Ibid., 618.
34. *Bowers* v. *Baystate Technologies*, 64 U.S.P.Q. 2d 1065 (CA FC 2002) (Fed. Cir. Aug. 20, 2002).
35. *State Street Bank & Trust Co.* v. *Signature Financial Group.* 49 F. 3d 1368 (Fed. Cir. 1998), *cert. denied* 119 U.S. 851 (1999). The decision widened patent protection to software that recited a mathematical algorithm, deployed business methods normally exempt from patent protection, and did not have physical aspects or perform physical transformations. The history of each consideration is described in I. Saladi, 'Computer Software: Patentable Subject Matter Jurisprudence comes of Age', 18 *John Marshall Journal of Computer and Information Law* 113 (Fall, 1999). The decision was extended in *AT&T Corp.* v. *Excel Communications, Inc.*, 172 F. 3d 1352 (Fed. Cir. 1999).
36. The point is persuasively made in Judge Pauline Newman's dissent in *Rite-Hite Corp.* v. *Kelly Co.*, 56 F. 3d 1358, 1578–9 (Fed. Cir.), *cert. denied*, 116 S. Ct. 184 (1995). The sale of packages that included infringed components caused actual damages in the sales of the whole package. *See also* L.C. Childs, 'Rite-Hite Corp. v. Kelley Co.: The Federal Circuit Awards Damages for Harm Done to a Patent not in Suit', 27 *Loyola University Chicago Law Journal* 665, 701 (1996).
37. *Grain Processing Corp.* v. *American Maize-Products Co.*, 979 F. Supp. 1233, 44 USPQ 2d 1782 (N.D. Ind. 1997), *affirmed* 185 F. 3d 1341 (Fed. Cir. 1999).
38. Ibid., *see also Panduit Corp.* v. *Stahlin Bros. Fibre Works, Inc.*, 575 F. 2d 1152, 197 U.S.P.Q. 726 (6th Cir. Mich. 1978).
39. 964 F. 2d 965 (9th Cir. 1992).
40. For example, the number of lives of the player's character, or the speed at which the character operates.
41. Ibid., 967.
42. 780 F. Supp. at 1291.
43. Supra note 41, at 970.
44. Supra note 42, at 1295.
45. Ibid., 1295.
46. 'An economic justification for depriving a copyright owner of this market entitlement exists only when the possibility of [an efficient] consensual bargain has broken down in some way' (W.J. Gordon, 'Fair Use as Market Failure: A Structural and Economic

Analysis of the Betamax Case and Its Predecessors', 82 *Columbia Law Review* 1600
(1982)). The author continues: 'Only where the desired transfer of resource use is unlikely
to take place spontaneously, or where special circumstances such as market flaws impair
the market's ordinary ability to serve as a measure of how resources should be allocated,
is there an economic need for allowing nonconcensual transfer' (at 1615).

47. 49 F. 3d 807 (1st Cir. 1995).
48. Ibid., 809.
49. 830 F. Supp. at 212.
50. *Lotus Dev. Corp.* v. *Paperback Software Int'l*, 740 F. Supp. 37, 68–70 (D. Mass. 1990).
51. *Lotus Dev. Corp.* v. *Borland Int'l, Inc.*, 799 F. Supp. 203 (D. Mass. 1992), *Lotus Dev.*
     Corp. v. *Borland Int'l, Inc.*, 831 F. Supp. 223 (D. Mass. 1993).
52. Supra note 47, at 815–16.
53. Ibid., 818.
54. Ibid., 821.
55. 513 U.S. 233 (1996).
56. The Supreme Court case attracted an amicus brief from 15 distinguished economists that
     identified additional network effects (infra note 151; *see also Apple Computer, Inc.* v.
     Microsoft Corp., 799 F. Supp. 1006, 1025 (N.D. Cal. 1992); *aff'd*, 35 F. 3d 1435 (9th Cir.
     1994)) that arise from the common interests of different users wanting access to the same
     platform. Continuing on Judge Boudin's theme, the amici argued that an early platform
     may enjoy considerable market power not due to superiority or lower price, but simply by
     a sequence of early events that led to positive bandwagon effects and resulting barriers to
     entry. In this respect, users who want to share macros will need compatible interfaces to
     facilitate the handoff. Indeed, several commentators have argued that IP should not protect
     interface components at all (J. Farrell, 'Standardization and Intellectual Property', 30
     Jurimetrics Journal 35, 38, 45–6; P.S. Menell, 'The Challenges of Reforming Intellectual
     Property Protection for Computer Software', 94 *Columbia Law Review* 2644, 2652–3
     (1994)).
57. F.R. Brooks, *The Mythical Man-Month*, 20 (Reading, MA:Addison-Wesley, 1975).
58. Brief Amicus Curaie, pp. 2–3
59. P. Samuelson, R. Davis, M.D. Kapor and J.H. Reichman, 'A Manifesto Concerning the
     Legal Protection of Computer Programs', 94 *Columbia Law Review* 2318, 2581 n. 12
     (1994).
60. Ibid., 2396, n. 356.
61. H. Demsetz, 'Why Regulate Utilities?', 11 *Journal of Law and Economics* 55 (1968).
62. P. Klemperer, 'Price Wars Caused by Switching Costs', 56 *Review of Economic Studies*
     405 (1989); B. Klein, 'Market Power in Antitrust: Economic Analysis after Kodak', 3
     Supreme Court Economic Review 43, 47–63 (1993).
63. D. Friedman, infra note 65, at 1121–2.
64. Y. Barzel, 'Optimal Timing of Innovations', 50 *Review of Economics and Statistics* 348
     (1968); P. Dasgupta and J. Stiglitz, 'Uncertainty, Industrial Structure, and the Speed of
     R&D', 11 *Bell Journal of Economics* 1 (1980).
65. From a free market point of view, producers who stop platform compatibility would create
     a healthy competition among contending standards, *see* A. Clapes, 'Confessions of an
     Amicus Curiae: Technophobia, Law and Creativity in the Digital Arts', 19 *University of*
     Dayton Law Review 903, 934 (1994); A. Miller, 'Copyright Protection for Computer
     Programs, Databases, and Computer Generated Works: Is Anything New since CONTU?',
     106 *Harvard Law Review* 977, 1029–32 (1993); D. Friedman, 'Standards as Intellectual
     Property: An Economic Approach', 19 *University of Dayton Law Review* 1109, 1110–11
     (1994); K. Dam, 'Some Economic Considerations in the Intellectual Property Protection of
     Software', 24 *Journal of Legal Studies* 321, 338 (1995).
66. H.A. Shelanski and J.G. Sidak, 'Antitrust Divestiture in Network Industries', 68 *University*
     of Chicago Law Review 8 (2001). This is to be compared with S.C. Salop and R.C.
     Romaine, 'Preserving Monopoly: Economic Analysis, Legal Standards, and Microsoft', 7
     George Mason Law Review 617, 654–5, 663–4, arguing generally that exclusionary
     conduct in high-tech network industries deserves heightened antitrust scrutiny because it

may deter innovation.

67. The details of the competition are described in *Paperback*, supra note 50, 65–6.
68. Case C-481/01, *NDC Health GmbH & Co. KG* and *NDC Health Corporation* v. *Commission and IMS Health Inc.*, Order of 11 April 2002, [2002] ECR I-3401.
69. Treaty Establishing the European Community as Amended by Subsequent Treaties, Rome, Article 82 (formerly 86) (25 March 1957).
70. Infra note 167.
71. R.G. Badal and H.E. Ware, 'U.S. Company Compelled to License its Software by E.U. Antitrust Authorities: The Case of NDC Health v. IMS Health', at http://www.hewm.com/use/articles/imshealth.pdf.
72. Ch D: Laddie J: 31 May 2002.
73. Ordnance Survey ('OS') was the government department responsible for the official definitive surveying and topographic mapping of Great Britain. Ordnance Survey had created a 'Master Map' framework for geographical data ('DNF') that consisted of several layers or themes (e.g., topographic, digital imagery, etc.). When made available on a web site, the MasterMap enabled Ordnance Survey's customers to look up a map and pull up the equivalent digital image showing features not on the map, such as trees. Ordnance Survey then planned to develop a one-stop shop, to allow customers to obtain all their mapping and imagery requirements from one web site. The claimant sought to place its own images on the web site as well in order to allow customers to access the images of both, and sought action when OS refused. The plaintiff contended that OS had abused its dominance in the map market to set up the one-stop shop contrary to Section 18 of the UK's Competition Act 1998. Justice Laddie ruled that it was not a per se abuse for a trader dominant in one market to use his financial muscle to enter a new market and enjoy a commercial advantage over others.
74. Misuse can reasonably be defined as the 'the use of a copyright [or patent] to secure an exclusive right or limited monopoly not granted by the [Copyright] Office and which it is contrary to public policy to grant' (*Lasercomb*, infra note 94, at 972).
75. *Morgan Envelope Company* v. *Albany Perforated Wrapping Paper Co.* (the Paper Roll case) 152 U.S. 425, 14 S.Ct. 627; 38 L. Ed. 500; 1894 U.S. LEXIS 2132 (1894). *See also Heaton-Peninsular Button-Fastener Co.* v. *Eureka Speciality Co.* (the Button Fastener case) 77 F. 288; 1896 U.S. App. LEXIS 2241 (6th Cir. 1896).
76. *Motion Picture Patents Co.* v. *Universal Film Mfg. Co.*, 243 U.S. 502; 37 S. Ct. 416; 61 L. Ed. 871; 1917 U.S. LEXIS 2017 (1917), *vacating Henry* v. *A.B. Dick Co.* (224 U.S. 1; 32 S. Ct. 364; 56 L.Ed. 645; 1912 U.S. LEXIS 2279 (1912)).
77. *Morton Salt Co.* v. *G.S. Suppiger Co.* 314 U.S. 488 (1942). The court declined to consider the merits of an antitrust plea upheld in the Circuit Court. 117 F. 2d 968 (7t Cir. 1941)
78. *U.S.* v. *Loews, Inc.* 371 U.S. 38, 45; 83 S. Ct. 97, 102; 9 L.Ed. 2d 11, 18 (1962). The court declared block booking of theater movies to be a copyright misuse that was per se illegal due to the presence of a copyright.
79. Patent misuse is easier to prove for three reasons. The definition is generally broader, key elements of an antitrust case are not essential (particularly if regarding monopolization under Section 2 of the Sherman Act) and the grieving party has standing regardless of whether it can demonstrate individual harm (M. Lemley, 'The Economic Irrationality of the Patent Misuse Doctrine', 78 *California Law Review* 1599, 1611 (1990)).
80. R.J. Hoerner, 'Patent Misuse: Portents for the 1990s', 59 *Antitrust Law Journal* 687, 688–90 (1991); P.A. Martone, W.J. Gilbreth and R.G. Gervase, 'The Patent Misuse Defense – Its Continued Expansion and Contraction', 1 *Intellectual Property Antitrust* 325, 350–51 (1966).
81. *Eastern R.R. Presidents' Conference* v. *Noerr Motor Freight*, 365 U.S. 127 (1961); *United Mine Workers* v. *Pennington*, 381 U.S. 657 (1965); *California Motor Transp. Co.* v. *Trucking Unlimited*, 404 U.S. 508 (1972).
82. Antitrust law allows for treble damages, but no party can collect damages unless directly affected by the anti-competitive behavior. Sherman Act 15 U.S.C. 4, 15 (2003). *See also* J.B. Kobak, Jr, 'The Misuse Doctrine and Intellectual Property Litigation', 1 *Boston University Journal of Science and Technology Law* 2, 2 (1995).

83. D.S. Chisum, *Patents: a Treatise on the Law of Patentability, Validity, and Infringement* Chapter 19, 5 (New York: Matthew Bender & Company, 1996). Patent rights can be restored when the misuse is discontinued and its consequences dissipated. *Morton Salt*, supra note 77, at 492.

84. P.E. Areeda and H. Hovenkamp, *Antitrust Law* 360, 200–202 (New York: Aspen Publishers, 1995).

85. *Cargill, Inc.* v. *Monford of Colo. Inc.*, 479 U.S. 104, 109–13 (1986), *Brunswick Corp.* v. *Pueblo O-Mat*, Inc., 429 U.S. 477, 489 (1977). 'The greater scope of the misuse doctrine may produce benefits by providing for increased judicial scrutiny of patent practices ... If a litigant can make a plausible argument that the restriction is anticompetitive – that is, harms innovation and negatively affects efficiency – then the courts should hear it.' Note: 'Is the Patent Misuse Doctrine Obsolete?', 110 *Harvard Law Review* 1922, 1939 (1997).

86. 'The doctrine of patent misuse has been described as an equitable concept designed to prevent a patent owner from using the patent in a manner contrary to public policy. This is too vague a formulation to be useful ... The doctrine arose before there was any significant body of federal antitrust law; taken seriously, it would put all patent rights at hazard, and in application the doctrine has largely been confined to a handful of specific practices by which the patentee seemed to be trying to extend his patent grant beyond its statutory limits ... The antitrust laws define a separate role for a doctrine also designed to prevent an anticompetitive practice – the abuse of a patent monopoly ... If misuse claims are not tested by conventional antitrust principles, by what principles shall they be tested? Our law is not rich in alternative concepts of monopolistic abuse; and it is rather late in the day to try to develop one without in the process subjecting the rights of patent holders to debilitating uncertainty' (*USM Corporation* v. *SPS Technologies*, 694 F. 2d 505 (7th Cir., 1982)).

87. *Brulotte* v. *Thys*, 379 U.S. 29, 13 L. Ed. 2d 99, 85 S. Ct. 176 (1964).

88. *Zenith Radio Corp.* v. *Hazeltine Research, Inc.*, 395 U.S. 100, 133–40, 23 L. Ed., 2d 129, 89 S. Ct. 1562 (1969).

89. Supra note 86, at 511.

90. A Patent Interference and Misuse Reform Act of 1988. Pub. L. No. 100-703, 102 Stat. 4674 (1988). While a Senate version (S 438) that would have judged all patent misuse by antitrust standards failed passage, 35 U.S.C. § 271(d)(5) was amended to protect patent owners from misuse charges in matters involving exclusive dealing and tying unless market power could be demonstrated. Legislative history shows that the requisite definition of market power was purposely left to later Court discretion. J.B. Kobak, Jr, 'The New Patent Misuse Law', 71 *Journal of the Patent [& Trademark] Office Society* 859 (1989).

91. This led four advocates to suggest a *sui generis* regime that would protect software for short periods of time but would also require full disclosure of the source code as consideration. Supra note 59.

92. B. Fischmann and D. Moylan, 'The Evolving Common Law Doctrine of Copyright Misuse: A Unified Theory and its Application to Software', 15 *Berkeley Technology Law Journal* 3 (2001).

93. O.E. Williamson, *The Mechanisms of Governance*, ch. 3 (Oxford: Oxford University Press, 1996).

94. 911 F. 2d 970, 976 (4th Cir. 1990).

95. Ibid., 979.

96. Lee Carl Bromberg (attorney for Lasercomb), personal note to author, March 23, 2003.

97. 166 F. 3d 772 (5th Cir.).

98. Ibid., 777–8.

99. Ibid., 779.

100. Ibid.

101. Ibid., 780–84.

102. Ibid., 789.

103. Ibid., n. 86.

104. Supra note 77.

105. Patent Misuse Reform Act, Pub. L. No. 100-73, 102 Stat. 4674 (1988), codified at 35 U.S.C. 271(d).

106. 35 U.S.C. 271(d)(5). ('No patent owner otherwise entitled to relief for infringement or contributory infringement of a patent shall be denied relief or deemed guilty of misuse or illegal extension of the patent right by reason of his having ... conditioned the license of any rights to the patent or the sale of the patented product on the acquisition of a license to rights in another patent or purchase of a separate product, unless, in view of the circumstances, the patent owner has market power in the relevant market for the patent or patented product on which the license or sale is conditioned' [emphasis mine]).

107. 121 F. 3d 516 (9th Cir. 1997), *cert. denied* June 26, 1998.

108. Ibid., 521.

109. 35 U.S.C. 101, 154 (1994); *see also U.S.* v. *Westinghouse*, 648 F. 2d 642, 647 (9th Cir. 1981) ('Once a patent is lawfully acquired, subsequent conduct that is permissible under patent law is the "untrammeled right of the patentee"'); *SCM* v. *Xerox*, 645 F. 2d 1195, 1204–5 (2d Cir. 1981) ('No court has ever held that the antitrust laws require a patent holder to forfeit the exclusionary power inherent in his patent the instant his patent monopoly afforded him monopoly power over a relevant product market'); *Zenith Radio Corp.* v *Hazeltine Research Inc.*, 395 U.S. 100, 135, 89 S. Ct. 1562, 1582 (1969) ('The heart of the patentee's legal monopoly is the right to invoke the State's power to prevent others from utilizing his discovery without his consent'). *Intergraph Corp.* v. *Intel Corp.*, 195 F. 3d 1346, 1362 (Fed. Circ. 1999) ('antitrust laws do not negate the patentee's right to exclude others from patented property').

110. Infra note 163, at 479, n. 29.

111. 'A [contractual] tying arrangement may be defined as an agreement by a party to sell one product but only on the condition that the buyer also purchases a different (or tied) product, or least agrees that he will not purchase that product from any other supplier.' *Northern Pacific RR. Co.* v. *United States*, 356 U.S. 1, 5 (1958).

112. 15 U.S.C. § 1,2.

113. *Response of Carolina, Inc.* v. *Leasco Response, Inc.* 537 F. 2d 1307, 1330 (5th Cir. 1976). The sole purpose standard seems to have been modified to a more balanced rule of reason in Microsoft, infra note 138, at 949–50. *See* K.N. Hylton and M. Salinger, 'Tying Law and Policy; A Decision Theoretic Approach', 69 *Antitrust Law Journal* 469, 479–84 (2001).

114. Supra note 78, at 45, 102, 18.

115. *International Business Machines* v. *US.*, 298 U.S. 131, 134–5, 56 S. Ct 701, 703; 80 L. Ed. 1085, 1088 (1936) (IBM's practice of tying sales of tabulating cards to lessees of its computer equipment was an infringement of Section 3 of the Clayton Act (15 U.S.C. 14)), *International Salt Co.* v. *US*, 332 U.S. 392, 396 (1947) (patents afforded no immunity from antitrust and tying represented a per se violation under Section 1 of the Sherman Act (15 U.S.C. 1)).

116. Infra note 138 and surrounding text.

117. Tying would be per se unlawful if 'the seller enjoys a monopolistic position in the market for the "tying" product, or if a substantial volume of commerce in the "tied" product is restrained. The per se rule of International Salt can apply only if both its ingredients are met' (*Times Picayune Publishing Co.* v. *United States*, 345 U.S. 594, 608–9, 73 S. Ct. 872, 880; 97 L. Ed. 1277, 1290 (1953)). 'First, there must be two separate products, with the sale of one conditioned upon the purchase of the other. Second, the seller must possess sufficient economic power in the tying market to restrain competition in the tied. Third, the amount of affected commerce in the tied market must be substantial' (*Northern Pacific RR. Co.* v. *United States*, 356 U.S. 1, 5 (1958)).

118. *Grappone, Inc.* v. *Subaru of New England, Inc.*, 858 F. 2d 792, 794–7 (1st Cir. 1988); *Data General Corp.* v. *Grumman Systems*, 36 F. 3d 1147, 1178 (1st Cir. 1994); *Microsoft*, infra note 139, at 85.

119. O'Connor conc. in *Jefferson Parish*, infra note 120, 34. The per se doctrine 'calls for the extensive and time consuming analysis characteristic of the rule of reason, but then may be interpreted to prohibit arrangements that economic analysis would show to be beneficial'. The time had come to 'abandon the per se label and refocus the inquiry on the adverse economic effects, and the potential economic benefits, that the tie may have'.

120. Defined alternatively as the power 'to force a purchaser to do something that he would not

do in a competitive market', and the 'ability of a single seller to raise price and restrict output'. *Jefferson Parish Hospital District No. 2* v. *Hyde*, 466 U.S. 2, 14 (1984). *Fortner Enterprises, Inc.* v *U.S. Steel Corp.*, 394 U.S. 495, 503 (1966).

121. *Jefferson Parish*, ibid., 19–21; *see also Times Picayune*, supra note 117, at 614; *Eastman Kodak*, infra note 162, 463; *Microsoft*, infra note 139, 135–36.

122. W.S. Bowman, 'Tying Strategies and the Leverage Problem', 67 *Yale Law Journal* 19 (1957).

123. The outcome is analytically different from tying with fixed proportions, where a monopoly provider of a tying good could expropriate no more profit from tied sales of a complement, all else held equal.

124. Sourcing in original *Bela Seating* v. *Poloron Prods., Inc.*, 438 F. 2d 733, 738 (7th Cir. 1971).

125. *USM Corporation* v. *SPS Technologies*, 694 F. 2d 505, 511 (7th Cir. 1982).

126. The sufficient economic power test here seems even more ambiguous than the outdated monopoly leveraging test of *Berkey Photo Inc.* v. *Eastman Kodak Co.*, 603 F. 2d 293 (2nd Cir. 1979), 'a firm that used its monopoly power in one market to gain a competitive advantage in another, albeit without an attempt to monopolize the second market' (603 F. 2d at 275). The Ninth Circuit had characterized the downstream monopoly requirement – 'to gain a competitive advantage' – as too loose (*Alaska Airlines, Inc.* v. *United Airlines, Inc.*, 948 F. 2d 536, 543 (9th Cir. 1991)).

127. C. Pleatsikas and D. Teece, 'The Analysis of Market Definition and Market Power in the Context of Rapid Innovation', 19 *International Journal of Industrial Organization* 665, 666 (2001).

128. The definition of market share encounters difficulties elaborated in US Department of Justice and Federal Trade Commission, supra note 4.

129. The demand elasticity represents the percentage decrease in quantity demand that is caused by a 1 percent increase in the relevant product price.

130. *Virtual Maintenance, Inc.* v. *Prime Computer Inc.*, 11 F. 3d. 660, 665. '[The copyright owner] Prime Computer has market power in the trivial sense that no one else makes [its product]. But true market power – power sufficient to change and sustain anticompetitive prices – cannot be inferred from this because were Prime to charge exorbitant prices for its software support, its customers would simply switch to some other manufacturer.'

131. H. Hovenkamp, *Economics and Federal Antitrust Law* at 219 (St. Paul, MN: West Publishing Co. 1985). 'Many patents confer absolutely no market power on their owners, and often patented products are not even marketable at their cost of production ... The economic case for "presuming" sufficient market power to coerce consumer acceptance of an unwanted tied product simply because the tying product is patented [or] copyrighted ... is very weak.'

132. *Will* v. *Comprehensive Accounting Corp.*, 776 F. 2d, 665, 672 (7th Cir. 1985). 'Unless barriers to entry prevent rivals from entering, even large market share does not establish the market power that is a requisite element of violation.' Common entry barriers include patents or other legal licenses, control of essential or superior resources, entrenched buyer preferences, high capital entry costs, and economies of scale.

133. Supra note 128.

134. *Brown Shoe Co.* v. *U.S.*, 370 U.S. 294, 325; 82 S. Ct. 1502, 1523; 8 L. Ed. 2d 510 (1962). The boundaries of such a market or submarket may be determined by examining such 'practical indicia as industry or public recognition of the market as a separate economic entity, the product's peculiar characteristics and uses, unique production facilities, distinct customers, distinct prices, sensitivity to price, and specialized vendors'.

135. F.M. Scherer, 'Panel Discussion, The Value of Patents and Other Legally Protected Commercial Rights', 53 *Antitrust Law Journal* 535, 547 (1985).

136. 'If a patent or other form of intellectual property does confer market power, that market power does not by itself offend the antitrust laws. As with any other tangible or intangible asset that enables its owner to obtain significant supracompetitive profits, market power (or even a monopoly) that is solely a "consequence of a superior product, business acumen, or historic accident" does not violate the antitrust laws' (supra note 4, section 2.2).

137. Supra note 78.
138. *Capital Temporaries, Inc. of Hartford* v. *Olsten Corp.*, 506 F. 2d 653, 663 (1974) ('The appellant misreads Loew's if he concludes that the mere existence of the copyrighted tying motion pictures was enough to create the tying.'); *In Re Data General Corp. Antitrust Litigation*, 490 F. Supp. 1089, 1112 (N.D. Ca. 1980) ('Notwithstanding implied suggestions to the contrary, the sole fact of the existence of a copyright notice has not been held to be sufficient to prove economic power.'); *3 P.M., Inc.* v. *Basic Four Corp.*, 591 F. Supp. 1350, 1359 (E.D. Mich. 1984) (copyright does not itself imply 'some advantage not shared by competitors in the market for the tying product'), *A.J. Root Co.* v. *Computer Dynamics, Inc.*, 806 F. 2d 673, 676 (6th Cir. 1986) (rejecting 'any absolute presumption of market power for copyright or patented product'). With regard to patents, see *Abbott Laboratories* v. *Brennan*, 952 F. 2d 1346, 1354 (1991); *American Hoist & Derrick Co.* v. *Sowa & Sons, Inc.*, 725 F. 2d 1350, 1367, 220 USPQ, 763, 776 (Fed. Cir. 1983), *cert. denied*, 469 U.S. 821, 105 S. Ct. 95, 83 L. Ed. 2d 41 (1984) ('patents are not legal monopolies in the antitrust sense of that word'); *Capital* v. *Olsten, see above*; *Carpa, Inc.* v. *Ward Foods, Inc.*, 536 F. 2d 39 (5th Cir. 1976); *Northern* v. *McGraw-Edison Co.*, 542 F. 2d 1336 (8th Cir. 1976), *cert. denied*, 429 U.S. 1097, 97 S. Ct. 1115, 51 L. Ed. 2d 544 (1977); *Town Sound* v. *Chrysler*, 959 F. 2d 468 (3rd Cir. 1990). With regard to trademarks, see *Capital* v. *Olsten, see above*; *Carpa, Inc.* v. *Ward Foods, Inc.*, 536 F. 2d 39 (5th Cir. 1976); *Northern* v. *McGraw-Edison Co.*, 542 F. 2d 1336 (8th Cir. 1976), *cert. denied*, 429 U.S. 1097, 97 S. Ct. 1115, 51 L. Ed. 2d 544 (1977).
139. 253 F. 3d 34 (2001).
140. 87 F. Supp. 2d 30, 35–51 (D.D.C. 2000); 97 F. Supp. 2d 59, 64–5 (D.D.C. 2000).
141. Ibid., 76–7.
142. Ibid.
143. Ibid., 94.
144. There are two elements to maintenance of monopoly in 15 U.S.C. § 2 – (p. 8). The Circuit Court found that Microsoft hindered the use of the competitive Netscape browser as well as Sun's Java Language. Both Netscape and Java were 'middleware' products that exposed alternative application program interfaces (APIs) to enable software designers to port applications to these new operating systems in a manner that could eliminate the monopoly of Microsoft's Windows operating system on personal computers (at 53, 55). These restrictions primarily implicated licensing agreements with desktop manufacturers that prevented the removal of a browser icon to IE, as well as alterations of the initial boot sequence of the appearance of the windows desktop. Other anticompetitive practices included exclusive licensing arrangements with internet access providers (at 67–71), independent software vendors (at 72), Apple Computer (at 72–4), and deceptive acts/agreements with Intel entered into during the buildout of a high-performance Java competitor (Java Virtual Machine) designed to compete with Sun (at 76–8). The court removed from the monopoly claim liability for technological bundling of IE and Windows (at 64–7), exclusionary deals with Internet content providers (at 71) and the deliberate introduction of incompatibility in JVM (at 74–5).
145. Supra note 139, at 58–9.
146. The court termed Microsoft's position that its licensing agreements were legally justified within the domain of a copyright owner a 'bold and incorrect position on the law ... Intellectual property rights do not confer a privilege to violate the antitrust laws' (ibid., at 63).
147. For related ideas, see R. Posner, 'The Next Step in the Antitrust Treatment of Restricted Distribution: Per Se Legality', 48 *University of Chicago Law Review* 6 (1981).
148. Plaintiff must prove that (1) defendant possessed monopoly power in the relevant market and (2) willfully acquired or maintained that power as distinguished from growth or development as a consequence of a superior product, business acumen, or historic accident. *U.S.* v. *Grinnell Corp.*, 384 U.S. 563, 570–71 (1966)
149. Plaintiff must prove that (1) the defendant engaged in predatory or anticompetitive conduct with (2) a specific intent to monopolize, and (3) a dangerous probability of achieving monopoly power. *Spectrum Sports, Inc* v. *McQuillan*, 506 U.S. 447, 456, 122 L. Ed. 2d

247, 113 S. Ct. 884 (1993).

150.　J.B. Baker, 'Fringe Firms & Incentives to Innovate', 63 *Antitrust Law Journal* 621, 639–41 (1995); R.J. Gilbert and S.C. Sunshine, 'The Use of Innovation Markets: A Reply to Hay, Rapp, & Hoerner', 64 *Antitrust Law Journal* 75, 76–8 (1995).

151.　M.A. Lemley and D. McGowan, 'Legal Implications of Network Economic Effects', 86 *California Law Review* 479 (1998).

152.　M. Katz and C. Shapiro, 'Network Externalities, Competition, and Compatibility', 75 *American Economic Review* 424, 424 (1985).

153.　Supra note 4, section 2.2.

154.　*Data General Corp.* v. *Grumman Systems*, 36 F. 3d 1147 (1st Cir. 1994).

155.　Grumman's 'antitrust claims are intriguing because they present a curious conflict, namely whether harm to the competitive process when such harm is caused by the otherwise lawful exercise of any economically potent monopoly in a copyrighted work' (ibid., 1152).

156.　Ibid., 1185.

157.　*Aspen Skiing Co.* v. *Aspen Highlands Skiing Corp.*, 472 U.S. 585, 86 L. Ed. 2d 467, 105 S. Ct. 2847 (1985). 'If [Aspen Skiing] stands for any principle that goes beyond its unusual facts, it is that a monopolist may be guilty of monopolization if it refuses to cooperate with a competitor in circumstances where some cooperation is indispensable to effective competition.' *Olympia Equip. Leasing Co.* v. *Western Union Telegraph Co.*, 797 F. 2d 370, 379 (7th Cir. 1986).

158.　Infra notes 162–6.

159.　989 F. Supp. 1131, 1132　(D. Kans. 1997). 'A copyright holder can exercise its right to exclude others from using the protected expression, even if the exclusion impacts [sic] competition in more than one relevant antirust market. A copyright holders' intent and any other alleged exclusionary acts are irrelevant in determining the lawfulness of a unilateral refusal to license a copyright' (ibid., 1144).

160.　Ibid., 1139.

161.　*Digidyne Corp.* v. *Data General Corp.*, 734 F. 2d 1336 (9th Cir. 1984). But see *Will* v. *Comprehensive Accounting Corp.*, 776 F. 2d 665 (7th Cir. 1985); F.H. Easterbrook, 'Intellectual Property is Still Property', 12 *Harvard Journal of Law and Public Policy* 108 (1990).

162.　125 F. 3d 1195 (1997).

163.　504 U.S. 451 (1992), 'Kodak's theory that its lack of market power in the primary equipment market precludes – as a matter of law – the possibility of market power in the derivative aftermarkets rests on the factual assumption that, if it raised its parts or service prices above competitive levels, potential customers would simply stop buying its equipment. Kodak's theory does not accurately describe actual market behavior, since there is no evidence or assertion that its equipment sales dropped after it raised its service prices.' *See also* 465–78.

164.　Ibid., 490–92, *citing Aspen Skiing Co.* v. *Aspen Highlands Skiing Corp.*, 472 U.S. 585, 597, 611 (1985). Kodak had earlier asserted that patent protection of its patented parts was a valid business justification about which the District Court failed to instruct the jury. The section 1 claim was dropped.

165.　Brief for the U.S. as Amicus Curaie 18.

166.　Supra note 163, at 485.

167.　*Radio Telefis Eireann* v. *European Commission*, Case C-241/91 P (1995); Case C-242/91 P (1995).

168.　Supra note 69. 'Any abuse by one or more undertakings by a dominant position within the common market or in substantial part of it shall be prohibited as incompatible with the common market in so far as it may affect trade between Member States.' Proscribed actions include unfair pricing or trading conditions, limiting production, discriminatory transactions and supplementary contractual obligations that have no connection with the subject of the contract.

169.　Decision 89/205/EEC (1988).

170.　Case T-69/89, *RTE* v. *Commission* (1991) ECR II-575; Case T-76/89, *ITP* v. *Commission* (1991).

171. Supra note 167.
172. Ibid., paragraphs 52–5.
173. Ibid., paragraph 56, sourcing Joined Cases 6/73 and 7/73, *Commercial Solvents* v. *Commission* [1974] ECR 223, paragraph 25.
174. [1997] ECR II 923.
175. 'The refusal to supply the applicant could not fall within the prohibition laid down by Article 86 unless it concerned a product or service which was either essential for the exercise or the activity in question, in that there was no real or potential substitute, or was a new product whose introduction might be prevented, despite specific, constant and regular potential demand on the part of consumers' (ibid., paragraph 131).
176. 499 U.S. 340 (1991).
177. 663 F. Supp. 214 (1987); 916 F. 2d 718 (1990).
178. Per Article 1 § 8, cl. 8. *See also Burrow-Giles Lithographic Co.* v. *Sarony*, 111 U.S. 53 (1884), L.R. Patterson and C. Joyce, 'Monopolizing the Law: The Scope of Copyright Protection for Law Reports and Statutory Compilations', 36 *UCLA Law Review* 719, 763, n. 155 (1989). ('The originality requirement is constitutionally mandated for all works.')
179. Ibid., 345.
180. Ibid., 348.
181. Ibid., 362.
182. Ibid., 352–4, *citing Miller* v. *Universal City Studios, Inc.*, 650 F. 2d, at 1372.
183. Ibid., 353. *See also Hutchinson Tel. Co.* v. *Frontier Directory Co.*, 770 F. 2d 128, 132 (8th Cir. 1985).
184. Ibid., *sourcing International News Service* v. *Associated Press*, 248 U.S. 215 (1918). ('The news element – the information respecting current events contained in the literary production – is not the creation of the writer, but is a report of matters that ordinarily are public juris; it is the history of the day.')
185. Ibid., 349.
186. 17 U.S.C. 102 (2003). Section 102(a) extends copyright protection only to 'original works of authorship'. Section 102(b) denies protection to 'any idea, procedure, process, system, method of operation, concept, principle, or discovery, regardless of the form in which it is described, explained, illustrated, or embodied in such work'. 'Section 102(b) is universally understood to prohibit any copyright in facts' (ibid., 360).
187. See Landes and Posner, in Chapter 2, n. 22, and surrounding text.
188. 737 F. Supp. at 612.
189. J.C. Ginsburg, 'Creation and Commercial Value: Copyright Protection of Works of Information', 90 *Columbia Law Review* 1865, 1873–93 (1990).
190. J.C. Ginsburg, 'No "Sweat"? Copyright and Other Protection of Works of Information after Feist v. Rural Telephone', 92 *Columbia Law Review* 338, 341 (1995). *See also International News Service*, supra note 184 (regarding Federal standards for misappropriation of fact-based intellectual property [i.e., news stories]).
191. Ibid., 387.
192. 86 F. 3d 1447 (7th Cir. 1996).
193. The license opened as follows: 'Please read this license carefully before using the software or accessing the listing contained on the discs. By using the discs and the listing licensed to you, you agree to be bound by the terms of this License. If you do not agree to the terms of this License, promptly return all copies of the software, listings that may have been exported, the discs, and the User Guide to the place where you obtained it' (908 F. Supp. 640, 644 (W.D. Wisc.)).
194. Ibid., 644, 647.
195. Supra note 192, at 1452–3.
196. Ibid., 1454.
197. Ibid., 1449.
198. Directive 96/9/EC of the European Parliament and of the Council of 11 March 1996 on the Legal Protection of Databases (1996), *Official Journal* No. L 77 of 27 March 1996, p. 20, Art. 7.1, Brussels.
199. Ibid., Art. 5.1.

200. Ibid., Art. 5.2.
201. Ibid., Art. 8.2.
202. Ibid., Art. 10.1.
203. Act of 8 July 1999, Staatsblad 1999, 303 effective 21 July 1999.
204. Memorandum in reply to Parliamentary Report of 22 December 1998, Second Chamber of Parliament, TK 26108 no. 6, p. 5.
205. *Algemeen Dagblad* v. *Eureka*, President District Court of Rotterdam, 22 August 2000, Mediaforum 2000, p. 344 [2000], AMI 205, note K.J. Koelman. ('It cannot be said that the newspapers have invested substantially in the contents of the lists of titles. Their investment is directed to gathering the reports and articles to fill the newspapers. The titles are invented as headlines.')
206. *NOS* v. *De Telegraaf*, Court of Appeals of the Hague, 30 January 2001 [2001], Mediaforum 90, note T.F.W. Overdijk; [2001] AMI 73, note H. Cohen Jehoram. ('The broadcasting organizations, having as their primary task to provide nationwide radio or television broadcasting, cannot fulfill this task without gathering program data and drawing up program listings; lacking probable evidence to the contrary, it must be accepted that the mere drawing up of program listing does not amount to (separate) substantial investments in time, money, or otherwise.')
207. *NVM* v. *De Telegraaf*, Supreme Court of the Netherlands, 22 March 2002, [2002], AMI 88, note D.G. Visser; [2002] IER 150, note H.M.H. Speyart; overruling Court of Appeal The Hague, 21 December 2000, [2001], Mediaforum 87, note M.M.M. van Eechoud.
208. B. Hugenholtz, 'Program Schedules, Event Data, and Telephone Subscriber Listings under the Database Directive: The Spinoff Doctrine in the Netherlands and elsewhere in Europe', 26 *AMI* (the Dutch Journal of Copyright Law) 161, 162 (2002).
209. In a related case involving horseracing data in the UK, Justice Laddie held for the defendant's right to extract data from British Horseracing Board's data listing. ('Of more significance to this dispute is the type of investment involved. As one would expect, effort put into creating the actual data which is subsequently collected together in the database is irrelevant. [There is] a distinction between rights in the database and rights in the data within the database ... For this reason, the costs and effort involved in BHB fixing the data of a racing register does not count toward the relevant investment to which database right is directed.') *British Horseracing Board* v. *William Hill*, High Court of Justice, Ch. Div., 9 February 2001, Case No. HC 2000 1335, §33–34.
210. S.M. Maurer, P.B. Hugenholtz and H.J. Onsrud, 'Europe's Database Experiment', *Science* 789–90 (2001).
211. Supra note 168–73 and surrounding text.
212. M.A. O'Rourke, 'Fencing Cyberspace: Drawing Borders in a Virtual World', 82 *Minnesota Law Review* 609, 615–19 (1998).
213. M.S. Nadel, 'Maximizing Consumer Benefits from E-commerce Competition: Emerging Obstacles & Policy Options', 14 *Harvard Journal of Law and Technology* (2001).
214. A.X. Fellmeth, 'Cyber Trespass Comes of Age', 19(2) *Intellectual Property Lawyer Newsletter* 8 (Winter, 2001).
215. 100 F. Supp. 2d 1058 (N.D. Ca. 2000); 2000 U.S. Dist. LEXIS 7287; 54 U.S.P.Q. 2D (BNA) 1798.
216. Carney Decl., 17.
217. Felten Decl., 33.
218. Johnson-Laird Decl., 64
219. Ibid., 81–5.
220. eBay's First Amended Complaint, 31–3.
221. Supra note 215, at 1066.
222. Ibid.
223. *Thrifty Tel, Inc.* v. *Bezenek*, 54 Cal. Rptr. 2d 468, 473–4 (Cal. Ct. App. 1996).
224. Ibid.
225. Ibid., 1072. Professor O'Rourke distinguishes this from the court's decision in *Ticketmaster* (infra note 228), where unauthorized use of a web site might have been a copyright violation.

226. R.H. Coase, 'The Problem of Social Costs', 3 *Journal of Law and Economics* 1 (1960); G. Calabresi and D. Melamed, 'Property Rules, Liability Rules, and Inalienability: One View of the Cathedral', 85 *Harvard Law Review* 1089 (1972); W.M. Landes and R.A. Posner, 'An Economic Analysis of Copyright Law', 18 *Journal of Legal Studies* 325, 357 (1989).
227. Admittedly in an ideal pricing system, the Court would have set BE's access fees equal to the incremental congestion costs imposed by a trespass that would have increased with general usage of eBay's system, including searches by other parties. The required measurement is impractical for a court to order and oversee.
228. 2000 U.S. Dist. LEXIS 4553 (C. D. Ca. Mar. 27, 2000).
229. 'The time, place, venue, price, etc. of public events are not protected by copyright even if great cost and expense is expended in gathering the information ... Thus, unfair as it may seem to TM, the basic facts that it gathers and publishes cannot be protected from copying' (ibid., *10). *See also* supra notes 176–85 and surrounding text.
230. 2000 U.S. DIST. LEXIS 4553, at 6.
231. Ibid., *15–16.
232. Ibid., *17.
233. Ibid., *18.
234. Ibid.
235. 280 F. 3d 1004 (9th Cir. 2002).
236. 77 F. Supp. 2d 1117 (N.D. Ca. 2000)
237. Ibid., 1116.
238. 'The image attributes page, however, raises other concerns. It allowed users to view (and potentially download) full-size images without necessarily viewing the rest of the originating Web page. At the same time, it was less clearly connected to the search engine's purpose of finding and organizing Internet content for users. The presence of the image attributes page in the old version of the search engine somewhat detracts from the transformative effect of the search engine' (ibid., 1120).
239. Ibid., 1121.

8. Open source and innovative copyright

8.1 INTRODUCTION

Open source is a term that comprises open standards, shared source code and collaborative development of computer software. Per the general terms of open source licenses,[1] operating code that is licensed under an open source contract is available for later modification and redistribution, so long as the same licensing terms are made available to later participants.[2]

Although conceived in 1968,[3] the first practical application of open software arose in 1985, when Richard Stallman of the Massachusetts Institute of Technology (MIT) developed a legal mechanism to preserve ongoing free access to software developed by programmer teams. Stallman took action after MIT licensed for institutional gain some computer codes that had been designed by a group of employed programmers, thereby restricting to the original group ongoing access to the code that they themselves had built.[4]

> [Stallman's] pioneering idea was to use the existing mechanism of copyright law to this end. Software authors interested in preserving the status of their software as 'free' software' could use their own copyright to grant licenses on terms that would guarantee a number of rights to all future users. They could do this by simply affixing a standard license to their software that conveyed these rights.[5]

In this respect, Stallman developed the General Public License (GPL, or Copyleft), which extends to programmers the right to use, study, or distribute modified or unmodified versions in a manner that safeguards ongoing access.[6] Not necessarily free of price, open source software is not the same as freeware (such as Adobe's file readers), which charge no price but may entail proprietary code that is made available in order to promote the sale of upgrades and related products.

Bruce Prens and Eric Raymond extended in 1998 Stallman's conception of free software to the virtually identical construct of open source programming.[7] The web site Sourceforge now lists 43 open source licenses that subsume nearly 40000 different projects.[8] Nearly 29000 of these projects use the GNU General Public License (GPL) of Stallman's Free Software Foundation. Over 4000 more use the GNU Lesser General Public License. Famous open source projects include Apache[9] (which has a 62 percent market share among programs for web servers[10]), Linux[11] (which now challenges Microsoft for leadership on network servers) and Sendmail (which routes 75 percent of emails[12]).

A spectacular open source success, Linux is a free Unixs-type operating system originally created by Linus Torvalds in 1991. Torvald wanted to run a Unix operating system with an Intel 386 processor, and found existing software to be too expensive. He developed his own operating system, and inconspicuously posted a request to a USENET newsgroup for assistance.[13] The rest is cyber-history. Now available with the GPL, Linux is the largest development project in number of programmers,[14] and accounts for a growing market share in both the server and desktop markets. With a resistance to crashing that greatly surpasses Microsoft's Windows NT[15] and costs of less than half,[16] Linux market share in the web server sector stands at approximately a third;[17] the company also accounts for 4 percent of the desktop market after sales grew 185 percent in 2002.[18] Internet service vendors now developing on Red Hat Linux include Adobe, Borland, Checkpoint, IBM, Lotus, Novell, Oracle and Veritas.[19]

Open source programming is reasonably associated with a 'hacker' culture where computer professionals have found 'it a normal part of their research culture to freely give and exchange software they had written, to modify and build upon each other's software both individually and collaboratively, and to freely give out their modifications in turn'.[20] Open source programming also is perceived less correctly as a 'gift culture' that enables programmers to make donations of code with an implied duty for reciprocation,[21] or a decentralized bazaar where players operate without hierarchy to maintain a spontaneous order that advances the social good.[22] In a few imaginations, the open source movement has apparently gained some countercultural mystique, implicating 'freedom, sharing, unrestricted exchange of information, anti-capitalism, or anti-imperialism [*sic*]'.[23]

As an economist, I shall argue that open source contract is a highly pragmatic mechanism that principally benefits programmers and institutions by reducing transactions costs and eliminating the threat of expropriation.[24] This point was wisely recognized in 1998 by Perns and Raymond themselves, who characterized the ideological differences between open source software and Stallman's Free Software movement; open source differed 'primarily on philosophical grounds, preferring to emphasize the practical benefits of such licensing practices over issues regarding the moral rightness and importance of granting users the freedoms offered by both free and open source software'.[25] However, in order to ensure the proper application of open source licenses, a strong system of intellectual property is necessary. Rather than oppose intellectual property, the open source movement is a particularly good testament to a creative application of the concept.

8.2 THE ELEMENTS OF OPEN SOURCE

Open source programs are kernels of code that are made available to and used by computer professionals on an ongoing basis; it implicates a specialized product used by programmers and not an item for mass consumer demand. As mentioned, each player in an open source project may download code from the posted web site and adopt it to his particular needs, so long as modifications are licensed to others under the same terms. Programmers may also post code back to the web site, where the program director or his lieutenants will decide whether to keep the suggested edit.[26]

Open source programs then are composed of interacting modules; 'it is [then] possible to change a part of a module or an entire module without knowing all information about the program that the module belongs to and without altering other modules or the overall purpose of the program'.[27] A strategy for managing complexity, modularity then permits customization, facilitates third-party add-on, and incorporates features and fixes from a wide range of users.

An open source project is begun typically by someone with a personal interest in a matter and a need for assistance to meet an unfilled need; 'every good work of software starts by scratching a developer's personal itch'.[28] The channels of the web and Internet are particularly convenient to posting code, which other programmers can download, tinker with and modify. Once a project is started, the initiator will usually control edits and project definition, a gain over content with no cost. However, careful judgment by the director is necessary, as programmers may jump ship and projects may 'fork' when project leaders follow a questionable course.[29] The consequent loss to a leader's reputation, and the professional gains that may follow, can be considerable.[30]

Since each programmer has the technical ability to modify a program for particular applications, there is no need to maintain a large central kernel of code. Indeed, coordination involves 'keeping the kernel small and limiting to a minimum the number of interfaces and other restrictions to its future development'.[31] This centrifugation of content contrasts with the design of program code that is released to the general public. Design of mass market programs, such as Microsoft Windows, must from the outset incorporate more functionality directly into the program kernel so as to meet the low technical abilities and diverse range of applications of unskilled buyers. Programming for the mass market then requires considerable more effort, particularly in debugging, in order to handle the many different permutations of events that may realistically ensue.[32] If the number of features in a program is M, there are 2^M use-combinations, some large sample of which must be debugged.[33]

In the disclosure–feedback approach of open source software, each innovator posts his work and subsequent recipients test and report bugs in ongoing trial-and-error: 'given enough eyeballs, all bugs are shallow'.[34] In contrast, proprietary programmers do not disclose source code to peers, but rely instead upon consumers of final products to report existing flaws.[35] Software development then involves substantial experimentation, as innovation builds incrementally on previous software and numerous individuals apply multiple approaches to the same problem.[36] Open source programming can then be viewed as a relay race, where each player can make sequential contributions, but no person's entry or continuation is certain.[37]

If programming is a relay race, a transfer mechanism must be designed to allow later contributors some ready ability to expend effort without fear of later expropriation.[38] Under such circumstances, enforcing prices and private property rights at each transaction could actually hinder ongoing product development. For if a uniform price were fixed for each transaction, certain programmers might be dissuaded entirely. And if entry fees were variable, the associated cost of negotiating terms for each admittance of code would be overbearing. The incremental worth of each new programmer would be uncertain, and each player would behave opportunistically so as to extract more favorable terms.[39]

As was Stallman's original intent,[40] a transfer mechanism must then be designed to allow programmers to invest efforts without fear of later expropriation; money is not the primary currency that is needed to enable exchange. The key elements of exchange are not prices, but preemptive assurances that can be made. 'Running an open source project under the GPL, or similar licensing agreements, sends a credible commitment to the investors in reputation that nobody will be able to cut them off from the stream of attention generated by their contributions'.[41] The open source contract then can be likened to a nonprofit institution, where the operating compact (or nondistribution constraint[42]) serves as the necessary assurance to donors that gains will not be expropriated at some point for private gain.[43]

The open source license then is a transactionally efficient contract that allows software professionals to program without need for constant renegotiation for rights to download the kernel, modify code or admit new modules. Each player participates at will, the ongoing path is refereed, and each programmer adapts code for private use so long as every variation of the source code is licensed in the same manner.

8.3   THE PROCESS OF OPEN SOURCE

Four related economic phenomena are of particular interest. First, better programming standards may expectedly eventuate in open source activities as more players come to participate. As long as program leaders edit efficiently, the program outcome is a network good with a value that increases with the number of participants; that is, each team member appreciates bandwagon effects from network externalities made possible from the cumulative intelligence of acceptance by a widening base.[44] The process then represents a virtuous cycle; value grows as more programmers are attracted to a project, and more individuals accordingly follow suit. In this respect, open source programmers then may attempt to dominate actions so to influence an informal industry standard in a manner that is beneficial to the private aims of their employer.[45]

Second, companies can profit from open source code by selling complementary programs or services. For example, Red Hat designs and upgrades application software for use with the Linux operating system, while IBM complements Linux with consulting and maintenance. By participating in open source projects, Red Hat and IBM help direct the path of the project, interact with talented programmers and access inexpensive code for their applications. Succinctly put, the additional revenues made possible by contributing to the open source project exceed the incremental costs of paid programmer time.

Third, professional programmers benefit considerably from personal enjoyment, professional interaction and reputation gains.[46] To the technically initiated, programming is as enjoyable as an ongoing game of chess, where teams play against nature for indefinite periods. Moreover, individual programmers may learn much from working with a group of talented programmers who communicate with one another in the hybrid language of source code and prose. Individual programmers can derive considerable status by demonstrating skill to the wider population of professionals,[47] and therefore earn a measure of professional worth that can advance careers, attract venture capital and promulgate residual claims. Quite properly put, 'hackers, programmers, and contributors are far from being benevolent benefactors operating in a gift economy whose only purpose is to share their own knowledge. [Rather], they are individualistic agents whose actions protect public goods that are a side-effect of their private behavior'.[48]

Fourth, the apparent 'free rider' problem[49] posed by takings by non-contributing programmers is actually no problem at all, but almost a preferred outcome. First, the costs of policing the system and excluding free riders would be quite high. Second, free riders who download programs cause no congestion or other forms of incremental harm to any individual. Indeed, a wider group of users can actually enhance chances for standardization that engaged companies may design. Finally, active players benefit considerably more from the project than do free riders; active players may direct the project, learn interactively from others and improve professional reputation.[50]

8.4 CONCLUSION

Generally, any open source project has five economic efficiencies: a wide talent pool, modular adaptation, transactional ease, easy standardization and reduced debugging. An open source network, then, is a self-organizing system with high levels of quality and performance that depend on repeated transactions that evolve in kind and which feature some limited hierarchy. The result is a 'self-correcting spontaneous' organization of work that is 'more elaborate and efficient than any amount of central planning could have achieved'.[51]

In some apparent respects, open source programs compare favorably with proprietary software, where only insiders have the code and the access needed to modify it.[52] While open projects necessarily maintain some hierarchy, proprietary programs restrict contributions to a much smaller team of programmers. These programmers must be recruited, trained, monitored and added to company overheads, presenting a management concern to their prospective employers that can serve as a bottleneck to growth as well.[53]

However, closed systems may have a countervailing advantage of dynamic commitment and clearer accountability. Open source projects entail informal teams of programmers who contribute to the project as the need and urge arises, but who individually have no commitment to certain desirable long-run goals, such as user-friendliness and attendance to the mundane tasks.[54] By contrast, proprietary programmers face the constraints of competition, consumer demand and future viability to maintain consumer quality, implement improvements and release new versions. The choice between open and closed software then crucially depends upon the targeted market.

Our present experience with open source systems can highlight conceptual problems now implicated by standard views on intellectual property (including, admittedly, the general views of the present author) that often suggest that private property rights are best enforced, and production incentives maximized, through ongoing market exchange. As pointed out above, this can be professionally limiting, transactionally difficult and productive of tactics that may establish proprietary interfaces. In some instances, the actual effect of software lockup can be an unintended reduction in secondary invention due to the difficulty of accessing and building from pre-existing code. Open source agreements allow programmers to resolve these matters procedurally, rather than with litigation.

Open source licensing, then, can be a particularly efficient way to build synergies and reduce transactions costs. However, nothing is possible unless expropriation is deterred. It is difficult to imagine any open source project continuing efficiently, or even initiating, if necessary protections are not clearly established from the outset. The open source process then resolves many outstanding matters of exchange that would otherwise hinder new innovation.

While not governed like traditional copyright, open source projects then certainly require only strong protection of efforts that are productive of new intellectual property, and can result only when IP contracts are respected and strongly enforceable. While open source licensing may question exchange-for-price, it nonetheless demonstrates that IP protection can be used to enable creative modes of institutional accommodations. More than anything, open source is a primary tribute to the power of the construct of intellectual property, and should be appreciated as such.

NOTES

1. Infra note 8.
2. T. O'Reilly, 'Lessons from Open Source Development Software', 41 *Communications of the ACM* 4:33 (1999).
3. J.C.R. Licklider and R.W. Taylor, 'The Computer as a Communications Device', at http://ftp.digital.com/pub/DEC/SRC/research-reports/SRC-061.pdf (retrieved June 1, 2003).
4. E. von Hippel and G. von Krogh, 'Exploring the Open-Source Software Phenomenon: Issues for Organization Science', unpublished paper, Massachusetts Institute of Technology, p. 5 (2002).
5. Ibid.
6. The current version of the GPL can be viewed at http://www.linux.org/info/gnu.html (retrieved June 1, 2003).
7. B. Prens, 'The Open Source Definition' (1998) at http://prens.com/Articles/OSD.html (retrieved June 1, 2003)
8. At http://sourceforge.net/softwaremap/trove_list.php?form_cat=14 (retrieved June 1, 2003).
9. Supra note 4, at 7–8.
10. Network Web Server Survey, May, 2003, at http://news.netcraft.com (retrieved June 1, 2003).
11. A. Metiu and B. Kogut, 'Distributed Knowledge and the Global Organization of Software Development', unpublished manuscript, University of Pennsylvania, 15, n. 4 (2001), at http://opensource.mit.edu/online_papers.php (retrieved June 23, 2003).
12. Infra note 23, at 3.
13. 'Hello netlanders. Due to a project I'm working in, I'm interested in the [Unix] standard definition. Could somebody please point me to a (preferably) machine readable format of the latest [Unix] rules. FTP-sites would be nice' (supra note 11).
14. Supra note 4, at 23.
15. Infra note 16.
16. The total cost of operation of GNU/Linux is roughly 40 percent of Windows NT. D. Wheeler, 'Why Open Source Software/Free Software (OSS/FS)? Look at the Numbers!', at http://www.dwheeler.com/oss_fs_why.html (retrieved June 1, 2003).
17. R. King, 'Linux Market Share Within Web Server Sector to Grow', at http://thewhir.com/features/linux-market-share.cfm (retrieved June 1, 2003).
18. At http://silicon.com/news/500011/1/3508.html?source=nh (retrieved June 1, 2003).

19. M. Webbink, Presentation, 'Open Issues on Open Source', unpublished document, Red Hat Inc., Charlotte, NC, Kaye Scholer LLP, New York, November 6, 2003.
20. Supra note 4, at 2.
21. S. Rota, A. von Wartburg and M. Osterloh, 'Trust and Commerce in Open Source: A Contradiction?' working paper, University of Zurich (2002), at http://www.wiwiss.fu-berlin.de/w3/w3sydow/EURAM/pdf_2002/EURAM%20Paper%20Rota%20et%20al.pdf (retrieved June 23, 2003).
22. E.S. Raymond, *The Cathedral and the Bazaar: Musings on Linux and Open Source by an Accidental Revolutionary* (Sebastopol: O'Reilly and Associates, 2001).
23. E. Franck, and C. Jungwirth, 'Reconciling Investors and Donors – The Governance Structure of Open Source', working paper, University of Zurich, p. 15 (2002), at http://opensource.mit.edu/online_papers.php (retrieved June 23, 2003).
24. Supra notes 4–5, and surrounding text.
25. Supra note 5.
26. Supra note 23, at 12.
27. H. Baetjer, 'Software as Capital: An Economic Perspective on Software Engineering', IEEE Computer Society (1998).
28. Supra note 22, at 32.
29. Supra note 23, at 12.
30. Ibid.
31. Infra note 49, at 18.
32. In one survey, testing, debugging, and program maintenance accounted for 82 percent of development costs. M.A. Cusamano, *Japan's Software Factories: A Challenge to American Management* 65 (Oxford: Oxford University Press, 1991). Microsoft in 1995 employed 3900 engineers for testing and customer support, but only 1850 engineers for software design. Many of these engineers had to spend some time debugging as well. M.A. Cusamano and R.W. Selby, *Microsoft Secrets: How the World's Most Powerful Software Company Creates Technology, Shapes Markets, and Manages People* (New York: Simon and Schuster: 1995).
33. Supra note 23, at 6.
34. Supra note 22, 'In the bazaar view, you assume that bugs are generally shallow phenomena – or at least that they turn shallow pretty quickly when exposed to a thousand eager co-developers pounding on every single new release. Accordingly, you release often in order to get more corrections, and as a beneficial side effect you have less to lose if an occasional botch gets out the door' (at 30–31).
35. Ibid., 7–8.
36. G. Garzarelli, 'Open Source Software and the Economics of Organization', unpublished paper, Universita degli Studi di Roma (2002), at http://opensource.mit.edu/online_papers.php (retrieved June 23, 2003).
37. The peculiar domain then presents a market where the users are the innovators, a situation reasonably compared with high-performance windsurfing, where sport participants determine the appropriate technology simply by attending events and learning to play the game. E. von Hippel, 'Innovation by User Communities: Learning from Open Source Software', *Sloan Management Review* July (2001).
38. Supra notes 4–5, and surrounding text.
39. See O.E. Williamson, 'Transaction Cost Economics', in *The Mechanisms of Governance*, (Oxford: Oxford University Press, 1996).
40. Supra notes 4–5 and surrounding text.
41. Supra note 23, at 14 .
42. H.B. Hansmann, 'The Role of Nonprofit Enterprise', 89 *Yale Law Journal* 835 (1980).
43. Supra note 23, at 16–17.
44. C. Shapiro and H.R. Varian, *Information Rules* (Boston, MA: Harvard Business School Press, 1999).
45. N. Gallini, 'Deterrence through Market-sharing: A Strategic Incentive for Licensing', 74 *American Economic Review* 5:931 (1984). See also J.M. Dalle and N. Jullien, 'Open Source v. Proprietary Software', working paper, Massachusetts Institute of Technology (2002)).

46. A survey in 2001 of programmers in 35 countries reports that the open source community mostly comprises highly skilled IT professionals who have on average over 10 years of programming experience. Participants generally noted extremely high levels of creativity in their projects. Having fun, enhancing skills, personal needs, and having access to source code are the primary motivators. Most participants dedicated at least 10 hours per week in their shared programming efforts. K. Lakhani and R. Wolf, 'Does Free Software Mean Free Labor: Characteristics of Participants in Open Source Communities' (Boston Consulting Group, 2001), at http://osdn.com/bcg (retrieved June 1, 2001).

47. N. Bezroukov, 'A Second Lack at the Cathedral and the Bazaar' (1999), at http://www.firstmonday.org/issues/issue4_12/bezroukov (retrieved June 1, 2001).

48. F. Iannacci, 'The Economics of Open Source Networks', unpublished paper, London School of Economics, pp. 6–7.

49. It is estimated that 10 percent of the authors write more than 70 percent of the produced code. Fifteen developers wrote 90 percent of Apache, and 52 programmers out of 301 wrote 80 percent of GNOME. A. Bonaccorsi and C. Rossi, 'Why Open Source Software can Succeed', unpublished manuscript, p. 16, Sant'Anna School of Advanced Studies, Pisa (2001).

50. In the Linux project, the kernel has a mailing list of 3500, but the real number of contributors is more like 500. For Apache, 15 programmers did much of the initial coding, but hundreds contributed to it while thousands customized code for private uses. A. Mockus, R.T. Fielding and J. Herbsleb, 'A Case Study of Open Source Software Development: The Apache Server' (2001), at http://opensource.mit.edu/online_papers.php (retrieved June 23, 2003). N. Franke and E. von Hippel; 'Satisfying Heterogeneous User Needs via Innovation Toolkits: The Case of Apache Security Software' (2000), at http://opensource.mit.edu/papers/frankevonhippel.pdf (retrieved June 1, 2003).

51. Supra note 22, at 52.

52. M.H. Meyer and L. Lopez, 'Technology Strategy in a Software Products Company', 12 *Journal of Product Innovation Management* 4:194 (1995); K.R. Conner and C.K. Prahalad, 'A Resource-based Theory of the Firm: Knowledge versus Opportunism', 7 *Organization Science* 5:477 (1996); G. Young, K.G. Smith, and C.M. Grimm, 'Austrian and Industrial Organization Perspectives on Firm Level Competitive Activity and Performance', 7 *Organization Science* 3:243 (1996).

53. F. Brooks, *The Mythical Man Month* (Reading, MA: Addison-Wesley, 1975); but see S. McConnell, 'Brooks' Law Repealed', *IEEE Software*, November–December, 6 (1999).

54. B. Fitzgerald, 'Open Source Software: More Placebo than Panacea?', University of Limerick (2002), at http://www.infonomics.nl/FLOSS/workshop/papers/fitzgerald.htm (retrieved June, 23, 2003).

References

Adler, Allan R, 'Statement before the Senate Judiciary Committee Concerning S.487: The Technology, Education, and Copyright Harmonization Act of 2001' (2001), March 13, 2001, at http://www.publishers.org/home/congrpt/s487testimony.htm (retrieved May 11, 2000).

Africa, Matthew, 'The Misuse of Licensing Evidence in Fair Use Analysis: New Technologies, New Markets, and the Courts', 88 *California Law Review* 1145 (2000).

Ames, E. Kenley, 'Note, Beyond Rogers v. Koons: A Fair Use Standard for Appropriation', 93 *Columbia Law Review* 1473 (1993).

Appel, Andrew W. and Edward W. Felten, 'Initial Comments, Rulemaking on Exemptions from Prohibition on Circumvention of Technological Measures that Control Access to Copyrighted Works' (2000), http://www.loc.gov/copyright/1201/comments (retrieved May 19, 2001).

Akerof, George A. et al., 'Brief as Amici Curaie', U.S. Court of Appeals for the D.C. Circuit, Eric Eldred v. John D. Ashcroft, May 20, 2002.

Areeda, P.E. and H. Hovenkamp, *Antitrust Law* 360, 200–202 (New York: Aspen Publishers, 1995).

ASCAP, 'Frequently Asked Questions about Internet Licensing', at http://ascap.com/weblicence/webfaq.html (retrieved December 13, 2001).

Badal, Robert G. and Hilary E. Ware, 'U.S. Company Compelled to License its Software by E.U. Antitrust Authorities: The Case of NDC Health v. IMS Health', at http://www.hewm.com/use/articles/imshealth.pdf (retrieved April 4, 2003).

Baetjer, Herbert, 'Software as Capital: An Economic Perspective on Software Engineering', IEEE Computer Society (1998).

Baker, Jonathan B, 'Fringe Firms & Incentives to Innovate', 63 *Antitrust Law Journal* 621 (1995).

Barzel, Yoram, 'Optimal Timing of Innovations', 50 *Review of Economics and Statistics* 348 (1968).

Beard, Joseph J., 'Clones, Bones and Twilight Zones: Protecting the Digital Persona of the Quick, the Dead, and the Imaginary', 16 *Berkeley Technology Law Journal* 1165, 1171–6, 1186–90 (2001).

Belczyk, Tamarah, 'Domain Names: The Special Case of Personal Names', 82 *Boston University Law Review* 485 (2002).

Bell, Tom W., 'Fair Use vs. Fared Use: The Impact of Automated Rights Management on Copyright's Fair Use Doctrine', 76 *North Carolina Law Review* 557 (1998).

Benkler, Yochai, 'From Consumer to Users: Shifting the Deeper Structures of Regulation Toward Sustainable Commons and User Access', 52 *Federal Communications Law Journal* 561 (2000).

Benkler, Yochai, 'The Battle over the Institutional Ecosystem in the Digital Environment', 44 *Communications of the ACM* 2 (2001).

Besen, Stanley R., 'Private Copying, Reproduction Costs, and the Supply of Intellectual Property', Rand Report No. N-2207-NSF (1984).

Besser, Howard, 'Intellectual Property: The Attack on Public Space in Cyberspace', *Processed World* (2001), at http://www.gseis.ucla.edu/~howard/Papers/pw-public-spaces.html (retrieved June 16, 2003).

Bezroukov, Nikolai, 'A Second Lack at the Cathedral and the Bazaar' (1999), at http://www.firstmonday.org/issues/issue4_12/bezroukov (retrieved June 1, 2003).

Bisceglia, Julia, 'Parody and Copyright Protection: Turning the Balancing Act into a Juggling Act', 34 *Copyright Law Symposium (ASCAP)* 1 (1987).

Bonaccorsi, Andrea and Cristina Rossi, 'Why Open Source Software can Succeed' (2001), at http://opensource.mit.edu/online_papers.php (retrieved June 23, 2003).

Bonn, Maria S., Wendy P. Lougee, Jeffrey K. MacKie-Mason and Juan F. Riveros, 'A Report on the Peak Experiment: Usage and Economic Behavior', 5 *D-LIB Magazine* 7/8 (1999), at http://www.dlib.org/dlib/july99/mackie-mason/07mackie-mason.html (retrieved June 5, 2001).

Bonn, Michael S., Wendy P. Lougee, Jeffrey K. MacKie-Mason and Juan F. Riveros, 'A Report on the PEAK Experiment: Content and Design', 5 *D-LIB Magazine* 6 (1999), at http://www.dlib.org/dlib/juje99/06bonn.html (retrieved June 6, 2001).

Bork, Robert A, *The Antitrust Paradox* (New York: Basic Books, 1976).

Borland, John, 'Apple Unveils Music Store', *Tech News*, CNET.com, April 28, 2003, at http://www.cnet.com (retrieved June 16, 2003).

Borland, John, 'Bands to Buy KaZaa Search Results, CNET NEWS.com, August 22, 2002, at http://www.cnet.com (retrieved June 16, 2003).

Borland, John, 'File-swapping tools are legal', CNET NEWS.com, April 25, 2003, at http://www.cnet.com (retrieved June 16, 2003).

Borland, John, 'Fingerprinting P2P pirates', CNET NEWS.com, February 20, 2003, at http://www.cnet.com (retrieved June 16, 2003).

Borland, John, 'Freenet Founder Launches P2P Product', CNET NEWS.com, April 30, 2002, at http://www.cnet.com (retrieved June 16, 2003).

Borland, John, 'Freenet Keeps File-trading Flame Burning', CNET NEWS.com, October 28, 2002, at http://www.cnet.com (retrieved June 16, 2003).

Borland, John, 'Judge: Napster Filtering Efforts "Disgraceful"', CNET NEWS.com, Apr. 10, 2001, at http://www.cnet.com (retrieved June 16, 2003).

Borland, John, 'KaZaa, Morpheus Legal Case Collapsing', CNET NEWS.com, May 22, 2002, at http://www.cnet.com (retrieved June 16, 2003).

Borland, John, 'Listen Aims for Living Room', *Tech News*, CNET.com, January 9, 2003, at http://www.cnet.com (retrieved June 16, 2003).

Borland, John, 'Listen.com Lands Last Big Five Label', *Tech News*, CNET.com, July 1, 2002, at http://news.com.com.2100-1023-963120.html?tag=fd_top (retrieved September 30, 2003).

Borland, John, 'Listen to Offer Legal CD-Burning', *Tech News*, CNET.com, October 23, 2002, at http://www.cnet.com (retrieved June 16, 2003).

Borland, John, 'Madster Told to Pull the Plug', CNET NEWS.com, December 3, 2002, at http://www.cnet.com (retrieved June 16, 2003).

Borland, John, 'Net Music Gets AOL Audition', *Tech News*, CNET.com, February 26, 2003, at http://www.cnet.com (retrieved June 16, 2003).

Borland, John, 'Networks Promise Unfettered File Swapping', CNET NEWS.com, June 19, 2001, at http://www.cnet.com (retrieved June 16, 2003).

Borland, John, 'New KaZaa Likely to Raise Labels' ire', CNET NEWS.com, September 22, 2002, at http://www.cnet.com (retrieved June 16, 2003).

Borland, John, 'Paid Content Comes to KaZaa', CNET NEWS.com, May 19, 2002, at http://www.cnet.com (retrieved June 16, 2003).

Borland, John, 'Spike in "Spyware" Accelerates Arms Race', CNET NEWS.com, February 24, 2003, at http://www.cnet.com (retrieved June 16, 2003).

Borland, John, 'Stealth P2P Network Hides Inside KaZaa', CNET NEWS.com, April 1, 2002, at http://www.cnet.com (retrieved June 16, 2003).

Borland, John, 'Suit Hits Popular Post-Napster Network', CNET NEWS.com, October 3, 2001, at http://www.cnet.com (retrieved June 16, 2003).

Borland, John, 'Sun's Joy Rapturous over Jxta', CNET NEWS.com, June 6, 2001, at http://www.cnet.com (retrieved June 16, 2003).

Borland, John, 'The Brains Behind KaZaa', CNET NEWS.com, December 29, 2002, at http://www.cnet.com (retrieved June 16, 2003).

Borland, John, 'Verizon Gets 14 Days to ID File-swapper', CNET NEWS.com, April 24, 2003, at http://www.cnet.com (retrieved June 16, 2003).

Borland, John, 'Pressplay to Offer Unlimited Downloads', *Tech News*, CNET.com, July 31, 2002, at http://www.cnet.com (retrieved June 23, 2003).

Borland, John and S. Olsen, 'RealNetworks Seeks Listen.com Buyout', *Tech News*, CNET.com, April 21, 2003, at http://www.news.com.com/2100-1027-997704.html (retrieved September 30, 2003).

Bowman, Lisa M., 'Are File Traders Next?', CNET NEWS.com, April 25, 2003, at http://www.cnet.com (retrieved June 16, 2003).

Bowman, Lisa M., 'Consumer Claims Victory in CD Lawsuit', *Tech News*, CNET.com, February 22, 2002, at http://www.cnet.com (retrieved June 16, 2003).

Bowman, Lisa M., 'MusicNet, Pressplay Closing in on Labels', *Tech News*, CNET.com, October 15, 2002, at http://www.cnet.com (retrieved June 23, 2003).

Bowman, Lisa M., 'Napster Orders Strict Service Upgrade', CNET NEWS.com, June 28, 2001 at http://www.cnet.com (retrieved June 16, 2003).

Bowman, Lisa M., 'Sony to Send Songs via Scour', *Tech News*, CNET.com, May 14, 2002, at http://www.cnet.com (retrieved June 16, 2003).

Bowman, Ward S., 'Tying Strategies and the Leverage Problem', 67 *Yale Law Journal* 19 (1957).

Bresler, Judith, 'Begged, Borrowed, or Stolen: Whose Art is it Anyway?' presented to the New York Chapter of the Copyright Society of America, January 16, 2003, unpublished manuscript.

Breyer, Stephen, 'The Uneasy Case for Copyright: A Study of Copyright in Books, Photocopies, and Computer Programs', 84 *Harvard Law Review* 281 (1970).

Brooks, Frederick, *The Mythical Man Month* (Reading, MA: Addison-Wesley, 1975).

Buchanan, James M. and Yong J. Yoon, 'Symmetric Tragedies: Commons and Anti-Commons', 43 *Journal of Law and Economics* 1 (2000).

Calabresi, Guido and John T. Hirschoff, 'Toward a Test for Strict Liability in Torts', 81 *Yale Law Journal* 1055 (1972).

Calabresi, Guido and Douglas Melamed, 'Property Rules, Liability Rules, and Inalienability: One View of the Cathedral', 85 *Harvard Law Review* 1089 (1972).

Cha, Ariana Eunjung, 'Harry Potter and the Copyright Lawyer' (2003) at http://www.washingtonpost.com/wp-dyn/articles/A7412-2003june17.html (retrieved June 30, 2003).

Chessen, J., 'Information and Privacy', American Bankers Association, Washington, DC (2000).

Childs, Lisa C., 'Rite-Hite Corp. v. Kelley Co.: The Federal Circuit Awards Damages for Harm Done to a Patent not in Suit', 27 *Loyola University Chicago Law Journal* 665 (1996).

Chisum, Donald S., *Patents: A Treatise on the Law of Patentability, Validity, and*

Infringement (New York: Matthew Bender & Company, 1996).

Clapes, Anthony, 'Confessions of an Amicus Curiae: Technophobia, Law and Creativity in the Digital Arts', 19 *University of Dayton Law Review* 903 (1994).

Clarke, Ian, 'A distributed decentralized information storage and retrieval system', MS thesis, Division of Informatics, University of Edinburgh (1999).

Clarke, Ian, Oskar Sandberg, Brandon Wiley and Theodore W. Hong, 'Freenet: A Distributed Anonymous Information Storage and Retrieval System', *ADAISARS in Designing Privacy Enhancing Technologies: International Workshop on Design Issues in Anonymity and Unobservability*, LNCS 2009 (ed. by Hannes Federrath, New York: Springer 2001).

Coase, Ronald H., 'The Nature of the Firm', 4 *Economica* 386 (1937).

Coase, Ronald H., 'The Federal Communications Commission', 2 *Journal of Law and Economics* 1 (1959).

Coase, Ronald H., 'The Problem of Social Costs', 3 *Journal of Law and Economics* 1 (1960).

Cohen, Julie E., 'A Right to Read Anonymously: A Closer Look at Copyright Management in Cyberspace', 28 *Connecticut Law Review* 981 (1996).

Committee on the Judiciary House of Representative, 'Testimony, 97th Cong., Home Recording of Copyrighted Works', April 12, 1982.

Computer Science and Telecommunications Board, National Research Council, *The Digital Dilemma: Intellectual Property in the Information Age* (Washington, DC: National Academy Press, 2000).

Conner, K.R. and C.K. Prahalad, 'A Resource-based Theory of the Firm: Knowledge versus Opportunism', 7 *Organization Science* 5:477 (1996).

Coombe, Rosemary J., 'Author/izing the Celebrity: Publicity Rights, Postmodern Politics, and Unauthorized Genders', 10 *Cardozo Arts and Entertainment Law Journal* 365, 370–73 (1992).

Cooter, Robert, 'Unity in Tort, Contract, and Property: The Model of Precaution', 73 *California Law Review* 1 (1985).

Cooter, Robert and Thomas Ulen, *Law and Economics* 145 (Reading, MA: Addison-Wesley, 1988).

Copyright Clearance Center, 'Comments: Promotion of Distance Education through Digital Technologies', US Copyright Office, Docket No. 98-12A, February 5, 1999.

Cranor, Laurie F. and Joel R. Reidenberg, 'Can User Agents Accurately Represent Privacy Notices?' Discussion Paper 1.0 (2002), Telecommunications Policy Research Conference, Washington, DC, unpublished manuscript.

Crews, Kenneth D., 'Copyright at a Turning Point: Corporate Response to the Changing Environment', *Intellectual Property Law* 277 (1996).

Cusamano, Michael A., *Japan's Software Factories: A Challenge to American Management* (Oxford: Oxford University Press, 1991).

Cusamano, Michael A. and Richard W. Selby, *Microsoft Secrets: How the World's Most Powerful Software Company Creates Technology, Shapes Markets, and Manages People* (New York: Simon and Schuster, 1995).

Dalle, James M. and Nicholas Jullien, 'Open Source v. Proprietary Software' (2002), at http://opensource.mit.edu/online_papers.php (retrieved June 23, 2003).

Dam, Kenneth, 'Some Economic Considerations in the Intellectual Property Protection of Software', 24 *Journal of Legal Studies* 321 (1995).

Dam, Kenneth, 'Self Help in the Digital Jungle', 28 *Journal of Law and Economics* 393 (1999).

Dasgupta, Partha and Joseph Stiglitz, 'Uncertainty, Industrial Structure, and the Speed of R&D', 11 Bell *Journal of Ecomics* 1 (1980).

Demsetz, Harold, 'When Does the Rule of Liability Matter?', 1 *Journal of Legal Studies* 13 (1972).

Demsetz, Harold, 'Why Regulate Utilities?', 11 *Journal of Law and Economics* 55 (1968).

Douglas, Jeanne-Vida, 'Altnet Tops 2 Million Downloads', CNET NEWS.com, July 2, 2002, at http://www.cnet.com (retrieved June 16, 2003).

Easterbrook, Frank H., 'Intellectual Property is Still Property', 12 *Harvard Journal of Law and Public Policy* 108 (1990).

Electronic Privacy Information Center, 'Pretty Poor Privacy: An Assessment of P3P and Internet Privacy', at http://www.epic.org/reports/prettypoorprivacy.html (retrieved October 19, 2002).

Ellickson, Robert C., *Order Without Law: How Neighbors Settle Disputes* (Cambridge, MA: Harvard University Press, 1991).

European Parliament and the Council of 11 March 1996, Directive 96/9/EC on the Legal Protection of Databases (1996), *Official Journal* No. L77 of 27 March 1996, p. 20, Art. 71, Brussels.

European Parliament and the Council of the European Union, Common Position (EC) No. 48/2000, 47, 28 September (2000).

Farrell, Joseph, 'Standardization and Intellectual Property', 30 *Jurimetrics Journal* 35 (1989).

Federal Trade Commission, 'Privacy Online: Fair Information Practices in the Electronic Marketplace: A Federal Trade Commission Report and Congress', May, 2000, at http://www.ftc.gov/opa/2001/10/privacyagenda.html (retrieved October 19, 2002).

Fellmeth, Aaron X., 'Cyber Trespass Comes of Age', 19(2), *Intellectual Property Lawyer Newsletter* (Winter, 2001).

Felten, Edward, 'Another DMCA Attack on Interoperation', at http://www.freedom.to.tinker.com/archives/000253.html (retrieved June 29, 2003).

Fessenden, Gloria, 'Peer-to-Peer Technology: Analysis of Contributory Infringement and Fair Use', 42 *Idea* 391 (2002).

Fischmann, Brett and Dan Moylan, 'The Evolving Common Law Doctrine of Copyright Misuse: A Unified Theory and its Application to Software', 15 *Berkeley Technology Law Journal* 3 (2001).

Fisher, William W., 'Reconstructing the Fair Use Doctrine', 101 *Harvard Law Review* 1661 (1988).

Fitzgerald, Brian, 'Open Source Software: More Placebo than Panacea?', University of Limerick (2002), at http://www.infonomics.nl/FLOSS/workshop/papers/ fitzgerald.htm (retrieved June 23, 2003).

Franck, Egon and Carola Jungwirth, 'Reconciling Investors and Donors – The Governance Structure of Open Source', working paper, University of Zurich, p. 15 (2002), at http://opensource.mit.edu/online_papers.php (retrieved June 23, 2003).

Franke, Nikolaus and Eric von Hippel, 'Satisfying Heterogeneous User Needs via Innovation Toolkits: The Case of Apache Security Software' (2000), at http://opensource.mit.edu/papers/frankevonhippel.pdf (retrieved June 1, 2003).

Fried, I., 'Apple Plants Seed of iTunes for Windows', *Tech News*, CNET.com, April 30, 2003, at http://www.cnet.com (retrieved June 16, 2003).

Friedman, David, 'Standards as Intellectual Property: An Economic Approach', 19 *University of Dayton Law Review* 1109 (1994).

Friedman, David, 'In Defense of Private Orderings', 13 *Berkeley Technology Law*

Journal 3 (1998).

Gabszewicz, Jean, Lynne Pepall and Jacques-Francoise Thisse, 'Sequential Entry with Brand Loyalty Caused by Consumer Learning by Using', 40 *Journal of Industrial Economics* 397 (1992).

Gallini, Nancy, 'Deterrence through Market-sharing: A Strategic Incentive for Licensing', 74 *American Economic Review* 931 (1984).

Garzarelli, Giampaolo, 'Open Source Software and the Economics of Organization', unpublished paper, Universita degli Studi di Roma (2002), at http://opensource.mit.edu/online_papers.php (retrieved June 23, 2003).

Gasaway, Laura M., 'Values Conflict in the Digital Environment: Librarians versus Copyright Holders', 24 *Columbia Journal of Law and the Arts* 115 (2000).

Gervais, Daniel J., 'E-Commerce and Intellectual Property: Lock it Up or License?', at http://www.copyright.com/News/AboutArticlesIntellectualProp.asp (retrieved June 15, 2001).

Ghosh, Shubha, 'The Merits of Ownership', 15 *Harvard Journal of Law and Technology* 453 (2002).

Giacoppo, Erin, 'Avoding the Tragedy of Frankenstein: The Application of the Right of Publicity to the Use of Digitally Reproduced Actors in Film', 48 *Hastings Law Journal* 601, 604–8 (1997).

Gilbert, Richard J. and Michael L. Katz, 'When Good Value Chains Go Bad: The Economics of Indirect Liability for Copyright Infringement', 52 *Hastings Law Journal* 961 (2001).

Gilbert, Richard J. and Steven C. Sunshine, 'The Use of Innovation Markets: A Reply to Hay, Rapp, & Hoerner', 64 *Antitrust Law Journal* 75 (1995).

Gilles, Stephen G., 'Negligence, Strict Liability, and the Cheapest Cost-Avoider', 78 *Virginia Law Review* 1291 (1992).

Ginsburg, Jane C., 'Authors and Users in Copyright', 45 *Journal of the Copyright Society of the U.S.A.* 1 (1997).

Ginsburg, Jane C., 'From Having Copies to Experiencing Works: The Development of an Access Right in U.S. Copyright Law', *U.S. Intellectual Property: Law and Policy* (Hugh Hansen, ed, London: Sweet and Maxwell, 2000).

Ginsburg, Jane C., 'Can Copyright Become User-Friendly? Essay Review of Jessica Litman', 25 *Columbia Journal of Law and the Arts* 71 (2002).

Goldstein, Paul, *Copyright's Highway: From Gutenberg to the Celestial Jukebox* (Palo Alto, CA: Stanford University Press, 1994).

Gordon, Wendy J., 'Fair Use as Market Failure: A Structural and Economic Analysis of the Betamax Case and its Predecessors', 82 *Columbia Law Review* 1600 (1982).

Gordon, Wendy J., 'An Inquiry into the Merits of Copyright: The Challenges of Consistency, Consent, and Encouragement Theory', 41 *Stanford Law Review* 1343 (1989).

Gordon, Wendy, 'Intellectual Property as Price Discrimination: Implications for Contract', 73 *Chi-Kent Law Review* 1367 (1998).

Grady, Mark F., 'A Positive Economic Theory of the Right of Publicity', 1 *UCLA Entertainment Law Review* 97 (1994).

Grandpre, Vincent M. de, 'Understanding the Market for Celebrity: An Economic Analysis of the Right of Publicity', 12 *Fordham Intellectual Property, Media and Entertainment Law Journal* 73, 114 (2001).

Griffin, Jim, Statement, 'The Future of Digital Music: Is there an Upside to Digital Downloading?', Senate Judiciary Committee, Washington, DC, July 11, 2000.

Haddock, Donald D. and Frederick S. McChesney, 'Do Liability Rules Deter

Takings?', in *The Economic Consequences of Liability Law: In Defense of Common Law Liability* (ed R.E. Meiners and B. Yandle, New York: Quorum Books, 1991).

Hansen, Evan, 'Microsoft Prepares Reply to iTunes', *Tech News*, CNET.com, May 23, 2003, at http://www.cnet.com (retrieved June 16, 2003).

Hansen, Evan and Lisa M. Bowman, 'Court: Napster filters must be foolproof', CNET NEWS.com, July 12, 2001, at http://www.cnet.com (retrieved June 16, 2003).

Hansen, Evan and Jim Hu, 'RealNetworks Plugs in MusicNET', *Tech News*, CNET.com, December 4, 2001, at http://www.cnet.com (retrieved June 23, 2003).

Hansmann, Henry B., 'The Role of Nonprofit Enterprise', 89 *Yale Law Journal* 835 (1980).

Healey, John, 'Microsoft using KaZaa as a Marketing Portal', *L.A. Times*, September 22, 2002.

Heeger, George A., 'University of Maryland University College, Testimony, Concerning the Technology, Education, and Copyright Harmonization Act of 2001', House Judiciary Committee, U.S. House of Representatives, Washington, DC, March 13, 2001.

Hoerner, Ronald J., 'Patent Misuse: Portents for the 1990s', 59 *Antitrust Law Journal* 687 (1991).

Hoppin, Jason, 'Judge Leaning Studios' Way in DMCA Fight', The Recorder, IP Law Practice Center, May 16, 2003, at http://www.cnet.com (retrieved June 16, 2003).

Hovenkamp, Herbert, *Economics & Federal Antitrust Law* (St. Paul, MN: West Publishing Co., 1985).

Hu, Jim, 'Pressplay Comes to Life after Long Wait', *Tech News*, CNET.com, December 19, 2001, at http://news.com.com/2100-1023-277176.html (retrieved September 30, 2003).

Hu, Jim, 'AOL Fills Bargain Bin with New Music', *Tech News*, CNET.com, June 18, 2002, at http://www.cnet.com (retrieved June 16, 2003).

Hu, Jim, 'KaZaa Picks Up the Speed with Update', CNET NEWS.com, February 11, 2002, at http://www.cnet.com (retrieved June 16, 2003).

Hu, Jim, 'Liquid Audio to Evaporate', *Tech News*, CNET.com, December 6, 2002, at http://www.cnet.com (retrieved June 16, 2003).

Hu, Jim, 'Listen.com Inks Broadband Deals', *Tech News*, CNET.com, July 31, 2002, at http://www.cnet.com (retrieved June 23, 2003).

Hu, Jim, 'Napster: Gimme Shelter in Chapter 11', CNET NEWS.com, June 3, 2002, at http://www.cnet.com (retrieved June 16, 2003).

Hu, Jim, 'Pressplay Bid Points to Napster Remix', *Tech News*, CNET.com, May 19, 2003, at http://www.cnet.com (retrieved June 23, 2003).

Hu, Jim, 'Warner Whistles a New Digital Tune', *Tech News*, CNET.com, September 23, 2002, at http://www.cnet.com (retrieved June 16, 2003).

Hugenholtz, Bernt, 'Program Schedules, Event Data, and Telephone Subscriber Listings under the Database Directive: The Spinoff Doctrine in the Netherlands and elsewhere in Europe', 26 *AMI* (the Dutch Journal of Copyright Law) 161 (2002).

Hylton, Keith N. and Michael Salinger, 'Tying Law and Policy: A Decision Theoretic Approach', 69 *Antitrust Law Journal* 469 (2001).

Iannacci, Federico, 'The Economics of Open Source Networks' (2001), at http://opensource.mit.edu/online_papers.php (retrieved June 23, 2003).

Information Infrastructure Task Force, *Intellectual Property and the National Information Infrastructure: The Report of the Working Group on Intellectual Property Rights*, 177 (Washington, DC: US Department of Commerce, 1995).

Jaszi, Peter, 'Testimony, Exemption to Prohibition on Circumvention of Copyright

Protection Systems for Access Control Technologies' (2000), at http://www.copyright.gov/1201/hearings (retrieved June 16, 2001).

Johnson-Laird, Andrew, 'Software Reverse Engineering in the Real World', 19 *University of Dayton Law Review* 843 (1994).

Jung, Gregory K., 'Dr. Seuss Enterprises v. Penguin Books', 13 *Berkeley Technology Law Journal* 119 (1998).

Junnarkar, Sandeep, 'P2P boost for Microsoft's Net?', CNET NEWS.com, September 16, 2002, at http://www.cnet.com (retrieved June 16, 2003).

Kane, M., 'Liquid Audio finds a Buyer', *Tech News*, CNET.com, June 13, 2002, at http://www.cnet.com (retrieved June 16, 2003).

Kanellos, M., 'Gateway tests Waters of Music Business', *Tech News*, CNET.com, April 26, 2002, at http://www.cnet.com (retrieved June 16, 2003).

Katz, Michael and Carl Shapiro, 'Network Externalities, Competition, and Compatibility', 75 *American Economic Review* 424 (1985).

Katz, Michael and Carl Shapiro, 'Systems Competition and Network Effects', *Journal of Economic Perspectives* 8 (1994).

King, Rawlston, 'Linux Market Share Within Web Server Sector to Grow' (2003), at http://thewhir.com/features/linux-market-share.cfm (retrieved June 1, 2003).

Kitch, Edmund W., 'The Nature and Function of the Patent System, 20 *Journal of Law and Economics* 265 (1977).

Kitch, Edmund W., 'Can the Internet Shrink Fair Use?', 78 *Nebraska Law Review* 880 (1999).

Klein, Benjamin, 'Market Power in Antitrust: Economic Analysis after Kodak', 3 *Supreme Court Economic Review* 43 (1993).

Klemperer, Paul, 'Price Wars Caused by Switching Costs', 56 *Review of Economic Studies* 405 (1989).

Kobak, James B., 'The New Patent Misuse Law', 71 *Journal of the Patent and Trademark Office Society* 859 (1989).

Kobak, James B., 'The Misuse Doctrine and Intellectual Property Litigation', 1 *Boston University Journal of Science and Technology Law* (1995).

Kohn, Bob, 'A Primer on the Law of Webcasting and Digital Music Delivery', at http://www.kohnmusic.com/articles/newprimer.html (retrieved June 29, 2003)

Kozinski, Alex and Christoper Newman, 'What's So Fair about Fair Use?', *Journal of the Copyright Society of the U.S.A.* 513 (2000).

La Monica, Martin, 'Microsoft Makes P2P Play', CNET NEWS.com, February 26, 2003, at http://www.cnet.com (retrieved June 16, 2003).

Lakhani, Karim and Robert Wolf, 'Does Free Software Mean Free Labor: Characteristics of Participants in Open Source Communities' (Boston Consulting Group, 2001), at http://osdn.com/bcg (retrieved June 1, 2001).

Landes, William M. and Richard A. Posner, *Economic Structure of Tort Law*, (Cambridge, MA: Harvard University Press, 1987).

Landes, William M. and Richard A. Posner, 'Trademark Law: An Economic Perspective', 30 *Journal of Law and Economics* 265, 269–70 (1987).

Landes, William M. and Richard A. Posner, 'An Economic Analysis of Copyright Law', 18 *Journal of Legal Studies* 325 (1989).

Landes, William M. and Richard A. Posner, 'Indefinitely Renewable Copyright', July 18, 2002, at http://www.ssrn.com (retrieved June 23, 2003).

Lange, David, 'Recognizing the Public Domain', 44 *Law and Contemporary Problems* 147 (1981).

Lee, Mark S., 'Agents of Chaos: Judicial Confusion in Defining the Right of Publicity-free Special Interface', 23 *Loyola of Los Angeles Entertainment Law Journal* 471, 478 (2003).

Lemley, Mark, 'The Economic Irrationality of the Patent Misuse Doctrine', 78 *California Law Review* 1599 (1990).

Lemley Mark A., 'The Economics of Improvement in Intellectual Property Law', 75 *Texas Law Review* 989 (1997).

Lemley, Mark A. and David McGowan, 'Legal Implications of Network Economic Effects', 86 *California Law Review* 479 (1998).

Lessig, Lawrence, *Code and Other Laws of Cyberspace* (New York: Basic Books, 2001).

Lessig, Lawrence, *The Future of Ideas: The Fate of the Commons in a Connected World* (New York: Basic Books, 2002).

Leval, Pierre N., 'Toward a Fair Use Standard', 103 *Harvard Law Review* 1105 (1990).

Lewis, O. Yale, 'Personality, Persona, and Publicity Rights', at http://www.hllaw.com/a_personality.html (retrieved June 16, 2003).

Licklider, J.C.R. and R.W. Taylor, 'The Computer as a Communications Device', at http://ftp.digital.com/pub/DEC/SRC/research-reports/SRC-061.pdf (retrieved June 1, 2003).

Liebowitz, Stanley J., 'Copying and Indirect Appropriability: Photocopying of Journals', *Journal of Political Economy* 945 (1985).

Lindblom, Charles E., 'The Science of Muddling Through', 19 *Public Adminstration Review* 79 (1959).

Loren, Lydia P., 'Redefining the Market Failure Approach to Fair Use in an Era of Copyright Permission Systems', 5 *Journal of Intellectual Property Law* 1 (1997).

MacKie-Mason, Jeffrey K. and A.L. Jankovich, 'PEAK: Pricing Electronic Access to Knowledge', at http://www-personal.umich.edu/~jmm/papers/PEAK (retrieved June 5, 2001).

Madow, Michael, 'Private Ownership of the Public Image: Popular Culture and Publicity Rights', 81 *California Law Review* 125, 139 (1993).

Magaziner, Ira, 'Creating a Framework for Electronic Commerce', Progress and Freedom Foundation, at http://www.pff.org/ira_magaziner.htm (retrieved June 4, 2002).

Mann, C.C., 'The Heavenly Jukebox', *Atlantic Monthly*, September (2000).

Mariano, Gwendolyn, 'Audiogalaxy to ask first, trade later', CNET NEWS.com, June 18, 2002, at http://www.cnet.com (retrieved June 16, 2003).

Mariano, Gwendolyn, 'BMG to Offer Tunes on the Go', *Tech News*, CNET.com, January 28, 2002, at http://www.cnet.com (retrieved June 16, 2003).

Mariano, Gwendolyn, 'Full Audio Gets New Music, Funding', *Tech News*, CNET.com, June 18, 2002, http://www.cnet.com (retrieved June 16, 2003).

Mariano, Gwendolyn, 'Gateway Grooves to Emusic', *Tech News*, CNET.com, April 29, 2002, at http://www.cnet.com (retrieved June 16, 2003).

Mariano, Gwendolyn, 'Muze Attracts Fourth Major Label', *Tech News*, CNET.com, June 11, 2002, at http://www.cnet.com (retrieved June 16, 2003).

Mariano, Gwendolyn, 'Off-key Efforts Hinder Paid Net Music', *Tech News*, CNET.com, June 5, 2002, at http://www.cnet.com (retrieved June 16, 2003).

Mariano, Gwendolyn, 'Rival Services Prepare for Napster Onslaught', *Tech News*, CNET.com, March 1, 2001, at http://www.cnet.com (retrieved June 16, 2003).

Mariano, Gwendolyn, 'Universal Licenses Music to Streamwaves', *Tech News*, CNET NEWS.com, June 4, 2002, at http://www.cnet.com (retrieved June 16, 2003).

Mariano, Gwendolyn, 'Universal, Sony to Trim Download Prices', *Tech News*,

CNET.com, June 12, 2002, http://www.cnet.com (retrieved June 16, 2003).

Martone, Patricia A., William J. Gilbreth and Richard G. Gervase, 'The Patent Misuse Defense – Its Continued Expansion and Contraction', 1 *Intellectual Property Antitrust* 325 (1996).

Maurer, Stephen M., P. Bernt Hugenholtz and Harlan J. Onsrud, 'Europe's Database Experiment', 294 *Science* 789 (2001).

McConnell, Steve, 'Brooks' Law Repealed', *IEEE Software*, November–December, 6 (1999).

McCullagh, Declan, 'Lexmark invokes DMCA in Toner Suit', CNET.com, January 8, 2003, at http://www.news.com.com/2100-1023-979791.html (retrieved June 29, 2003).

McCullagh, Declan, 'Judge: KaZaa can be sued in U.S.', CNET NEWS.com, January 10, 2003, at http://www.cnet.com (retrieved June 16, 2003).

McGowan, David, 'Innovation, Uncertainty, and Stability in Antitrust Law', 16 *Berkeley Technical Law Journal* 729 (2001).

Menell, Peter S., 'The Challenges of Reforming Intellectual Property Protection for Computer Software', 94 *Columbia Law Review* 2644 (1994).

Merges, Robert P., 'Intellectual Property and Costs of Commercial Exchange: A Review Essay', 93 *Michigan Law Review* 1570 (1995).

Merges, Robert P., 'Contracting into Liability Rules: Intellectual Property Rights and Collective Rights Organizations', 84 *California Law Review* 1293 (1996).

Merges, Robert P., 'The End of Friction? Property Rights and Contract in the Newtonian World of On-Line Commerce', 12 *Berkeley Technology Law Journal* 115 (1997).

Merrill, Thomas W., 'Trespass, Nuisance, and the Costs of Determining Property Rights', 14 *Journal of Legal Studies* 13 (1985).

Metiu, Anca and Bruce Kogut, 'Distributed Knowledge and the Global Organization of Software Development', unpublished manuscript, University of Pennsylvania, 15, n.4 (2001), at http://opensource.mit.edu/online_papers.php (retrieved June 23, 2003).

Meyer, M.H. and L. Lopez, 'Technology Strategy in a Software Products Company', 12 *Journal of Product Innovation Management* 4:194 1995).

Miller, Arthur, 'Copyright Protection for Computer Programs, Databases, and Computer Generated Works: Is Anything New since CONTU?' 106 *Harvard Law Review* 977 (1993).

Mirchin, David, 'Statement, Rulemaking on Exemptions from Prohibition on Circumvention of Technological Measures that Control Access to Copyrighted Works' (2000), at http://www.loc.gov/copyright/1201/hearings (retrieved May 19, 2001).

Mockus, Audris, Roy T. Fielding, and James Herbsleb, 'A Case Study of Open Source Software Development: the Apache Server' (2001), at http://opensource.mit.edu/online_papers.php (retrieved June 23, 2003).

Muris, Timothy, 'Protecting Consumers' Privacy: 2002 and Beyond', The Privacy 2001 Conference, Cleveland, Ohio, October 4, 2001, at http://www.ftc.gov/speeches/muris/privisp1002.htm (retrieved June 4 2002).

Nadel, Mark S., 'Maximizing Consumer Benefits from E-commerce Competition: Emerging Obstacles & Policy Options', 14 *Harvard Journal of Law and Technology* (2001).

Nelson, Richard and Robert Merges, 'On Complex Economics of Patent Scope', 90 *Columbia Law Review* 839.

Netanel, Neil W., 'Copyright and a Democratic Society', 106 *Yale Law Journal* 283 (1996).

Network Web Server Survey, May, 2003, at http://news.netcraft.com (retrieved June 1, 2003).

Nimmer, David, 'Ignoring the Public, Part I: On the Absurd Complexity of the Digital Audio Transmission Right', 7 *UCLA Entertainment Law Review* 189 (2000).

Nimmer, Melville B., 'The Right of Publicity', 19 *Law and Contemporary Problems* 203, 215–18 (1954).

Nimmer, Melville, 'Does Copyright Abridge the First Amendment Guarantees of Free Speech and Press?', 17 *UCLA Law Review* 1180 (1970).

Nisbet, Miriam M., 'Initial Comments', at http://www.loc.gov/copyright/1201/ comments (retrieved May 19, 2001).

O'Reilly, Timothy, 'Lessons from open source development software', 41 *Communications of the ACM* 4:33 (1999).

O'Rourke, Maureen A., 'Fencing Cyberspace: Drawing Borders in a Virtual World', 82 *Minnesota Law Review* 609 (1998).

Ochoa, Tyler, 'Dr. Seuss, The Juice, and Fair Use: How the Grinch Silenced a Parody', 45 *Journal of the Copyright Society of the U.S.A.* 546 (1998).

Odlyzko, Andrew, 'Stronger Copyright Protection for Cyberspace: Desirable, Inevitable, and Irrelevant', at http://www.research.att.com/~amo (retrieved June 26, 2001).

Odlyzko, Andrew, 'Tragic Loss or Good Riddance? The Impending Demise of Traditional Scholarly Journals', *International Journal of Human Computer Studies*, 42, 71 (1995).

Okerson, Ann S., 'Buy or Lease? Two Models for Scholarly Information at the End (or the Beginning) of an Era', 125 *Daedalus* 55 (1996) at http://www.library.yale.edu/~okerson/daedalus.html (retrieved June 26, 2001).

Okerson, Ann, 'The Transition to Electronic Content Licensing: The Institutional Context in 1997', Scholarly Communication and Technology Conference of the Andrew W. Mellon Foundation, Emory University, April 24–25, 1997, 1, at http://www.library.yale.edu/~okerson/mellon.html (retrieved March 23, 2003).

Olsen, Mancur, *The Logic of Collective Action* (Cambridge, MA: Harvard University Press, 1972).

Olsen, Steven, 'MusicMatch in Tune with Labels', *TechNews*, CNET.com, November 13, 2002, at http://www.cnet.com (retrieved June 16, 2003).

Owen, Bruce M. and Steven S. Wildman, *Video Economics* (Cambridge, MA: Harvard University Press, 1992).

Parchomovsky, Gideon and Peter Siegelman, 'Towards an Integrated Theory of Intellectual Property', 88 *Virginia Law Review* 1455 (2002).

Patterson, L. Ray and Craig Joyce, 'Monopolizing the Law: the Scope of Copyright Protection for Law Reports and Statutory Compilations', 36 *UCLA Law Review* 719, 763, n.155 (1989).

Prens, Bruce, 'The Open Source Definition' (1998) at http://prens.com/Articles/ OSD.html (retrieved June 1, 2003).

Perlman, Victor S., 'Reply Comments. Rulemaking on Exemptions from Prohibition on Circumvention of Technological Measures that Control Access to Copyrighted Works' (2000), at http://www.copyright.gov/1201/reply (retrieved May 19, 2002).

Philp, Daniel, 'Who Owns Satellite Transmissions?', at www.cs.dartmouth.edu/ ~dphilp/paper2.html (retrieved February 12, 2003).

Plant, Arnold, 'The Economic Aspects of Copyright in Books', 1 *Economica* 167

(1934).

Pleatsikas, Christopher and David Teece, 'The Analysis of Market Definition and Market Power in the Context of Rapid Innovation', 19 *International Journal of Industrial Orgasnization* 665, 666 (2001).

Posner, Richard, 'The Economics of Privacy', *Papers and Proceedings*, American Economic Association, May, 1981.

Posner, Richard, 'The Next Step in the Antitrust Treatment of Restricted Distribution: Per Se Legality', 48 *University of Chicago Law Review* 6 (1981).

Posner, Richard A., 'When is Parody Fair Use?', 21 *Journal of Legal Studies* 67 (1992).

Prosser, William L., 'Privacy', 48 *California Law Review* 383, 389 (1954).

Raymond, Eric S., *The Cathedral and the Bazaar: Musings on Linux and Open Source by an Accidental Revolutionary* (Sebastopol: O'Reilly and Associates, 2001).

Reichman, Jerry H., 'Computer Programs as Applied Scientific Know-How: Implications of Copyright Protection for Commercialized University Research', 42 *Vanderbilt Law Review* 639 (1989).

Reidenberg, Joel R., 'Privacy in the Information Economy: A Fortress or Frontier for Individual Rights', 44 *Federal Communications Law Journal* 195 (1992).

Reidenberg, Joel R. and Francois Gamet-Pol, 'The Fundamental Role of Privacy and Confidence in the Network', 30 *Wake Forest Law Review* 105 (1995).

Reuters, 'IMG Snaps up Peer-to-Peer Service, *Tech News*, CNET.com, July 30, 2002, at httl://www.cnet.com (retrieved June 16, 2003).

Reuters, 'KaZaa Nears Download Record', CNET NEWS.com, May 22, 2003, at http://www.cnet.com (retrieved June 16, 2003).

Reuters, 'Listen.com Discounts CD-copying Fee', *Tech News*, CNET.com, February 13, 2003, at http://www.cnet.com (retrieved June 16, 2003).

Reuters, 'Net Music Giveaway Plays Encore', *Tech News*, CNET.com, January 20, 2003, at http://www.cnet.com (retrieved June 16, 2003).

Rose, B. and L. Rosin, 'Internet V: Startling New Insights About the Internet and Streaming' (New York: Arbitron/Edison Media Research, 2000).

Rota, Sandra, Marc von Wartburg and Margit Osterloh, 'Trust and commerce in open source: A contradiction?', working paper, University of Zurich (2002), at http://www.wiwiss.fu-berlin.de/w3/w3sydow/EURAM/pdf_2002/EURAM%20Paper%20Rota%20et%20al.pdf (retrieved June 23, 2003).

Saladi, Indira, 'Computer Software: Patentable Subject Matter Jurisprudence comes of Age', 18 *John Marshall Journal of Computer and Information Law* 113 (1999).

Saliba, Claire, 'MP3.com Inks Tentative Licensing Pact', *Wireless News Factor*, October 18, 2000, at http://www.wirelessnewsfactor.com/perl/story/4575.html (retrieved June 1, 2003).

Salop, Steven C. and R. Craig Romaine, 'Preserving Monopoly: Economic Analysis, Legal Standards, and Microsoft', 7 *George Mason Law Review* 617 (1999).

Samuelson, Pamela and Suzanne Scotchmer, 'The Law and Economics of Reverse Engineering', 111 *Yale Law Journal* 1575 (2002).

Samuelson, Pamela, Randall Davis, Mitchell D. Kapor and Jerry H. Reichman, 'A Manifesto Concerning the Legal Protection of Computer Programs', 94 *Columbia Law Review* 2318 (1994).

Scherer, Frederick M., 'Panel Discussion, The Value of Patents and Other Legally Protected Commercial Rights', 53 *Antitrust Law Journal* 535 (1985).

Schmalensee, Richard, 'Monopolistic Two-Part Pricing Arrangements', 11 *Bell*

Journal of Economics 445 (1981).

Schumpeter, Joseph A., *Capitalism, Socialism, and Democracy* (New York: Harper & Brothers, 1947).

Scotchmer, Suzanne, 'Standing on the Shoulders of Giants: Cumulative Research and the Patent Law', 5 *Journal of Economic Perspectives* 29 (1991).

Shapiro, Carl and Hal R. Varian, *Information Rules* (Boston, MA: Harvard Business School Press, 1999).

Shapiro, Michael L., 'An Analysis of the Fair Use Defense in Dr. Seuss Enterprises v. Penguin', 28 *Golden Gate University Law Review* 1 (1998).

Sharfman, Keith, 'A New Procedure for Resolving Valuation Disputes', unpublished manuscript, Rutgers University School of Law (2003).

Shavell, Steven, 'The Fundamental Divergence between the Private and the Social Motive to Use the Legal System', 26 *Journal of Legal Studies* 575 (1997).

Shelanski, Howard A. and J. Gregory Sidak, 'Antitrust Divestiture in Network Industries', 68 *University of Chicago Law Review* 1 (2001).

Simon, Herbert, *The Sciences of the Artificial* (Cambridge, MA: MIT Press, 1996).

Spence, A. Michael, 'Nonlinear Prices and Welfare', 8 *Journal of Public Economics* 66 (1979).

Sterk, Stewart E., 'Rhetoric and Reality in Copyright Law', 94 *Michigan Law Review* 1197 (1996).

US Copyright Office, 'A Review of Copyright Licensing: Retransmission of Broadcast Signals' (1997), at http://www.loc.gov/copyright/reports (retrieved January 24, 2002).

US Copyright Office, 'Digital Millenium Copyright Act Section 104 Study' (2001), at http://www.copyright.gov/reports/studies/dmca/dmca_study.html (retrieved June 16, 2002).

US Copyright Office, 'Exemption to Prohibition on Circumvention of Copyright Protection Systems for Access Control Technologies: Final Rule', 65 *Federal Register* 64555 (2000), at http://www.copyright.gov/fedreg/2000/65fr64555.pdf (retrieved July 22, 2001).

US Copyright Office, 'Public Performance of Sound Recordings: Definition of a Service', 65 *Federal Register* 77292 (2001).

US Copyright Office, 'Report on Copyright and Digital Distance Education' (1999), at http://www.loc.gov/copyright/docs/de_rprt.pdf (retrieved May 19, 2001).

US Department of Justice and Federal Trade Commission, *Antitrust Guidelines for the Licensing of Intellectual Property*, Washington, DC: Government Printing Office (1995).

US Department of Justice, Antitrust Division, 'Second Amended Final Judgment: U.S. v. ASCAP' (2001), at http://www.usdoj.gov/atr/cases/f63000/6395.html (retrieved May 5, 2001).

University of Maryland University College, 'Comments, Promotion of Distance Education through Digital Technologies', (1999) at http://www.loc.gov/copyright/disted/comments.html (retrieved May 19, 2001).

Vaughan, J.C., Association of American Universities, et al., 'Comments: Rulemaking on Exemptions from Prohibition on Circumvention of Technological Measures that Control Access to Copyrighted Works' (2000), at http://www.loc.gov/copyright/1201/hearings (retrieved May 19, 2001).

Vogel, Jason M., 'The Cat in the Hat's Latest Bad Trick', 20 *Cardozo Law Review* 287 (1998).

Volokh, Eugene, 'Freedom of Speech and Intellectual Property after Eldred, 44 Liquormart, Saderup, and Bartwick', forthcoming, *Houston Law Review* at IV.C.2 (2003).

von Hippel, Eric, 'Innovation by User Communities: Learning from Open Source Software', *Sloan Management Review* July (2001).

von Hippel, Eric and Georg von Krogh, 'Exploring the Open-Source Software Phenomenon: Issues for Organization Science', 5 (2002), at http://opensource.mit.edu/online_papers.php (retrieved June 23, 2003).

Weaver, Jane, 'Compact disc sales slid in 2002', MSNBC.NEWS.com, February 29, 2003, at http://www.cnet.com (retrieved June 16, 2003).

Webbink, Mark, Presentation, 'Open Issues on Open Source', unpublished document, Red Hat Inc., Charlotte, NC, presented at Kaye Scholer LLP, New York, November 6, 2003.

Weinrib, Lloyd, 'Copyright for Functional Expression', 111 *Harvard Law Review* 1149 (1998).

Weinrib, Lloyd L., 'Fair's Fair: A Comment on the Fair Use Doctrine', 103 *Harvard Law Review* 1137 (1990).

Wheeler, David, 'Why Open Source Software/Free Software (OSS/FS)? Look at the Numbers!', at http://www.dwheeler.com/oss_fs_why.html (retrieved June 1, 2003).

White, Michelle J. and Donald Wittman, 'Long Run versus Short Run Remedies for Spatial Externalities: Liability Rules, Pollution Rules, and Zoning', in *Essays on the Law and Economics of Local Governments* (Daniel L. Rubinfeld ed., Washington, DC: Urban Institute, 1979).

Wilcox, Joe and Evan Hansen, 'Apple's music: Microsoft's sour note?', *Tech News*, CNET.com, April 30, 2003, at http://www.cnet.com (retrieved June 16, 2003).

Wilcox, Joe, 'Microsoft protecting rights – or Windows?', CNET NEWS.com, February 3, 2003, at http://www.cnet.com (retrieved June 16, 2003).

Wilcox, Joe, 'Microsoft Expands Rights Management Tool', CNET NEWS.com, February 21, 2003, at http://www.cnet.com (retrieved June 16, 2003).

Williamson, Oliver E., *The Economic Institutions of Capitalism* (Glencoe, NY: Free Press, 1985).

Williamson, Oliver E., 'Transaction Cost Economics', *The Mechanisms of Governance* (Oxford: Oxford University Press, 1996).

Williamson, Oliver E., *The Mechanisms of Governance* (Oxford: Oxford University Press, 1998).

Williamson, Oliver E., 'Transaction Cost Economics: The Governance of Contractual Relations', 22 *Journal of Law and Economics* 233 (1979).

Winslow, Annastasia P., 'Rapping on a Revolving Door: An Economic Analysis of Parody and Campbell v. Acuff Rose', 69 *Southern California Law Review* 767 (1996).

World Intellectual Property Organization, Copyright Treaty, Article 11; Performances and Phonogram Treaty, Article 18; adopted December 20, 1996, Geneva, Switzerland.

Young, G., K.G. Smith and C.M. Grimm, 'Austrian and Industrial Organization Perspectives on Firm Level Competitive Activity and Performance', 7 *Organization Science* 3:243 (1996).

Zimmerman, Diane, 'The More Things Change, The Less They Seem "Transformed"; Some Reflections on Fair Use', *Journal of the Copyright Society of the U.S.A.* 251 (1998).

Zimmerman, Diane L., 'Competing Perspectives and Divergent Analyses Fitting Publicity Rights into Intellectual Property and Free Speech Theory', 10 *Journal of Art and Entertainment Law* 283, 301–2 (2000).

Legal references

Index